Jon Naunton

# Head for Business

## Upper-Intermediate Student's Book

**OXFORD**

UNIVERSITY PRESS

# Contents

# Contents

# 11

## Look before you leap

# 12

## Reputations

## Tapescript

## Glossary

# 1 Target markets

## Talking business

**1** Look at the cartoon. What is it trying to say? How possible is it to sell anything to anyone?

**2** Read about OGO. Is Hammond's task easier or more difficult than the refrigerator salesman's? Do you share his optimism?

> Two Dutch entrepreneurs are trying to sell oxygen in a can. The product, called OGO, costs about £8.99 and gives five minutes' worth of oxygen. Richard Hammond of Spirit, the advertising agency appointed to handle OGO's launch in the UK, is confident of success. He says that bottled water was once considered unmarketable because water was freely available from the tap. He points out: 'The mineral water market didn't exist fifteen years ago and now it is worth $25bn worldwide.'

*The Independent*

## Listening

### Ad makers

**1** Janet White, an account director from a top British advertising agency, is being interviewed about her job.

- What do advertising agencies do?
- What qualities do you think you need to work in an advertising agency?

**2**  Listen to part A.

1 What different roles exist in a large agency?

2 Which people are actively involved in the creative side of the advertising business?

3 What is Janet's role, and why is it particularly important?

**3** In part B Janet describes the advertising process.

1 Look at these stages in the process and put them in the order (1–6) in which you think they would happen. Then listen to part B and check.

a The agency comes up with an advertising concept. ......

b The agency identifies which media are best. ......

c The agency has a meeting with the client to present its findings. ......

d The agency writes the advertisement. ......

e The client and agency refine the concept. ......

f The client tells the agency about the customers it wishes to target. ......

2 What different terms does she use to refer to the customers the advertisement will be aimed at?

3 How scientific does Janet say the process is?

4 Janet discusses two ways of finding out if an advertising campaign has been successful. Listen to part C and summarize it, using these notes to help you.

> Tracking studies let agencies know **1** ............... .
> One way you can find out if a campaign has been successful is by using before **2** ............... . This tells the agency if the target audience's attitudes **3** ............... .

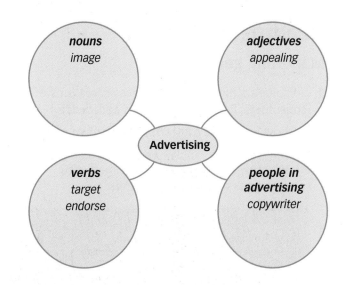

nouns
image

adjectives
appealing

Advertising

verbs
target
endorse

people in advertising
copywriter

5 Listen to part D. How does Janet's anecdote show that advertising is a stressful business?

6 Study the tapescript on page 152 and add words to do with advertising to the spidergram.

## Language study

### The present

1 Match the definitions of use (1–4) with the examples of use (a–d).

1 an activity starting in the past and continuing up to the present _d_

2 a routine action _a_

3 an activity in progress in the present _c_

4 an action at some time in the past with an effect in the present _b_

~~baglanti kurmak~~

a I liaise between the client and all the other aspects of the agency. _Simple Present_

b She has worked with some major clients. _Perfect_

c She is currently working at the New York office. _Simple continuous_

d We've been looking for a replacement. _Perfect Continuous_

2 Identify the tenses in a–d.

3 Turn to tapescript [1.1] on page 152. Find other examples of each tense and say why they are used in each case.

4 Discuss the difference in meaning between the pairs of sentences below.

1 a What do you do? _asking the Job_
  b What are you doing? _at the moment what she's doing_

2 a What do you think? _opinion_
  b What are you thinking?

3 a You're unreasonable. _always_
  b You're being unreasonable. _at the moment_

4 a We have lost market share. _we lost market share_ _it effects us now_
  b We've been losing market share. _we are losing_

(g) Grammar guide, page 148

5 Complete the sentences by choosing the correct form in _italics_.

1 Your advertising plan (sounds) / is sounding interesting.

2 High wages generally (cause) / are causing inflation.

3 They've been interviewing / interviewed new copywriters all morning.

4 Fiona usually is working / (works) at the London office, but she (is working) / works in New York for a few months.

5 How long has she written / (been writing) the report?

6 I (don't know) / 'm not knowing what these survey results (mean) / are meaning.

7 I can't come to Friday's meeting, I'm going / go to Madrid.

8 How often have you visited / ~~been visiting~~ the Brazilian market?

6 Work in pairs. Student A, turn to File 30 on page 135. Student B, turn to File 34 on page 136.

# Reading

## Marketing generations

1 Sociologists have identified three generations of US consumers. Read the definitions and decide:

- how well these categories fit your own country and society
- why this analysis could worry marketing managers of established brands.

### Marketing generations in the USA

Baby Boomers: 72 million babies were born in the baby boom in the USA between 1946 and 1964. Marked by their strong ideals and love of family, they are fearful of the future and socially liberal.

Generation X: 17 million were born between about 1965 and 1978. Generation Xers live in the present and like to experiment. They are selfish and cynical.

Generation Y: 60 million were born between 1979 and 1994. Materialistic, selfish and disrespectful, they are very aware of the world and technologically literate. They are trying to grow up too fast.

2 Read paragraphs 1–3 of the article.

1 What do Laura Schaefer and Lori Silverman tell us about changes in fashions between generations?

2 How has this affected companies like Nike and Pepsi? Sime

3 How are Generation Yers different from Generation Xers who preceded them? In what way are they more important?

4 How is Generation Y different from the Baby Boomer generation?

3 Now read the second part of the article.

1 Mark statements a–f true (T) or false (F) giving reasons for your answers. Generation Yers:

a like celebrity endorsements. F
b enjoy humour and irony in advertisements. T
c distrust slogans and image-building campaigns. T
d aren't brand conscious. F
e belong to different ethnic groups. T
f rely on TV to find out about fashion. F

2 How are some brand leaders trying to find out what Generation Yers want?

# Generation Y

All across America, a new generation of consumers is making its presence felt. In one shopping mall, clerk Laura Schaefer has been handling returned goods. 'They say "My mom and dad got me these".' Parents in Nikes sit quietly while their teenage daughters try on massive platform shoes. Asked what brands are cool, these teens give a list of names their parents have never heard of. Which brands are over? Now the names are familiar: Levi's, Converse, Nike. 'They just went out of style,' shrugs Lori Silverman, 13. Labels that have shaped popular tastes since the Baby Boomers were young simply aren't producing the same excitement with today's kids. PepsiCo. Inc. has struggled to build loyalty among teens, Nike Inc.'s sales are tumbling as the brand sinks in teen popularity polls, while Levi Strauss & Co. is fighting falling market share. Meanwhile, newcomers in entertainment, sports equipment and fashion have become hot names.

Today's kids aren't Baby Boomers. They're part of Generation Y which rivals the baby boom in size and will soon rival it in buying power. Marketers haven't been given an opportunity like this since the baby boom. Yet for a lot of established brands, Generation Y presents huge risks. Boomer brands flopped in their attempts to reach Generation X, but with only 17 million that was tolerable. This is the first generation big enough to hurt a Boomer brand simply by ignoring it – and big enough to launch rival brands.

Companies unable to connect with Generation Y will lose out on a vast new market. Along with cynicism,

Generation Y is marked by a distinctly practical world view. Raised in dual income and single-parent families, they've already been given substantial financial responsibility. Surveys show they are deeply involved in family purchases, be they groceries or a new car. Most expect to have careers and are already thinking about home ownership.

Nike has found out the hard way that Generation Y is different. Although still popular among teens, the brand has lost its tight hold on the market in recent years. Nike's slick national ad campaigns, emphasizing image and celebrity, helped build the brand among Boomers, but they have backfired with Generation Y. 'It doesn't matter to me that Michael Jordan has endorsed Nikes,' says Ben Dukes, 13. Instead Generation Yers respond to humour, irony, and the truth. Sprite has scored with ads that make fun of celebrity endorsers and carry the tagline 'Image is nothing. Obey your thirst.'

This doesn't mean that Generation Yers aren't brand-conscious. But marketing experts say they form a less homogeneous market than their parents. One factor is their racial and ethnic diversity. Another is the breaking up of media, with network TV being replaced by cable channels. Most important is the rise of the Internet, which has sped up the fashion life cycle by letting kids everywhere find out about even the most obscure trends as they emerge. It's the Generation Y medium of choice, just as network TV was for Boomers. Marketers who don't learn the interests and obsessions of Generation Y will meet a wall of cynicism and distrust. To break through this, marketers are making their campaigns more subtle and more local. A growing number, including Universal Studios, Coca-Cola and McDonald's are using 'street teams'. Made up of young people, the teams hang out in clubs, parks and malls talking to teens about everything from fashion to finance. Will the labels that grew up with Baby Boomers re-invent themselves for Generation Y, or will the new brands of the millennium bear names that most of us have not yet heard of?

*Business Week*

4 Look at the article again. Find words and expressions which:

1 express the idea of being very big.
2 deal with success.
3 deal with failure and hardship.

## ❙Television drives homogeneity, the Internet drives diversity.❙

**Mary Slayton**, global director for consumer insights for Nike

5 Read the situation and, in groups, discuss questions 1–3.

> You have just joined the marketing department of a famous sportswear firm which is finding it harder than before to attract younger consumers. It is producing a new range targeted at teenagers. Traditionally, the firm has used big advertising companies and celebrity endorsements to run its campaigns.

1 What do you think of the firm's promotions policy?
2 How will you encourage your boss to read the article you have just read?
3 How will you find out what young people really want?

6 Work in groups. You have been put in charge of the promotion of the new sportswear. You have a budget of 12 points to spend. Think carefully of the age and interests of the group you wish to target, and decide how to spend your budget most effectively.

> – sponsorship of musical and sporting events (5 points)
> – advertising on the Internet (3 points)
> – advertising on network TV (7 points)
> – product placement in teen TV shows and movies (3 points)
> – free gifts of clothes to pop singers and teen idols (1 point)
> – street poster campaign (5 points)
> – publicity stunts; for example, a parachuting team dressed in your brand's clothes (2 points)
> – advertisements in selected teen magazines (4 points)
> – celebrity endorsement for a poster or TV campaign (3 points)

## Language in use

### Giving opinions

1 **1.2** Three people are discussing an advertisement showing children doing dangerous activities. Listen to their conversation and decide who you agree with most.

2 Listen again and fill in the gaps.

Martin: So ¹_____ this kids' commercial, then?

Carol: I ²_____ . It's a lot of fuss about nothing.

Martin: I ³_____ , Carol. ⁴_____ , advertising is just a bit of fun.

Carol: Yes, ⁵_____ we should be more worried about the TV programmes themselves.

Martin: You're very quiet. ⁶_____ , Megan?

Megan: Well, I suppose so, ⁷_____ .
⁸_____ , but don't you think advertisers should be more careful? Kids can be very influenced by advertisements.

Martin: ⁹_____ ! Even children don't believe everything they see on TV.

3 Which expressions are used to:

1 introduce our opinions?

2 invite other people's opinions?

3 agree and disagree?

4 acknowledge another person's opinion?

4 What other ways of introducing opinions can you add to the list?

### Pronunciation: linking

1 In connected speech words run together, which can make it difficult to tell where one word ends and the next begins. Read the following sentence aloud, taking care to link the words as marked.

*That's‿an‿interesting point.*

2 Mark the linked words in these sentences and phrases from **1.2** . Then listen again and check.

1 I think it's absolutely ridiculous.

2 As far as I'm concerned ...

3 In my opinion ...

4 Don't you agree, Megan?

5 up to a point.

3 Now mark the words you think should be linked in the following sentences. Then say them aloud.

1 What on earth are you saying?

2 Come off it, Anna!

3 On the other hand, they could be right.

4 Wouldn't you accept that position?

5 What an awful thing to suggest!

6 There are two other points I'd like to make.

4 **1.3** Listen and check.

5 Work in groups of three and practise giving and exchanging opinions. Discuss these three topics and take it in turns to be A, B, or C.

- An animal rights campaigner claims that animals are often injured in TV commercials

- A public figure says TV commercials should be banned.

- You think research proves that people buy things they don't need because of advertising.

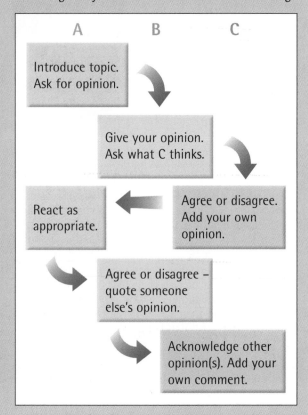

A    B    C

Introduce topic. Ask for opinion.

Give your opinion. Ask what C thinks.

Agree or disagree. Add your own opinion.

React as appropriate.

Agree or disagree – quote someone else's opinion.

Acknowledge other opinion(s). Add your own comment.

# Speaking

## An eye on advertising

1 In Britain advertising is regulated by an independent organization called the Advertising Standards Authority (ASA). Look at their basic principles.

 – All advertisements should be legal, decent, honest and truthful.
 – All advertisements should be prepared with a sense of responsibility to consumers and to society.
 – All advertisements should respect the principles of fair competition generally accepted in business.

 1 The ASA issues guidelines and encourages self-regulation. It does not have the power to make laws. Why do you think it is set up in this way?

 2 What controls exist in your country? Can you think of any advertisements which break the ASA's guidelines?

2 Adbusters is a pressure group based in Canada. It campaigns against big-brand advertising and the over-consumption of developed countries.

 1 Look at this 'un-commercial' which is trying to encourage people to turn their TVs off for a week. What other meaning of 'turn off' is used in the commercial?

 a How do you think Adbusters calculated the number of commercials the child will watch?

 b In your opinion, how many commercials will her brain really absorb?

 c How easy do you think it is to influence children with advertising?

 d Do you think TV advertising can be a force for good?

 2 How far do you agree with Adbusters' message?

 3 How different is its role from the ASA's?

3 Look at this second un-commercial from Adbusters. What do you think it is trying to say about consumers in a modern consumer society?

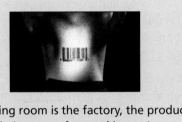

'The living room is the factory, the product being manufactured is you.'

**www.adbusters.org**

4 Divide into two groups. Group A, think of arguments in support of what the advertisement says. Group B, think of arguments against it. When you are ready, find a partner from the other group and give each other your opinions.

5 Study these quotes on the theme of advertising. Work in groups and discuss which ones you most, or least, agree with.

❝I regard a great ad as the most beautiful thing in the world.❞
**Leo Burnett**, ad agency founder

❝Advertising is only evil when it advertises evil things.❞
**David Ogilvy**

❝Word of mouth is the best (advertising) medium of all❞
**William Bernbach**

'By the time this child graduates from high school, her brain will have absorbed 350,000 television commercials, 100,000 alcohol ads and a daily barrage of sex and violence. If that doesn't turn you off, nothing will.'

**www.adbusters.org**

TV TURNOFF WEEK
April 24 - 30
a message from the media foundation 1-800-663-1243

# Writing

## Promotional copy

1  In advertising and marketing, what do AIDA and USP stand for? Turn to File 2 on page 126 to check your answers.

2  BMW, better known for its performance cars and motorcycles, has introduced a City Scooter, its Urban Personal Commuter, to the market. Study the product information. What are the City Scooter's obvious USPs?

**Car Magazine**

'[The C1] could be the answer to your commuting nightmare.'

'The C1 removes most of the normal hassles involved with commuting on a scooter – exposure to the elements, the danger of falling off, the need to don protective clothing – but retains a scooter's priceless ability to nip around queues of traffic as if they weren't

**Evening Standard**

'It's the perfect gift for the capital commuter who has tried everything and still can't get to work on time ...'

'Designed by BMW to combine car-like safety and comfort with the speed and manoeuvrability of a motorcycle, it is poised to become the latest "must have" item ...'

3  Work in pairs or groups. Decide which features would most appeal to the following people:
   - professionals who travel to work in a big city and who need to look smart
   - fashion conscious students who travel to and from college
   - parents who worry about the dangers of ordinary motorcycles.

4  Work in three groups. Following the AIDA principle, write some advertising copy for:

   **Group A:** a business magazine for young urban professionals. Turn to File 25 on page 134 for your Marketing Research information.

   **Group B:** the motoring section of a Sunday newspaper. Turn to File 22 on page 133 for your Marketing Research information.

   **Group C:** a magazine for students. Turn to File 37 on page 137 for your Marketing Research information.

5  Compare your copy with members from other groups and suggest improvements.

**Features of the C1**

→ stylish and different / a new concept
→ offers all-weather protection: full-size windscreen and windscreen wipers
→ weighs around 170 kg
→ 125 cc engine: will be cheap for tax, insurance and servicing
→ fuel consumption is 18–20 km per litre
→ environmentally clean
→ people will be able to use it on an ordinary car driving licence
→ gives users the pleasure of riding a motorized two-wheel vehicle
→ high standard of passive safety, as safe as a small modern car
→ aluminium space-frame providing maximum protection if the vehicle overturns
→ seat belts
→ a rear seat for a passenger or luggage
→ optional extras: ABS, heated handlebars, navigation system, radio, CD player

# In conversation

## Meeting and greeting

**1** The words we use to greet people depends on who we are talking to and how formal we wish to be.

   **1** Look at these greetings. Mark each one *F* (more formal) or *I* (less formal).

      a  Hi. .....

      b  Hello. .....

      c  Pleased to meet you. .....

      d  How do you do? .....

      e  How's it going? .....

      f  How are you? .....

      g  How are you doing? .....

   **2** Think of a suitable response to each one.

**2**  [1.4]  Listen to the first situation and use the phrases from the box below to complete the conversation.

> I'm very pleased to meet you at long last
> I don't believe you've met
> this is my third time
> the pleasure is all mine
> communicated by e-mail
> Is this your first visit?

Laurence: Katie, there's someone ¹................. Katie Crown, this is Dr Kowalska from the Warsaw office.

Dr Kowalska: No, but we've ²................. How do you do, Ms Crown?

Katie: How do you do, Dr Kowalska. ³...................

Dr Kowalska: Thank you, ⁴...................

Katie: So. ⁵...................?

Dr Kowalska: Well, actually, ⁶...................

**3** Practise the conversation in groups of three.

**4** Re-order these sentences 1–9 to form a more informal conversation.

   a  Phil: I must introduce you to Sonia. Sonia, come and say hello to Dieter. Dieter is from the Munich office. You haven't met before, have you? .....

   b  Dieter: Good things I hope. .....

   c  Dieter: Oh, you know, I can't complain. .....

   d  Dieter: Hi! Phil, long time no see. You're looking good. .....

   e  Sonia: Of course, he's a great fan of yours! So, Dieter, this is your first time over here isn't it? .....

   f  Dieter: No, but we've spoken on the phone. Pleased to meet you, Sonia. .....

   g  Phil: Hi Dieter. It's great to see you again. So, how's it going? .....

   h  Dieter: No, it's my second time, actually. .....

   i  Sonia: Likewise. It's great to put a face to a voice. I've heard so much about you from Phil. .....

**5**  [1.5]  Listen and check your answers.

**6** Work in groups of three and role-play the following two dialogues.

   **1** **Student A:** You are Jill Maxwell. You are the managing director of Cleveland Plastics. You are with Mr Yoshi Tanaka, a production engineer.

      **Student B:** You are Mr Tanaka. You have never met Clive Grey but you know from Ms Maxwell that he is Cleveland Plastics' best technician. He will be assisting you with the installation.

      **Student C:** You are Clive Grey. You know that Mr Tanaka is a respected production engineer. You have not met him before but you are looking forward to working with him.

   **2** **Student A:** You are Finbow Carter. You are a geologist with an oil exploration company. You meet your old friend and former colleague, Jo Norris, at a drinks party. You want to introduce your colleague, Gus Walsh, to Jo.

      **Student B:** You are Jo. You are really pleased to see Finbow again.

      **Student C:** You are Gus Walsh. You have spoken to Jo before and have read about him in the company magazine.

# Case study

## The Boston Matrix

**1** Nearly all products follow a typical life cycle. Study the graph opposite.

1 Describe the usual relationship between a product's sales and its age.

2 Decide where these stages belong on the graph.

| | | |
|---|---|---|
| decline | launch | death |
| re-launch | growth | maturity |

**2** The Boston Matrix is a way of classifying a company's product range.

1 Read about the four categories the matrix uses. How do they relate to the product life cycle?

2 How effective or memorable is this way of describing a company's product portfolio?

3 The blue circles in the matrix represent a company's product range. What does it tell us about the health of its products' portfolio?

### The Boston Matrix

**Stars**
These are new products which have a large market share in a growing market. However, their profits will be quite low because of the need to continue spending on development and promotion.

**Cash cows**
These are well-established products which have a large market share in a market with low growth. These products are in the mature stage of the product life cycle and are very profitable. Organizations love cash cows but have nightmares about them becoming dogs!

**Question marks**
Products where market growth is high but where market share is still low. New products which you hope will quickly become stars and highly profitable cash cows! Question marks are still at the introductory stage, with everybody keeping their fingers crossed.

**Dogs**
Dogs are products which have a low market share and little or no chance of growth. They may yield a little profit but these products are very near the end of their life cycle. Dogs can be ex-cash cows or other products which simply did not succeed.

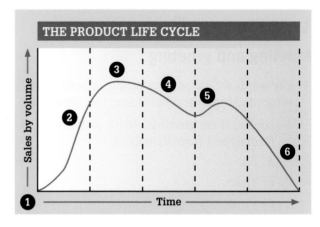

THE PRODUCT LIFE CYCLE

**3** Some companies continuously relaunch brands of products such as cereal and soap powder to appeal to new generations of consumers.

– Think of a well-established business or organization from your country and brainstorm where its products or services might fit on the Boston Matrix.

– How do you think this company may have adapted its range to meet the needs of different marketing generations?

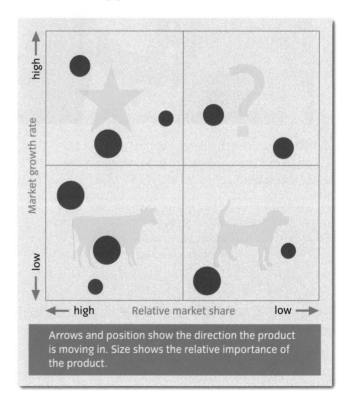

Arrows and position show the direction the product is moving in. Size shows the relative importance of the product.

4 **1.6** Stevens is a manufacturer of boxed board games. These are its key products:

- Gangstaz: a game based on criminals and the police
- Wordsters: a vocabulary and word-based game
- Sherlock: a mystery-murder board game
- Sketchit: a game based on drawing

1 Listen to members of Stevens' marketing department discussing the games, and decide where each one should belong on the Boston Matrix.

2 Listen again and complete the descriptions of the four products below.

Gangstaz:
a deserves a re-launch.
b could easily find a buyer.
c has never met expectations.

Wordsters:
a is in a saturated segment of the market.
b has a bright future ahead of it.
c has been a disappointment from the beginning.

Sherlock:
a has maintained its high levels of sales.
b makes Stevens a lot of money.
c no longer needs to be promoted.

Sketchit:
a needed a little explanation.
b could be a longer-term winner.
c only sells in English-speaking markets.

3 Turn to the tapescript on page 153. How do the speakers make suggestions and discuss options?

5 Read the information about three other games Stevens produces.

**Empire**

Players have to conquer their enemies and rule the world by throwing dice. A board map of the world is divided into different countries. Each player tries to accumulate armies by invading other players' countries and conquering them.

**Who's there?**

A logic-based guessing game where two players compete to work out the identity of a character. Two players sit opposite each other. Each player has a set of cards with people's faces the other cannot see. The winner is the first to guess the mystery person on a remaining card by asking questions and using a process of elimination.

**Bidders**

An auction game based on works of art and antiques. There are cards with pictures of objects on them, which players aim to win by bidding for them. The real value of the object is on the back of the card. The winner is the one who manages to buy the most valuable items by spending the least money.

1 Work in groups of three. Student A, turn to File 4 on page 127; Student B, to File 28 on page 135; and Student C, to File 41 on page 138. Take turns to present the extra information you have about the game. As a group, decide in which part of the matrix each game belongs.

2 If you were managers at Stevens, how confident would you feel about its product range?

6 Brainstorm ways to handle the products in the best interests of the company.

# 2 Triumph and disaster

## Talking business

1 How do you feel about money? Answer the questionnaire by putting a circle around the expression that matches your attitude.

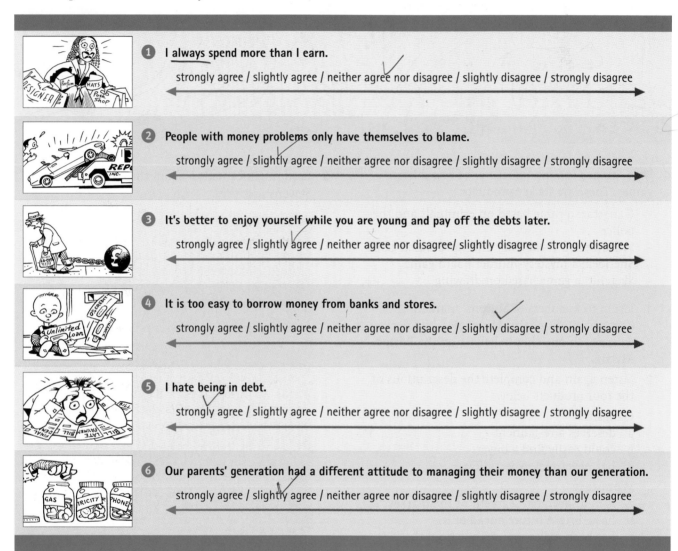

**1** I always spend more than I earn.

strongly agree / slightly agree / neither agree nor disagree / slightly disagree / strongly disagree

**2** People with money problems only have themselves to blame.

strongly agree / slightly agree / neither agree nor disagree / slightly disagree / strongly disagree

**3** It's better to enjoy yourself while you are young and pay off the debts later.

strongly agree / slightly agree / neither agree nor disagree / slightly disagree / strongly disagree

**4** It is too easy to borrow money from banks and stores.

strongly agree / slightly agree / neither agree nor disagree / slightly disagree / strongly disagree

**5** I hate being in debt.

strongly agree / slightly agree / neither agree nor disagree / slightly disagree / strongly disagree

**6** Our parents' generation had a different attitude to managing their money than our generation.

strongly agree / slightly agree / neither agree nor disagree / slightly disagree / strongly disagree

2 Discuss your answers with a partner.

3 Study the information about types of business in England. What are the equivalents in your country?

### Types of business

**sole trader:** An individual person who works on his or her own. Sole traders are liable for any debts they incur.

**partnership:** Where two or more people combine their capital and skills and share risks and profits. In the UK (except Scotland) partnerships are not legal entities so individuals are fully liable for any debts.

**limited company (Ltd)** A company whose owners have limited liability for the debts of their business. i.e. the company has a separate legal identity.

**public limited company (plc)** A company whose shares can be publicly traded. The letters 'plc' must follow its name.

# Listening

## Life after debt?

**1** You are going to listen to interviews with two people who advise on debt.

  **1** How different do you think the problems are which individuals and businesses suffer?

  **2** What kind of advice do you think they are likely to receive?

**2** Before you listen, match the words in the box with their definitions 1–9.

| | | |
|---|---|---|
| hire purchase | mortgage | instalment |
| outgoings | overheads | assets |
| cash flow | premises | bankrupt / insolvent |

  **1** the property and equipment owned by an individual or company *assets*

  **2** a way of buying an expensive item such as a car, by paying for it over a number of months *hire purchase*

  **3** the movement of money coming into and leaving a company *cash flow*

  **4** no longer able to trade because you have no more money *bankrupt*

  **5** a long-term loan which is used to buy a home *mortgage*

  **6** the fixed costs such as rent, electricity, and salaries which a business has to support *overheads*

  **7** a regular payment of money to pay off a debt *instalment*

  **8** the place where you conduct your business *premises*

  **9** the opposite of income *outgoings*

**3** [2.1] Listen to each interview and complete the columns in the table.

**4** How far should business people be responsible for their business debts?

**5** English has many idiomatic expressions for talking about money. Find the following expressions in tapescript [2.1] (Interview 2) on page 153. What do they mean?

  – *live within their means*

  – *make ends meet*

**6** Now match 1–6 with a–f below to form sentences containing further expressions.

  **1** Business is booming so we mustn't take a holiday now; we ... *d*

  **2** This is our *bread and butter* business; ... *f*

  **3** The firm is just about *keeping its head above water*, ... *c*

  **4** I know we're going through a difficult period, but we ... *b*

  **5** It's best to *save something for a rainy day* ... *e*

  **6** After years of trying to *stay afloat*, ... *a*

  **a** ... the business finally went under during the recession of the 1980s.

  **b** ... should be able to *weather the storm* if we cut our costs.

  **c** ... but it hasn't been easy lately.

  **d** ... should *make hay while the sun is still shining*.

  **e** ... rather than spending all your money at once.

  **f** ... without it we'd be in trouble.

**7** Work in pairs. You are going to role-play two situations involving debt counselling. Student A, turn to File 5 on page 127. Student B, turn to File 40 on page 138.

| | Interview 1 | Interview 2 |
|---|---|---|
| Roles | | |
| Type of client | Small shop keepers.... | |
| Cause of the client's problems | Cash, new overheads, Bankrupt | |
| Practical advice | • be aware of business environment • control the costs | |
| One client's story | • owned a cd shop, a big chain opened a branch next door. | |

# Reading

## Santa inspires Gadget Shop founder

1 You are going to read an article about a man who has made his fortune as an entrepreneur. Does the title help you predict how he did this?

2 Read the text and discover how the items in the pictures helped Jonathan to prepare for success.

3 Find evidence in the text which shows that he:
1 understands his customers.
2 thinks problems through carefully.
3 isn't afraid to take risks.
4 is persuasive.
5 is prepared to learn from other people.
6 is ambitious.

4 What have been the most critical points of Jonathan's career so far? When could his success so easily have turned to disaster?

Jonathan Elvidge could not find a store that sold innovative presents, so he decided to open his own. Today he runs a chain of twenty-five. Elvidge wanted to run his own company as a boy and he began his business career selling brushes. At seventeen he appeared on television after winning an award for co-designing kitchen scales for the blind. 'I knew we had a better chance if we created something worthy,' he says. 'It's all about identifying whom you target.'

He *came across* an idea he could make into a proper business some years later. He had been looking for Christmas presents, and was trying to find a retailer that stocked a large range of innovative presents. He found none and realized there was a gap in the market. After two years of research, he decided to start such a business himself and opened the first Gadget Shop. Before the end of the year he had opened two more and he now has twenty-five.

His aspiration to be an entrepreneur came after a number of diversions and make-or-break situations. He didn't take his final school exams, joining instead the local telephone department as an apprentice

telephone engineer while he decided what to do. While he was digging holes he had to be rescued when the pneumatic drill he had been using carried him down the road. He learned another lasting lesson climbing up telegraph-poles. He discovered that if you stand in dirt on the way up, then you get it on your hands on the way down. 'Holes and poles taught me to understand people from the ground up,' he says.

Elvidge worked his way around the company and eventually moved to sales. 'Selling was not new to me. The brush business had sharpened my communication skills and confidence.' He rose to be a star salesman, but found inspiration for his own plans from books about how entrepreneurs started in business.

His plans for the gift shop were accelerated when he *fell out with* a manager. He drew up a business plan for his new venture, spending his holidays at gift conventions. 'People used to think, "here comes the imaginary shop man again",' he says. 'I got friends at work to *carry out* market research and used the office laser printer to make letter headings with my new logo.'

Elvidge's persistence *paid off*. He re-mortgaged his home, raising enough money to fund his first shop. However, a newspaper article alerted his employers to what he was up to and he was told to choose between the jobs. He chose to leave the company, but when his initial launch was delayed, he hit a crisis. '*I missed out on* the Christmas sales, which dented my cash flow projection, I needed to raise a further £20,000 or face *going under* before I had even opened my doors.' He *found out about* government NatWest loan guarantees and *talked* NatWest bank *into* helping him.

'From the day it opened, The Gadget Shop was a success,' he says. After five months he made a small profit but he did not want to be just a shopkeeper. He found a partner who invested capital to help the business expand, and soon the company was making healthy profits. Elvidge says being ordinary and in tune with his customers is the key to his success. 'There is no such thing as a half-hearted entrepreneur,' he says. 'You have to be prepared to lose everything and remember that the biggest risk is not taking any risk.'

**5** Match the infinitive form of the phrasal verbs in italics in the text with their definitions below.

1 fail

2 persuade

3 find by chance

4 discover a piece of information

5 have an argument with someone

6 perform a task

7 produced good results

8 lose an opportunity

# Language study

## Past forms

**1** Identify the past forms in italics in sentences 1–5.

1 Selling *was* not new to me. The brush business *had sharpened* my communication skills.

2 He *had been looking for* Christmas presents.

3 While he *was digging* holes he had to be rescued.

4 Elvidge *worked* his way around the company and eventually *moved* to sales. He *rose* to be a star salesman.

5 His initial launch *was delayed*.

Ⓖ Grammar guide, page 147

**2** Which past form is used to describe:

a an action which was in progress when another action happened?

b a sequence of completed actions in the past?

c something that happened earlier than a stated point in the past?

d an action which was in progress up to a point in the past?

e a completed action in the past which happened to someone or something?

**3** Complete the text by changing the verbs in brackets into a suitable past narrative form.

Even as a child Jane Cavanagh **1** _____ (be) more at home with the circuit boards from her father's electronics business than dolls' houses. At the age of seventeen, she **2** _____ (demonstrate) her entrepreneurial capabilities by buying two cars at an auction. She **3** _____ (spend) half the summer renovating them, and afterwards she **4** _____ (sell) them at a profit. Some years later while she **5** _____ (work) for Telecom-Soft, a division of BT, she **6** _____ (give) the task of developing its computer games brands. She **7** _____ (travel) to

Japan and **8** _____ (build up) a portfolio of products for BT to sell. At this time, games consoles **9** _____ (become) increasingly popular and she **10** _____ (realize) the sector's enormous potential. She **11** _____ (still work) for BT when she **12** _____ (approach) by FIL, a division of the French conglomerate Thomson. For some time, FIL **13** _____ (look for) someone with good contacts in Japan to expand their games development. FIL **14** _____ (offer) her the job of negotiating the rights of arcade games which could be converted into computer games. However, it **15** _____ (always be) at the back of Cavanagh's mind to start her own business. She **16** _____ (start) SCI and was in profit from day one. But she **17** _____ (operate) for less than a year when disaster **18** _____ (strike). Thomson **19** _____ (decide) to wind up FIL.

**4** A narrative text may use forms other than narrative tenses to provide a variety of style.

1 In this sentence from the text, which verb form does the present participle *joining* replace?

*He didn't take his final school exams, **joining** instead the local telephone department.*

2 Find further examples of present participle clauses in the rest of the text.

**5** Use the prompts below to continue Jane's story, using present participle clauses.

1 FIL owed her £20,000. Six half finished games were left. She made several trips to France and visited FIL's liquidator who agreed to let her have the rights to the games.

2 She was given the rights to the games in progress . This transformed SCI from an agent into the owner of intellectual property.

3 SCI now publishes its own games. It sells them in 60 markets worldwide.

**6** Work in pairs. Student A, turn to File 6 on page 127. Student B, turn to File 31 on page 135.

## Language in use

### Apologies, criticism, and deductions

1 What do the words and expressions in the box mean?

> a misunderstanding    a slip-up
> to mislay something    to make a gaffe
> an oversight    to offend someone
> to put your foot in it    a mix-up
> to make a fool of yourself    to upset someone

2 When things go wrong, how easy do you find it to say sorry, or accept apologies from other people?

3 Read sentences 1–8 and say which are:

  a  apologies.

  b  criticisms.

  c  deductions.

  1  She must have been really embarrassed.

  2  I am so sorry for the misunderstanding.

  3  He can't have been very pleased.

  4  Oh dear, you really should not have said that.

  5  I do hope you will forgive me for the other evening.

  6  I would like to apologize for what happened.

  7  We ought to have briefed them better.

  8  Why weren't you there?

4 Look at responses 1–8 and decide which ones are used to:

  a  accept an apology.

  b  politely refuse responsibility.

  1  Fine, but it would have been better if it hadn't happened.

  2  It really doesn't matter.

  3  Don't worry, it's just one of those things.

  4  I'm sorry, but I didn't realize that I was supposed to (do that).

  5  It couldn't be helped, these things happen.

  6  I'm sure you didn't mean to (upset her).

  7  I wouldn't worry about it if I were you.

  8  I appreciate you're annoyed, but (this is not my responsibility).

### Pronunciation: contracted forms

1 Contractions are a feature of connected speech or informal writing. Look at **3** again and read sentences 1–8 aloud. What additional contractions can you make?

2  **2.2**  Listen and check. Identify the words which are contracted and underline them, as in the example.

*She <u>must have</u> been really embarrassed.*

3 Listen again. What do you notice about the pronunciation of the words *been* and *for*?

4 Work in pairs. Create some exchanges by taking sentences from **3** and responding with an answer from **4**.

5 In pairs, create mini-dialogues around situations 1–6.

  1  You have just discovered that you have overcharged a client.

  2  You have had a complaint about the rude treatment a guest received from a trainee receptionist at your hotel.

  3  A colleague has badly damaged the photocopier by trying to photocopy onto a sheet of plastic which has melted inside the machine.

  4  A colleague tells you that they have just been speaking to someone who was sent the wrong order not just once, but three times!

  5  A colleague tells you that they have left their car in the managing director's parking space. You know that the MD will be angry!

  6  You asked a junior colleague to complete some important documents for you. Unfortunately he or she has made a mess of it and is very upset. You realize that it was really your fault because you didn't explain carefully what to do.

# Speaking

## Who's responsible?

1  Read about Sexton's shoes. Who do you think was responsible for what happened? Rank the people involved from 1 (most responsible) to 5 (least responsible).

..... the group leader

..... the group of visitors

..... the driver of the fork-lift

..... the manager who authorized the visit

..... the employee who was acting as a guide

Sexton's shoe factory often conducts tours for visitors from its retail outlets in various countries to see the shoe production process. Normally such visits are without incident, but last week a group was walking through a storage area where an accident with a fork-lift truck occurred. Some drums of dangerous chemicals were spilt, resulting in the evacuation of much of the factory. No-one was hurt but the fire brigade had to be called to clear up the mess and there was some bad publicity for Sexton's in the local news.

2  Discuss your ranking with a partner.

3  Work in groups of four. Each person should choose one of the roles below.

1  Read your information carefully and prepare your case for a meeting between those involved in the incident.

2  When you are ready, have a group meeting. Use as many expressions from the 'Language in use' section as you can.

### THE MANAGER

There was a mix-up over the time of the visit. You asked an inexperienced member of staff to accompany the visitors. However, you didn't imagine that he / she would take the group into one of the most dangerous parts of the factory. The fork-lift truck driver has been involved in a number of other accidents. The level of damage suggests he was driving it too fast.

### THE GUIDE

The manager asked you to conduct the visit even though you'd never done this before. You didn't know that the warehouse was 'off-limits'. You found the group difficult to control, particularly when their leader left to make a telephone call. You are very upset by what happened.

### THE FORK-LIFT TRUCK DRIVER

There is a strict one-way system in the factory. You lost control of the fork-lift truck when a group of people unexpectedly walked across your path. You crashed into the drums of chemicals. You don't want to be made a scapegoat for what happened.

### THE GROUP LEADER

You were expecting the visit to be better organized. The guide was obviously inexperienced and not used to dealing with large groups. No-one was hurt, in fact they thought it was an exciting and interesting experience. You had to make an urgent phone call during the visit and feel partly responsible for what happened.

# Writing

## Good netiquette

1 In a recent survey, two people out of five said a superior had used e-mail to criticize them. How appropriate a medium is e-mail for giving out criticism?

2 Study these rules of netiquette. Are there any others that you would like to add?

> ★ Don't forget you're dealing with people.
>
> ★ Behave on-line as you would in a face-to-face situation.
>
> ★ Resist the temptation to 'flame' or criticize.
>
> ★ Don't spread gossip or rumours – you have no control over it.
>
> ★ Remember that a deleted e-mail can always be retrieved.
>
> ★ In a work situation check that a message is necessary and relevant before sending it.
>
> ★ Don't use e-mail as a way of avoiding taking action.

3 Match the e-mails below to their replies.

4 Which of the rules do they break or illustrate? How would you edit them to make them more appropriate?

A
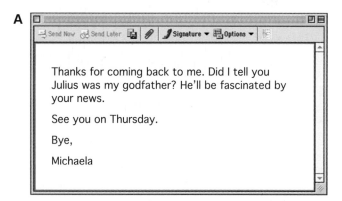

Thanks for coming back to me. Did I tell you Julius was my godfather? He'll be fascinated by your news.

See you on Thursday.

Bye,

Michaela

B
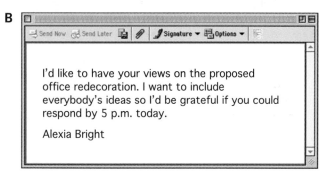

I'd like to have your views on the proposed office redecoration. I want to include everybody's ideas so I'd be grateful if you could respond by 5 p.m. today.

Alexia Bright

C
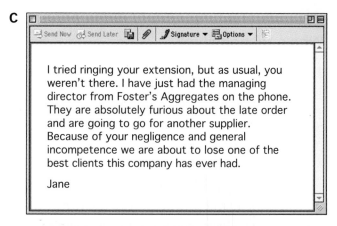

I tried ringing your extension, but as usual, you weren't there. I have just had the managing director from Foster's Aggregates on the phone. They are absolutely furious about the late order and are going to go for another supplier. Because of your negligence and general incompetence we are about to lose one of the best clients this company has ever had.

Jane

D
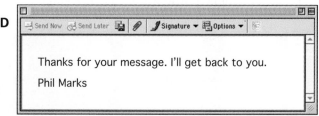

Thanks for your message. I'll get back to you.

Phil Marks

E
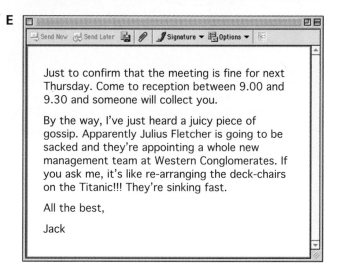

Just to confirm that the meeting is fine for next Thursday. Come to reception between 9.00 and 9.30 and someone will collect you.

By the way, I've just heard a juicy piece of gossip. Apparently Julius Fletcher is going to be sacked and they're appointing a whole new management team at Western Conglomerates. If you ask me, it's like re-arranging the deck-chairs on the Titanic!!! They're sinking fast.

All the best,

Jack

F

From: Howard Anderson
To: All staff
Cc:
Bcc:
Subject: Fw: Fire alarms
Attachments: none

FYI

Howard

Please note that the fire alarms will be tested at 3 p.m. this afternoon.

Bill Webster

Health and Safety Officer

**G**

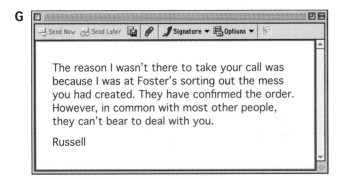

The reason I wasn't there to take your call was because I was at Foster's sorting out the mess you had created. They have confirmed the order. However, in common with most other people, they can't bear to deal with you.

Russell

**H**

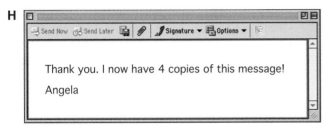

Thank you. I now have 4 copies of this message!
Angela

**5** Work in pairs. Look at the situations below.

1 Would any be unsuitable to send as e-mail messages?

  a You are angry about some new car parking regulations which have just been introduced. You'd like to find out what other colleagues think of them.

  b There has been a problem with an important order. You are e-mailing the person you think may be responsible for it.

  c Your dog has just had puppies and you would like to find homes for them.

  d You have heard an embarrassing story about a colleague you don't like.

  e You want to inform people about a change in offices.

  f Your secretary is back from holiday. You want him / her to produce some copies of a report as soon as possible.

2 What precautions would you have to take when preparing the messages?

3 Work in groups of three. Choose one of the situations and write a message to the two other members of your group.

4 Deliver your e-mail messages and write suitable replies to the ones you receive.

5 Compare the answers you receive.

# In conversation

## Triumphs and disasters

**1** Match sentences 1–10 below with an appropriate comment or reply (a–j). Sometimes more than one response is possible.

1 They've offered me the job!
2 What a disappointment!
3 How has she been since she heard the news?
4 Alex has left me.
5 He's only forty-five.
6 It was bad luck about your job.
7 I was sorry to hear about Felix.
8 I finally got my promotion.
9 We've just had a daughter.
10 Oh no, I've failed the practical.

a Oh, he didn't deserve you. You're better off without him.
b Oh, hard luck, I'm sure you'll pass next time.
c Life can be so unfair.
d Congratulations. What are you going to call her?
e He'll get over it.
f Well done! You deserve it.
g That's brilliant news! When do you start?
h Sad, but life goes on, you know.
i Yes, he was a lovely cat. I'll really miss him.
j Well, it's just one of those things, I suppose.

**2** **2.3** Listen and compare your answers. What has happened in each case?

**3** Work in pairs. Tell each other about your, or a friend's, recent triumphs or disasters. Respond appropriately and sympathetically.

23

# Case study

## Decisions, decisions

1 How do you usually make decisions? Which statement best matches your own?

- – I always trust my instincts and make up my mind straight away!
- – I like to sleep on any important decisions. Things often look different in the morning.
- – I like to analyse difficult decisions carefully and look at all the options.
- – I always distrust obvious answers to problems.
- – I am better at making important decisions at work than in my private life.

2 Study the information about the decision-making process. Is it just common sense?

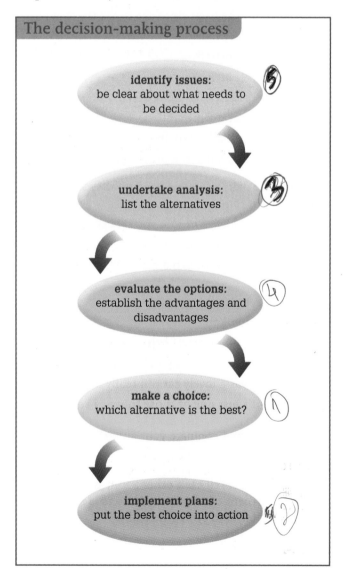

**The decision-making process**

**identify issues:** be clear about what needs to be decided

**undertake analysis:** list the alternatives

**evaluate the options:** establish the advantages and disadvantages

**make a choice:** which alternative is the best?

**implement plans:** put the best choice into action

3 Chapple and Scott's is a growing advertising agency which has just moved to larger premises in London. Every two years it holds a party for its most important and loyal clients. They have been discussing what they should do about this year's event. Look at comments 1–5 and decide which part of the decision-making process they belong to.

1 'So on balance, we've decided to go for the museum option. Although we're proud of the new premises, one set of offices looks very like another. After all, we're supposed to be a creative agency and this would be something that people would remember for a long time to come.'

2 'Right, now that we've made up our minds, we need to make it happen. Helen, we've discussed the budget, so could you get hold of the museum straight away and see what options they have for catering?'

3 A: 'Well, let's brainstorm the choices, shall we? We could hold it here; that way everyone would get to see the premises.'
   B: 'Or else we could have a reception in a hotel.'
   C: 'I've also heard that you can hire rooms at the museum. Just imagine chatting to people surrounded by paintings of skeletons of dinosaurs! Wouldn't that be fun?'

4 'There's no doubt that it would be cheaper to hold it here, and we do have a number of large rooms that we could use. A hotel could end up being extremely expensive and could give the wrong message to our clients. Provided we choose the right setting, the museum is a definite possibility.'

5 'We really need to think carefully about why we're holding this event. Is it to impress people with our new premises, or to thank them for their loyalty over the past couple of years? Personally, I think our aim should be to cement good relations with our key customers.'

4 Can you think of any decisions you have made which you later regretted?

5 Sometimes life is compared to a maze where we make choices which are difficult or impossible to reverse and which have important consequences. Has this ever happened to you?

Nibbler Eurer

**6** You and your partner are students at art college. For the last two winters you have had holiday jobs as skiing instructors. Two seasons ago you started to sell distinctive items of jewellery made to your own design. They were very popular and you have earned £3,000. You are now deciding what you should do.

You are going to make a series of business decisions which will lead to triumph, disaster, or a mixed triumph. Working in groups, make your first decision. Then go to point 10 or 15 depending on your choice and follow the instructions there. Points 1–14 are below; the rest are in File 7 on pages 128–9.

**1** If you stop now you will miss a once-in-a-lifetime business opportunity.
You should give up your art course and concentrate on the jewellery business. **Go to 10**.

You should carry on with your art course and graduate in two years' time. Afterwards you can always go back to the jewellery business. It will still be there. **Go to 15**.

**2** The department store says it will carry on buying your jewellery on condition that they sell it under its name (you will have to remove any details of your company from boxes and packaging).
You like the idea of a guaranteed income which will help your company grow. You accept their offer. **Go to 13**.

You insist on your independence and look for other customers. You turn down the offer. **Go to 21**.

**3** Your fragrances and clothes are a complete flop and damage your reputation. You are lucky enough to have another offer from the Luxury Label. However, the offer is greatly reduced. You still have enough to pay off your debts and walk away with enough money to start again.
*Mixed triumph*

**4** The department store buyers like your designs but think they need more work. However, you have spent most of your bank loan and need to raise some more money.
You go back to the bank and ask for a new loan. **Go to 28**.

You abandon your ambitious plans and sell the car. You invest the last of your money on a new workshop and perfecting your designs. **Go to 17**.

**5** Your shop in le Marais becomes very successful. You are still quite ambitious for further success.
You open shops in St Petersburg and Palm beach. **Go to 30**.

You decide to stretch your brand and produce accessories such as belts and leather goods carrying your logo and jewellery. **Go to 25**.

**6** The franchise is a limited success but takes all your energy and creativity. You haven't become rich but at least you are comfortably off.
*Mixed triumph*

**7** Your customer accepts the new deal you offer them. They recognize that your goods offer quality and good value for money. The business grows and you develop a wider customer base. You now aim to establish your jewellery as a recognizable brand.
You spend a large amount of money on advertising in fashion magazines. **Go to 27**.

You convince well-known celebrities to wear your jewllery and focus on product placement on TV programmes. **Go to 17**.

**8** You meet a small but successful firm of jewellery makers at the fair. They are very excited by your designs and the quality of your work. They invite you to go into partnership in the States. This will mean sharing the secret of your techniques. You decide to trust them and take up their offer. **Go to 14**.

You are flattered by their offer but think the risk is too great. **Go to 19**.

**9** The department store's offer guarantees you an income for the next two years. On the strength of this you become a limited company. You can now plan your next step. You continue to design and develop your range. You employ more people. **Go to 2**.

You focus on finding new customers for your existing designs .**Go to 21**.

**10** You realize that you need more money than your £3,000 to expand your business.
You go to the bank and ask them for a loan. **Go to 18**.

You approach family and friends to see if they are willing to finance you. **Go to 23**.

**11** Congratulations! The bank has accepted your business plan. You now have enough money to invest in your company's future.
You invest in a new workshop and equipment and work on perfecting your designs and a characteristic new logo. **Go to 17**.

You buy a smart car, invest in brochures, and entertain buyers in department stores. **Go to 4**.

**12** There is no snow this winter in the resorts where the chain has its shops. They return all their goods to you and you cannot meet your liabilities. You go bankrupt and lose everything.
*Disaster*

**13** The department store can now dictate terms to you. However, they promise continued business.
You stay with the store's exclusive contract and plan for the future. **Go to 35**.

You decide to leave the rat race and explore other options. **Go to 27**.

**14** Well done for trusting your judgement. Your acquaintances become dynamic business partners. You become an overnight success. You open a chain of jewellery shops and become rich, successful and happy.
*Triumph*

## Talking business

1 Fifty years ago, experts predicted that in the future people would work less, and have more free time for themselves and their families.

– As far as you know how true has this become?

– How likely is this to change in the future?

2 What are the consequences of a shorter working week likely to be on the following?

– salaries                  – competitiveness
– employment           – workers' timetables

3 How many hours a week do you think it is reasonable to work? What is a healthy balance between free time and the time we spend working?

## Listening

### Time for work

1 **3.1** Five people talk about a subject related to work. Listen and decide which person 1–5 is speaking in passages A–E.

| Person | Passage |
|---|---|
| 1 a project manager | ~~B~~ C |
| 2 a time-management expert | ~~C~~ B |
| 3 someone who has a job-share | ~~X~~ A |
| 4 an accountant / financial controller | E |
| 5 a company representative / salesperson | D |

rep. → kısaltılmış

2 Listen again, and answer questions 1–5 by choosing a, b, or c.

1 Which sentence best describes how the job-share works?
a One person works mornings and the other afternoons.
b They work alternate days.
c They each work half a week.

2 The time management expert says we should:
a deal with messages and phone calls immediately.
b avoid distractions during 'prime time'.
c take regular breaks.

3 The project manager:
a thinks they'll have to change the schedule.
b is determined to finish the project on time.
c doesn't want to disappoint an old customer.

4 The representative:
a found the meeting unsatisfactory.
b postponed the meeting to a later date.
c was late.

5 The accountant:
a is annoyed with his colleague.
b had checked the customer's bank references.
c asked for payment with the order.

3 In groups, discuss how you would handle the following situations diplomatically.

1 You had an important appointment for ten o'clock but it is now ten thirty and you are still sitting in reception. How can you show that you are unhappy, without getting angry or making yourself look foolish?

2 You have started working from home. Unfortunately, friends and family keep coming to see you during your working time. How can you prevent these interruptions, without upsetting anyone?

3 A new customer has placed a big order with a company. How can the company make sure it will be paid, without appearing suspicious or questioning the good faith of the new customer?

## Ways of expressing the future

1 Complete sentences 1–6 by selecting the most suitable form in italics for expressing the future.

1 Just look at this traffic! We *will / are going to* be late.

2 He *will / is going to* study sales and marketing.

3 What time *will / does* the next flight leave?

4 A: There's someone at the door.

   B: Oh, that *is going to / will* be the postman.

5 A: Can I phone for a taxi?

   B: Don't bother, I *'m going to / 'll give* you a lift.

6 She *will meet / is meeting* her new boss tomorrow at three o'clock.

2 Identify the forms which are used to:

a talk about timetables.

b make predictions.

c talk about a future plan which has already been decided.

d talk about arrangements.

e make a spontaneous decision / offer.

f make a deduction based on evidence.

ⓖ Grammar guide, page 143

3 There are further ways of expressing the future. Decide in which sentences a–f below the words in italics:

1 describe an action in progress in, or around a time in the future.

2 make a prediction based on usual or expected behaviour.

3 are followed by the present simple with a future meaning.

4 describe an activity that will be completed or achieved by a point in the future.

5 introduce something which was still in the future viewed from an earlier event.

6 express a plan or arrangement.

a If you'd like to wait, Mrs Wallace *should be* here in the next ten minutes.

b Can you deal with all my phone calls tomorrow? I*'ll be interviewing* all day.

c I *hope* she gets the job.

d The CEO *is to open* the new plant.

e At last! We*'ll have finished* by this time next week.

f I'm sorry, but we didn't think this decision *was going to* cause a problem.

4 Certain adjectives can convey a future meaning. Replace the words in italics with *bound*, *likely*, or *due*.

1 The presentation is *arranged* to begin at eleven o'clock.

2 It's *quite possible* that we won't get the components in time.

3 They are *certain* to blame us for their delivery problems.

5 Turn to tapescript [3.1] on page 154. Find other examples of forms used to express the future and say why they are used.

6 Look at the list of possible life and career milestones in the box below.

1 Choose six and add any others you wish. Which of these do you expect to have achieved in one, five, and ten years from now?

> finish higher education
> set up my own business
> marry a millionaire
> go into politics
> have a baby
> have a company car
> float my company on the stock exchange
> start a completely new career
> become famous
> write a book

2 Discuss with a partner, using an appropriate form of the future to say what:

– will be in progress

– you expect to happen

– you will have already achieved / done.

# Reading

## Beat the clock

1 How good do you think you are at managing your time? Do you always complete tasks before they are due, or do you leave everything until the last minute?

2 You are going to read an article by an expert on time management. Read the introduction and find out, according to the writer:

1 what problems poor time management can cause.

2 who is usually responsible for wasting our time.

> Time, like money is a limited resource. However, although it is possible to make more money, unfortunately you can't create more time; there are only twenty-four hours in a day. The inability to manage time effectively is often a big source of stress. Although frequently we may blame others for wasting our time, the most guilty party is usually ourselves.

3 The writer goes on to discuss the problems of three stereotypes of poor time managers.

1 Match the stereotypes to their definitions (a–c).
- 'Tomorrows'
- Disorganized types
- Poor delegators

a people who do not prepare
b people who insist on doing everything themselves
c people who never do anything straight away

2 What practical suggestions do you think the writer will give to help each of these three types?

4 Now read the article and see how many of your predictions were correct.

> *Work expands to fill the time available for its completion.*
> **C Northcote Parkinson**, academic and author

### Time wasters fall into a number of categories.

#### 'TOMORROWS'

'Tomorrows' cause themselves problems because they prefer to think about work rather than doing it. Such individuals *postpone* decisions so that, consequently, tomorrow becomes the busiest day of the week. Here are some tips for this type.

- Break huge tasks into smaller jobs. Set a *deadline* for completing the entire task and work on it a little bit every day.
- Draw up a 'to do' list of all the tasks you need to complete in the short term (i.e. within the next week), medium term (i.e. the next month), and the long term. Then each day, draw up a list of the things that you need 'to do today'.
- When planning your work *schedule*, attempt to balance *routine* tasks with the more enjoyable jobs. Combat paper shuffling by resolving to handle each piece of paper only once. Read it, act on it, file it or throw it away.

#### 'DISORGANIZED TYPES'

These individuals are immediately recognizable by the piles of paper on their desks. They are never on time for meetings and often spend a large part of their day hunting for files on their desks, and for messages and telephone numbers written on bits of paper scattered all over the office. This means they are always trying to make up for the time they have wasted. Typically they believe that creative minds are rarely tidy. Here are some tips for them.

- Plan your workload every day by *prioritizing* your work. Set up a system by colour-coding files and investing in a weekly, monthly and yearly planner chart.
- Create a 'to do' list at the start of each day. Review the list at the end of the day.
- Stick to one task at a time and make sure you finish it. If you fall behind, do what you can to catch up.
- Identify your best time for working, when your energy levels are high and during those periods carry out your complex tasks. Save the trivial, routine tasks for non-prime time.
- Make sure all messages, notes, and telephone calls are recorded in one place.
- Try to batch phone calls or group trivial and routine tasks and tackle them as one task.

### 'POOR DELEGATORS'

These are individuals who waste time doing work that could easily be done by someone else.

Typically this is because they lack trust in others and the ability to say 'no' and so take on too much. For people working from home and on their own, there is a need for them to set up a network of people who might help them with routine, trivial tasks or less important tasks. Some of the following might help in this process.

- Remember that delegation does not equal abdication.
- Having delegated a job, leave the person to get on with it.
- Always take time to explain what is required. Check the other person is clear about what they need to do and ask if they anticipate any problems.
- As soon as you become aware that a deadline is unrealistic, re-negotiate, *delegate* or let someone know.
- Avoid taking on unnecessary work and learn to say 'no' politely and assertively.

*The Sunday Times*

5  What kind of person might be speaking in sentences 1–9?

1  If you want a job done well then you have to do it yourself. ................

2  Now where did I put that address? I wrote it on a cigarette packet, so it must be somewhere. ................

3  I'm not sure what to do with this letter. I'll look at it again later. ................

4  I don't feel like doing the accounts today; let's make a start tomorrow. ................

5  Some days I leave work and I wonder what I have achieved. ................

6  It's such a big job; I really don't know where to begin. ................

7  Well, I'm really busy but I'll do it if you think nobody else can. ................

8  What I like best is visiting customers but I hate sending out letters and bills. ................

9  I must have a quick look at my e-mail; it'll only take a minute. ................

6  Which personality type best describes you? Which tips would help you manage your own time better?

7  Match the definitions below to the words in italics in the text.

1  the very last date by which a task must be completed ................

2  give some of one's own responsibilities to someone else, e.g. a subordinate ................

3  selecting the most important or urgent things to do first ................

4  delay an event until a later date ................

5  involving a programme of stages or commitments with fixed times and objectives ................

6  a regular, predictable order of activities ................

8  Complete the sentences below by using an appropriate form of the phrasal verbs in the box.

| set up | catch up | break down |
|---|---|---|
| fall behind | draw up | put off |
| take on | get on with | make up |

1  We have ................ far too much work lately; I just don't know how we are going to manage.

2  The bad weather means that we have ................ schedule on the building contract.

3  I think we should ................ a meeting as soon as possible. Could you fix a suitable date?

4  It's time we let them know about the delays, it's embarrassing, but we can't ................ it ................ any longer.

5  If everyone works extra shifts we should be able to ................ .

6  Is it OK if I leave early today, Mrs Jones? I'll ................ the time on Monday.

7  I have ................ a list of things we need to do.

8  I've analysed the problem and have ................ it ................ into five different areas.

9  You should spend less time gossiping and ................ your work.

## Language in use

### Requests and offers

1 Complete the sentences below with expressions from the box. Which phrases can be used in more than one sentence?

> Do you think you could …
> I was wondering …
> So if you'd like to …
> I'd like you to …
>
> Could you ask …
> Would you mind …
> Can you ring …

1 ............... if you could spare me two minutes.

2 ............... help me sort out these invoices.

3 ............... Richard to organize coffee and biscuits for the conference room?

4 ............... them and tell them the order is on its way?

5 ............... organizing the collection for Mrs Bevan?

6 ............... deal with this straight away.

7 ............... ask Anna to make this a priority?

2 **3.2** Listen and check your answers.

1 Which questions involve telling someone else what to do?

2 Which of these questions would you use if you were afraid the answer might be 'no'?

3 Which phrases are followed by the *infinitive* (*to* +verb), the *base form* (verb without *to*), and the *gerund* (verb+–*ing*)?

4 Which request could you agree to by answering 'Of course not.'?

3 **3.3** Re-arrange the words to form offers and promises. Then listen and check your answers.

1 the – I'll – it – of – put – at – list – top – my.

2 you – would – me – it –to – like – handle?

3 with – immediately – shall – deal – I – it?

4 take – me – for – care – let – of – you – that.

5 about – that – how – if – I – with – deal?

6 I – why – sort – don't – out – it?

7 better – I'd – with – that – straight away – deal.

4 The following orders are not very polite.

1 Express each one as a polite request using the prompts in brackets.

a Post these letters! (think)

b File these documents! (mind)

c Tidy up the office! (I'd like)

d Answer this fax! (could)

e Sign this letter! (if / like)

f Take me to the airport! (wondering)

2 Now express each order as a polite offer.

3 Try to answer each request and offer appropriately.

5 Write down five or six tasks you'd like someone to do. Working in pairs, take it in turns to make and reply to requests.

### Pronunciation: stress of auxiliaries

1 Look at these replies. Which requests in **1** opposite do they answer?

1 I *am* rather busy. Could we meet later?

2 I *could*, but he doesn't like taking orders from me.

3 Actually I *would* mind. I hate asking people for money.

4 I *will*, just as soon as I've finished this.

2 **3.4** Listen. How are the words in italics pronounced?

3 Stressing words which are usually unstressed emphasizes them. Why do you think the words in italics are stressed?

4 In pairs, read the following mini-dialogues. Underline the words which change their pronunciation according to their stress.

1 A: Do you think we'll reach a decision today?
   B: Yes, I do. We have all the information we need now.

2 A: I'll have your report by the end of the day, won't I?
   B: Yes, you will. I'm finishing it off now.

3 A: I don't think he was there. I didn't see him.
   B: He was. He arrived late and sat at the back.

4 A: Can you show me how the fax machine works please? I haven't used this type before.
   B: Yes, of course I can. You press this button …

# Speaking

## Fire-fighting

1  It is Monday morning. Jude James is PA to the managing director of a London-based company. Study her diary and the notes on her desk and notice board and compile a 'to do' list of tasks.

**Monday**
Visitors from Brussels. Richard to meet Eurostar at 14.15.
Book restaurant for dinner. 7–8 people Da Cosimo? Talk to Mr Lemonnier about job ad.

**Tuesday**
Get card signed for Mrs Bevan. Buy present. (add £50 from petty cash). Brochure to printers – final deadline. Confirm flights for Astrid Winter. South American sales trip.

**Wednesday**
Deadline for job ad. Check details with Mr Lemonnier?

**Thursday**
Presentation in conference room P.M.

**Friday**
Mrs Bevan's leaving party.

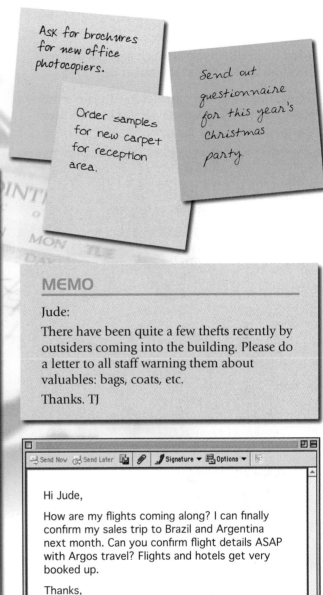

Ask for brochures for new office photocopiers.

Order samples for new carpet for reception area.

Send out questionnaire for this year's Christmas party.

**MEMO**

Jude:

There have been quite a few thefts recently by outsiders coming into the building. Please do a letter to all staff warning them about valuables: bags, coats, etc.

Thanks. TJ

Hi Jude,

How are my flights coming along? I can finally confirm my sales trip to Brazil and Argentina next month. Can you confirm flight details ASAP with Argos travel? Flights and hotels get very booked up.

Thanks,

Astrid.

2  Decide which three items on your list have to be dealt with immediately and which are less important.

3  Work in pairs. It's 9.30 on Monday morning.

**Student A:** You are the Office Manager. Jude is ill and won't be back for the rest of the week. You need to give instructions to a temporary secretary who has come to help out while Jude is away. Decide which tasks he / she can do and which ones will have to be delegated. Explain what to do and what the priorities are.

**Student B:** You are a temporary secretary from an employment agency. You have been called in to help out at Jude's office. Ask Student A to help you decide what your priorities are. Sound enthusiastic and ready to take charge of what needs to be done.

> **Plans are nothing; planning is everything.**
> **Dwight D. Eisenhower**, US president 1953–61

# Writing

## Can't pay, won't pay?

1 What is the difference between a debtor and a creditor? Which would you rather be?

2 Companies often have problems with late or non-payment of bills. Put these excuses in order from the most to the least creative.

1 I can't talk to you now ... we're having the office party.

2 The cheque's in the post.

3 You need to speak to Mr Rogers. I'm afraid he isn't in today.

4 I'm sorry, can you be patient a bit longer? I'm waiting for a client to settle his account with us.

3 Can you think of any other reasons for not paying a bill on time?

4 Read extracts A–C and find out:

1 who is writing to whom.

2 any terms and conditions connected with the supply.

5 Why do you think the invoice is still unpaid? How could the supplier have protected itself?

6 Which one is from:

1 a first letter of reminder?

2 a second letter of reminder and revised invoice?

3 a final demand for payment?

**A**

I am writing to you regarding our invoice JAC/638. According to our records the invoice, which fell due last Friday, is still outstanding. We feel sure that this is a simple oversight on your part.

As you will remember, we offered you 10% discount on condition that you paid our invoice within thirty days. Therefore, unless we receive payment within five working days we shall be obliged to issue a new invoice for the full amount of the goods supplied. We look forward to receiving your remittance.

If, in the meantime, you have already settled the original invoice please disregard this letter.

**B**

I am writing to you once again concerning the above invoice which remains outstanding. We have received no reply to our previous requests for payment dated 12 July and 19 July.

On purchasing the equipment you benefited from a 10% discount on our list price on condition that you undertook to settle within thirty days of receipt of our invoice. However, as of today, your account is ninety days in arrears.

As a gesture of goodwill I am prepared to give you a final opportunity to settle your account. However, unless we receive full payment within the next seven days, we will initiate proceedings to recover the debt, which will involve you in considerable legal costs.

**C**

I am writing once again regarding payment of our invoice which is now six weeks overdue. Both our original letter and letter of reminder have gone unanswered. However, if you are experiencing difficulty in paying your account, please contact me so that we may discuss alternative ways of settling it.

Under the terms of our contract you promised to clear the original invoice within thirty days. We supplied you with goods in good faith and are disappointed that you have not respected your side of the agreement. Accordingly, we have issued a new invoice for the full amount. We trust that you will give this matter your immediate attention and hope to hear from you within five working days.

**7** Read the extracts again.

1 Find the words and expressions which mean:

a became payable ...............

b a mistake by forgetting to do something
...............

c take no notice ...............

d agreed / promised ...............

e begin legal action to get our money back
...............

f proof of my good intention ...............

g kept your part of the deal ...............

h sincerely believe ...............

i the subject under discussion ...............

2 Which deal with the idea of:

a being late?

b paying?

c contract conditions?

**8** The letters are all formal. However, the tone changes from sympathetic to threatening. Find examples in the text to support this.

**9** You are going to write a series of letters to a client who has not paid an outstanding invoice or account. Work in groups of three or four.

1 Make notes and decide:

– what business you are in

– what goods or services you supplied

– when they were supplied and under what circumstances

– what the terms and conditions of the sale were; e.g. length of credit, special discounts

– the time that has passed since you supplied the goods

– how long you have been dealing with the client

– what relationship your companies have previously had

– if you think the non-payment is deliberate or simply a mistake

– what action you are prepared to take to have your account settled.

2 Alternatively, turn to File 1 on page 126. In your groups write the first letter accompanying your original invoice. Then decide who will write the first reminder, the second reminder, and the final demand.

# In conversation

## A matter of time

**1** Complete the exchanges by matching each sentence (1–7) with a reply (a–g).

1 Hi, Gerald, I haven't seen you for ages.

2 Is this the first time you've been to New York?

3 I've spent hours preparing for this meeting.

4 How much longer do you need?

5 How long does it take to get there?

6 It really is time we left.

7 How long does it last?

a Haven't you heard? It's been called off.

b It starts at 8.00 and finishes at 10.30.

c But check-in isn't for another three hours.

d No, I spent three years here as a student.

e Yes, it's been years, hasn't it?

f Well it took me about five hours by car last time.

g I should have finished it by tomorrow.

**2** **3.5** Listen and check your answers. Think of a context for each of the exchanges.

**3** Which question in **1** asks about:

1 the amount of time someone needs to finish a task? ......

2 the time needed to complete a journey? ......

3 the duration of a performance? ......

**4** What is the difference between the use of the verbs *take*, *last* and *spend*?

**5** Working in pairs, create mini-dialogues for 1–6.

1 You want to know the duration of a flight to Berlin. What do you ask the travel agent?

2 You bump into someone you last saw at school. How do you greet the person?

3 You left a CD player to be repaired but it isn't ready. You want to know how much more time is needed to complete the work.

4 You are speaking to a visitor to your country and you want to know if this is their first visit.

5 You realize someone has just told you a lie. How do you say you no longer trust him / her?

6 You think the class deserves a coffee break straight away.

# Case study

## Just in time

1 Read the information about critical path analysis and study the diagram. How useful is this technique for the following everyday tasks?

- cooking a three-course meal in the shortest possible time
- planning a route to work
- washing, ironing, and doing the housework
- decorating a room

### Critical path analysis

This is a technique for timing and organizing projects.

- Divide the project into different subject areas.
- Break each subject area into its different stages.
- Decide how long each stage will take and the order of the stages.
- Decide which things from each stage can be done at the same time.
- Identify when the quiet or 'dead' periods will be in the schedule.
- Work backwards from a future date to see if the plan is realistic / achievable.
- Work forwards from a current date to see when the project will be completed.

2 Read the situation. What things could possibly go wrong?

You specialize in organizing conferences. The World Video Games Confederation wants you to organize next year's award ceremony. This event is considered in the industry as the Oscars of computer games. The WVGC has asked you to find a suitable venue, such as a hotel or famous building, and to arrange entertainment and a charity dinner on the night of the ceremony. Tickets cost $2,000 each and about 800 guests are expected. The event will be hosted by the famous comedian Sammy Webb.

3 Work in groups and study the 'to do' list. After each item is an estimate of the time which it will take.

1 Produce a schedule which shows how the event can be organized in the most efficient way.

2 When will you need to start in order to keep the preparation period as short as possible?

* send out requests for prize nominations (2 weeks)
* deadline for nominations (6 weeks after requests sent out)
* print invitations for celebrities (2 weeks)
* make a shortlist of venues (2 weeks)
* make final selection of venue with sponsor (1 week)
* book venue (8 months notice usually required)
* approach caterers to tender for charity dinner (2 months before the event)
* decide menu and check with sponsors (2 weeks)
* produce and print tickets and programmes (3 weeks)
* invite celebrities to present the different awards (6 months before the event)
* send out tickets and programmes (8 weeks before event)
* decorate and arrange venue (1 week)
* contact TV chains about filming awards (as soon as the date and venue are known)
* visit venues and ask for quotations (6 weeks)
* advertise event in trade magazines (5 months before the event)

4 Present your critical path analysis to another group.

5 Read about Murphy's law. Do you have an equivalent saying in your country?

Murphy's law says that anything that can go wrong will go wrong at the worst possible time.

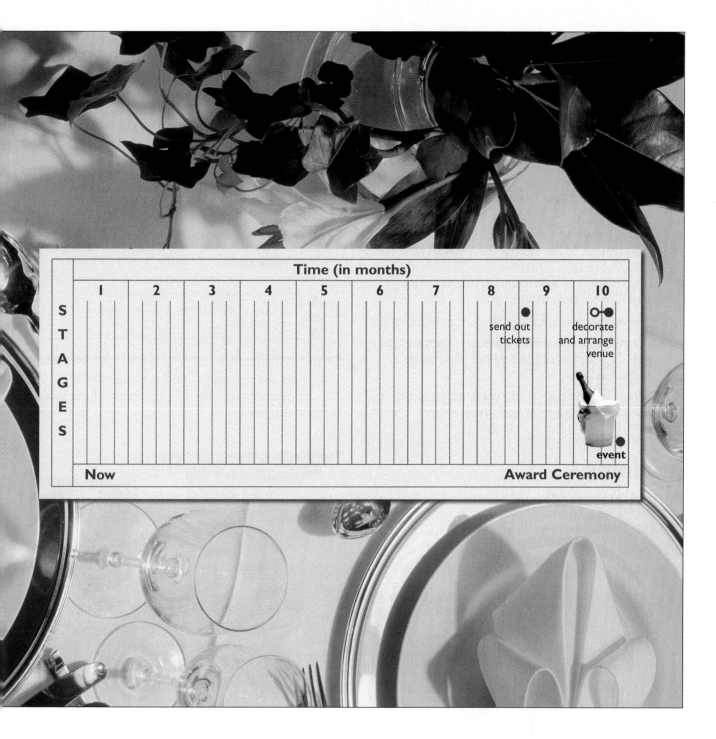

6  [3.6]  Listen to four problems which have come up with the organization of the ceremony.

1  Summarize each in your own words.

| Timing | Problem |
|---|---|
| 1  (4 months before) | |
| 2  (2 months before) | |
| 3  (6 weeks before) | |
| 4  (1 week before) | |

2  Discuss the problems and put them in order from the most to the least serious. How much difference does the timing make?

3  How will these problems affect your planning of the event? What could you do to minimize or deal with the difficulties they cause?

# 4 Going global

## Talking business

1   In the age of the multi-national corporation, more and more people are expected to work abroad.

  - Which three countries would you most / least like to work in?
  - What three things in your country would you miss most?
  - What would be the maximum time you would be prepared to live outside your country?

2   Doing business in a different culture or language can lead to misunderstandings.

  1   Try and work out the answers to the cultural quiz.
  2   Compare answers with a partner. Then turn to File 20 on page 133 to find out what really happened.
  3   What lessons can companies wanting to export to different countries learn from this?

 **A**   Why do you think one particular airline had problems predicting numbers of passengers on flights from Japan to Hawaii?

 **B**   Why do you think Coca-Cola found it difficult to introduce two-litre bottles in Spain?

 **C**   What do you think went wrong when Kentucky Fried Chicken's slogan *'finger lickin' good'* was translated into Chinese and then back into English?

 **D**   Why shouldn't you give handkerchiefs or cutlery as gifts in many Latin American countries?

4   How can companies find out more about consumer preferences? What research methods could they use?

## Listening

### Perfect placement

1   Read the text about fung shui.

  1   How well-known is it in your country?
  2   What is your immediate reaction to it?

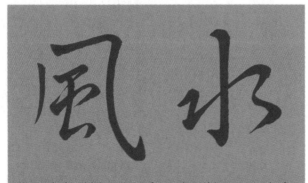

Fung shui, which comes from the Chinese words for 'wind' and 'water', has been described as the 'art of perfect placement'. It is over 4000 years old but its principles are still important today. Fung shui is a system of principles which may be taken into account when designing or positioning buildings. Fung shui experts, called geomancers, are often consulted before new buildings are built. They check the flow of energy in relation to spatial arrangement and orientation.

2   **4.1**   Anne Baldwin is talking to Nancy Chou, a fung shui expert. Listen to part A and answer questions 1–4.

  1   How does Nancy say fung shui may be useful?
  2   What example does she give?
  3   What is special about Hong Kong?
  4   How did some people react to the new airport?

**3** Listen to part B and mark the statements below true (*T*) or false (*F*). Explain your answers.

1 Property developers should remember the beliefs of their clients. .....

2 Some new buildings in Taipei have stayed empty because they are too expensive. .....

3 A restaurant failed to attract customers because of poor advertising. .....

4 Although fung shui is popular in the West, nobody has used it seriously in business. .....

**4** In part C, Nancy talks about how to arrange your office following the principles of fung shui. Listen to what she says, then look at the picture opposite. In what ways does it obey / break the rules of fung shui?

**5** Fung shui became popular in Britain in the 1990s.

1 Can you think of any other aspects of Eastern culture which are well established in the West?

2 Why do you think Westerners have adopted them?

## Language study

### Routines and habits

**1** To express routine in the present, we use the present simple along with a frequency expression. Put these words and phrases in order of frequency.

| | | |
|---|---|---|
| hardly ever | from time to time | rarely |
| as a rule | seldom | most of the time |
| generally | now and again | once in a while |

**2** *Always* has a number of uses. Complete sentences 1–3 with endings a–c. Which verb form accompanies *always* in each sentence?

1 He *always* cycles to work ... .....

2 We could *always* take a taxi, ... .....

3 She's *always* parking in my space, ... .....

a ... if you'd rather not walk.

b ... which is extremely annoying.

c ... for the exercise.

**3** Which sentence:

1 describes a frequently-repeated action?

2 describes an everyday habit or routine?

3 introduces a possible alternative?

**4** *Will* and *would* are used to describe characteristic behaviour. Which sentence (1–3) describes:

a an everyday habit or routine?

b expected behaviour based on past experience?

c habitual action during a specified period in the past?

1 She'll talk on the phone for hours at a time.

2 When I was a student I *would* work very late in the evenings.

3 He *will* ask difficult questions, so make sure you're well prepared.

**5** To describe past habit and routines, we can also use forms of *used to*.

1 Match the examples of *used to* in sentences a–c to their meanings in the box below.

| |
|---|
| become accustomed |
| a discontinued past habit or state |
| be accustomed to something |

a People *used to* build on the south side of a hill.

b Foreign developers will have to get *used to* following local customs.

c I'm *used to* working in chaos.

2 What form of the verb follows each example of *used to*?

3 In which sentence(s) is *used to* an adjective?

ⓖ **Grammar guide, page 149**

**6** Rewrite the sentences using a form of *used to*.

1 In the old days, everyone wore jackets and ties to work.

2 When Markus first lived in England, he found driving on the left difficult.

3 I don't have much experience of dealing with computers.

4 I found it hard to adapt to the new computer system.

5 Isn't that the house where you once lived?

**7** Describe how business and the way of life in your country has changed in the last fifty years.

# Reading

## A world of beauty

**1**  Look at the business tip, then scan the text.

   1  Which western multinational companies does it mention?

   2  What is the significance of these numbers?

| 600 | $995 bn | £2.7 bn | 50 miles |
|---|---|---|---|
| 365 m | 235 | 80 m | 200 |

> ### Globalization
>
> A strategy in which companies aim to sell their products and services all around the world. Driven by the convergence of consumer tastes from Tbilisi to Timbuktu, globalization presents companies with opportunities of achieving economies of scale.

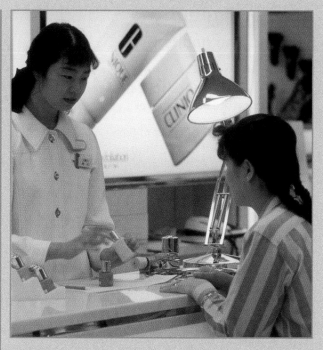

L'Oréal, the French cosmetics giant, is hoping to take advantage of one of the world's most fertile emerging markets. On the 20th floor of its China HQ in Shanghai is a bathroom where L'Oréal researchers have watched more than 600 women taking a shower. The study's purpose is to discover how Chinese consumers, unfamiliar until recently with western grooming, use the make-up and hair-and skin-care products the organization is introducing to a nation that has traditionally had little use for luxury.

'Pharmacies here have changed a lot over the past ten years,' says Paolo Gasparini, Managing Director of L'Oréal China. 'It used to be dried animals and plants, but it's moving very fast.' In the People's Republic, the use of deodorant and perfume is very unusual and pale skin is the beauty ideal women strive for. 'The people and culture are so different here that we have to be very prudent,' says Gasparini. But the company – with brands that include L'Oréal Paris, Giorgio Armani fragrances, Maybelline New York, and Lancôme make-up – is determined to be at the forefront of China's latest cultural revolution. Unlike other aspirational western brands such as Coca-Cola and McDonald's, which offer a single cultural icon, L'Oréal can offer Asian consumers French chic, New York attitude, and Italian elegance. Already about 80% of L'Oréal's £7.5 bn turnover is generated outside France and 40% outside Europe. L'Oréal, like many other businesses expanding into China, believes the market has outstanding potential.

The government's more open economic outlook, combined with a growing urban population which currently stands at 365 m, and a GDP put at $995 bn, have combined to produce a consumer base with disposable income and a taste for modern, western goods. Other western multinational corporations have been expanding throughout China too. Beijing has the distinction of being the site of the largest Kentucky Fried Chicken restaurant in the world. McDonald's, the rival fast-food chain, operates more than 235 outlets in 41 Chinese cities, and earlier this year hospitality group Hyatt opened the third tallest hotel in the world in Shanghai.

Last year, the Chinese cosmetics market was worth £2.7 bn and Gasparini estimates that in the People's Republic there are 80 m purchasers of L'Oréal products. At the same time, the company, together with other European businesses including Glaxo Wellcome and Siemens, has taken advantage of the new economic development zone 50 miles outside Shanghai, to build a production facility. The factory is the culmination of a push into China that began in 1993, when L'Oréal put together a small team in Hong Kong to test the Chinese market. The company had been evaluating the market for years, but until the early 1990s it considered average incomes too low, and distribution channels too poor, to merit a launch.

**2** Complete a–f in the chart below, showing how L'Oréal positions some of its products.

| Product | Image | Typical retail outlet |
|---------|-------|----------------------|
| L'Oréal Paris | a | b |
| Giorgio Armani | c | — |
| d | NY attitude | e |
| Lancôme | — | f |

**3** Read the text again and answer the questions.

1 What does L'Oréal's 'bathroom' research hope to achieve?

2 Why do you think Paolo Gasparini talks about Chinese pharmacies?

3 Why is China such an attractive market for foreign businesses?

4 What has China done to encourage foreign businesses to set up near Shanghai?

5 Why didn't L'Oréal enter the Chinese market earlier?

6 How did L'Oréal plan its entry into the Chinese market?

7 How useful has L'Oréal's joint venture with the Suzhou medical college been?

8 According to Paolo Gasparini, what is the difficulty and importance of recruiting good local staff?

**4** Match a word from box A with one from box B to form collocations from the text.

| A | | |
|---|---|---|
| outstanding | economic | production |
| distribution | development | consumer |
| joint | multinational | disposable |
| exclusive | | |

| B | | | |
|---|---|---|---|
| corporation | outlet | facility | outlook |
| base | income | venture | potential |
| channel | zone | | |

**5** Complete sentences 1–9 with an appropriate collocation from **4**.

1 The government has created a ..... / ..... to attract foreign investors to the region.

2 We really need to attract more customers; our ..... / ..... is simply too narrow.

3 They should only sell this perfume through ..... / ..... like top department stores.

4 We need to build another ..... / ..... to cope with the increased demand.

5 The ..... / ..... is poor; there is high inflation and fears of a recession.

6 After paying for food and rent, low-income earners have very little ..... / ..... for luxuries.

7 We should consider a ..... / ..... with a local partner as a way of entering the market.

8 The ..... / ..... is far too complicated, we should consider appointing a wholesaler.

9 This market shows ..... / ..... ; it's an opportunity we can't miss.

**6** Read the quotation below from Theodore Levitt.

1 What do you think he means by *idiosyncratic differences* and *universal drives*?

2 How far does what you have read prove or disagree with what he says?

3 What universal drives do companies L'Oréal, McDonald's and Coca-Cola satisfy?

> ❜Global companies must forget the idiosyncratic differences between countries and cultures and instead concentrate on satisfying universal drives.❜
>
> **Theodore Levitt**, marketing expert

---

In the following two years the company tested about 200 products and has recently launched a joint venture with the medical college in Suzhou. The research revealed some surprising results. For example, Asian hair is more porous than the European variety, so dye products need a different formulation. An extensive programme of research and development encouraged L'Oréal to launch both its international brands and more technical products throughout China. Maybelline is positioned as a mass-market name available in supermarkets and department stores. L'Oréal Paris is on offer in department stores only, while Lancôme is sold in just the most exclusive outlets.

Despite its success, L'Oréal, like other western investors, is facing commercial and cultural hurdles in China. 'This country is not familiar with marketing, so it is a huge job to train and keep clever young people,' says Gasparini. 'My priority is to take care of our staff; the battle will be won by the company with the best people.'

*The Sunday Times*

## Language in use

### Speaking with conviction

1 The Internet is probably the most important development in communication since the television.

 – How often do people in your class use e-mail and the Internet?

 – How have e-mail and the Internet changed the way we work and do business?

 – Have these changes always been for the better?

2 **4.2** John Green is taking part in a debate about the Internet in business: '*Is the Internet a blessing or a curse?*' He has just one minute to put his views across. Listen and decide which side of the debate John is on.

 1 According to John, what effect has the Internet had?

 2 What are his views on the Internet as a way of conducting business with the outside world?

 3 How does John feel about the amount of information that is available on the Internet?

3 Listen again and complete the sentences from the recording.

 1 So ............... for our everyday working lives?

 2 It means ............... ; the loss of ............... ; and ............... of information.

 3 I ............... that most natural business relationships are ............... , not ............... .

 4 ............... to measure and judge any future partner.

 5 ............... there are millions of impressive websites which provide useful information, ............... behind them?

 6 The web is susceptible to ............... and ............... .

 7 Providing personal details is risky if ............... .

 8 And finally, if we ask ourselves the question, '............... ?', the answer is 'nothing'.

 9 It's only a source of information, ............... , but much less reliable.

4 Read the business tip opposite about the art of rhetoric. Find examples in sentences 1–9 above.

5 Turn to the tapescript on page 156 and see if you can find other examples of these techniques.

### Pronunciation: /ʒ/, /ʃ/, /dʒ/, /tʃ/

1 **4.3** Listen to these four words from the listening passage and identify the easily confused sounds.

| /ʒ/ | /ʃ/ | /dʒ/ | /tʃ/ |
|---|---|---|---|
| inva**si**on | relation**ship** | **judge** | appro**ach** |
| | | | |
| | | | |
| | | | |
| | | | |

2 Unfortunately it is not always clear how a word should be pronounced from the way it is written. In pairs place each word from the box in the correct column of the table above according to the sound.

| | | | |
|---|---|---|---|
| virtual | sure | Asian | protectionism |
| encourage | question | urge | globalization |
| fortunately | message | information | |
| measure | future | television | |

3 **4.4** Listen and check your answers.

# Speaking

## One-minute debates

**1** You have to give a one-minute reply to John in which you present the advantages of the Internet. Using the notes to help you, brainstorm further arguments that you can use to put your case.

— stay in contact more easily

— do business more quickly

— faster than the post, more convenient than faxes, instant response

— on-line discussions cut down the need for face-to-face meetings

— paper-free offices

— allows people to tele-work

— good for customers and encourages competition

— cannot be 'un-invented', so needs to be used more wisely

**2** Now give your one-minute reply. Work in pairs. Your partner should listen and note which of the rhetorical devices you use from the business tip below.

### Rhetoric

**Persuasively presenting your views**

Speakers often use:

– lists of three
  e.g. *'Government of the people, by the people, for the people.'* (President Lincoln)

– rhetorical questions to produce an effect rather than to get an answer
  e.g. *'So what is to be done?'* (Lenin)

– adverbs to reinforce what they say
  e.g. *I strongly urge you to act now.*

– contrasting pair of ideas
  e.g. *'Man is born free and everywhere is in chains.'* (Jean-Jacques Rousseau)

– alliteration, where two or more words in succession begin with the same letter
  e.g. *the terrible twins*

– metaphors to make their language more memorable
  e.g. *The office was a beehive of activity.*

– similes to make their language more memorable.
  e.g. *His horse was as black as coal.*

**3** Read through the propositions below and decide whether you are broadly in favour or against them.

**1** In the long term, globalization will benefit everyone.
  for ☐  against ☐

**2** We worry too much about the environment and not enough about business.
  for ☐  against ☐

**3** It is the responsibility of government to control the activities of business.
  for ☐  against ☐

**4** Workers should be able to move freely between countries with no restriction.
  for ☐  against ☐

**4** Look at the business tip on debating techniques. For each proposition, find at least one other student who agrees with you and brainstorm ideas which will support your argument.

### Debating techniques

**Preparation**

– Be clear about which side of the argument you are on.

– Brainstorm the major points in support of your argument.

– Support your argument with strong statistics, examples and sources.

– Consider the arguments your opponent will put forward.

– Be ready to think quickly under pressure.

**During the debate**

– Listen carefully to your opponent.

– Have strong answers ready for each of the opponent's arguments.

– Address the chairperson and audience.

– Choose the right moment in the debate to present each of your points.

– Use persuasive and rhetorical language. Do not allow yourself to become emotional.

**5** Divide into groups for and against the first proposition. Then organize a debate. Use as many of the rhetorical devices as you can.

**6** Now do the same for the other propositions.

# Writing

## Positive spin

1 Adverbs can be used with verbs or adjectives to make language sound more convincing. Match the beginnings of sentences 1–5 with their endings a–e.

1 Both sides are *entirely* ... ......

2 They *wholeheartedly* ... ......

3 They apologized ... ......

4 The new guidelines which have been drawn up are *completely* ... ......

5 When I learnt that she had broken her side of the agreement, I *immediately* ... ......

a ... satisfied with the outcome of the negotiations.

b ... unsatisfactory and need to be rewritten.

c ... withdrew my offer.

d ... welcomed the new proposals.

e ... *profusely* for the misunderstanding.

2 In written or more formal English, adverbs are often used to introduce sentences. Replace the phrases in italics in 1–5 with one of the adverbs from the box.

| | | |
|---|---|---|
| admittedly | clearly | regrettably |
| accordingly | hopefully | |

1 *If all goes well*, you should receive the package early next week.

2 *It was a shame that* I didn't receive your message before leaving the office.

3 *It's obvious that* we should have checked their references before supplying them with the goods.

4 *We accept that* we were partly responsible for the misunderstanding.

5 *As a direct result* we decided to introduce new quality-control procedures.

3 Flavia's Natural Foods, FNF, produces a range of bottled sauces made from organically-grown vegetables. Its founder, Flavia Abrahams, is well-known for her environmental campaigns.

1 Recently Flavia contacted Carrie Phelps, a PR consultant. Read the press release which Carrie has written. What bad publicity has FNF received?

2 How does Carrie try to show that FNF is an ethical organization?

3 Now complete the text with adverbs from **1** and **2**.

As faithful customers, you will already be aware that we take great pride in our products, which we consider to be 1 ................ organic. We only use Mother Earth's resources as She intended them to be used.

2 ................ , we learnt recently that a small quantity of the tomatoes used in some of the pasta sauces in our Partnership range have been contaminated. This contamination was caused by chemical sprays blowing over from a neighbouring farm.

3 ................ , there is no excuse for the occurrence of such an incident, and strict measures are now being introduced to control the distance of our crops from non-organic ones. 4 ................ , in this way we will be able to ensure that this type of accident never happens again.

Even though 98% of our tomatoes were 5 ................ unaffected, we 6 ................ took action and have now withdrawn all the sauces from supermarket shelves. Products which may have contained even the slightest trace of chemicals have also been destroyed.

We, at FNF, would like to take this opportunity to thank Foodwatch for its vigilance and for bringing this story to everyone's attention, and we 7 ................ support this organization in its quest to improve what we have on our plates.

4 In her press release, Carrie has to explain some negative information to the public. How does she make the following negative facts more positive?

1 2% of FNF's tomatoes have been sprayed with chemicals.

2 Foodwatch has severely criticized FNF for selling 'organic' products sprayed with chemicals.

3 Contaminated products in the Partnership range have been sold to the general public.

**5** Carrie has now been asked to write a press release for Quayside Furniture, a company which received negative publicity in a recent TV documentary on working practices.

1 Work in pairs. Student A, turn to File 11 on page 129. Student B, turn to File 26 on page 134.

2 In pairs, compare your information. Find an argument in favour of Quayside for each of the criticisms made by the TV documentary.

3 Which facts might you include in a press release on behalf of the company? Are there any you would choose not to mention?

> **Positive spin**
>
> – Turn bad news into an opportunity for publicity and contact with the public.
>
> – Show that you are ready to admit mistakes and learn from them.
>
> – Emphasize what is being done to solve the problem.
>
> – Interpret the statistics so that they support your argument.

**6** Now write a press release to present Quayside in a better light using some of the techniques you have studied.

# In conversation

## Food and drink

**1** Label the pictures with the food preparation methods from the box below.

| fry | boil | grill | bake |
| chill | steam | freeze | |

**2** Look at the adjectives in the box below which are often used to describe food.

1 Can you add any to the list?

2 Which adjectives best describe your country's cuisine?

| sweet and sour | spicy | plain | rich |

**3** Study these exchanges. Which countries do you think they take place in?

1 A: Could you tell me what *crottins de chèvre chauds* is, please?

B: Yes, it's grilled goats cheese served on toast, with a side salad.

2 A: What's *tagliatelle alla matriciana*?

B: Well, it's a kind of pasta, like a flat spaghetti, with a spicy tomato sauce.

**4** What local dishes would you recommend visitors to your country? Describe them to a partner.

**5** Decide whether sentences 1–10. would be spoken by a host (*H*), a guest (*G*), or a waiter (*W*).

1 Can I tempt you with some cheese? .....

2 Mm, this is delicious! .....

3 And for your main course? .....

4 How is your meal, madam? .....

5 How would you like it done? .....

6 Shall I ask for the bill? .....

7 Still or sparkling, sir? .....

8 What would you like to drink with your meal? .....

9 Are you ready to order? .....

10 Do you fancy some oysters? .....

**6** Now match 1–10 with their replies (a–j). Then label the replies *H*, *G*, or *W*.

a It's really tasty, thank you. ..... .....

b A glass of dry white wine, please. ..... .....

c I think so, I'd like to start with the prawns. ..... .....

d I'm afraid they don't agree with me. ..... .....

e No thank you, I really couldn't manage anything else. ..... .....

f Still is fine thank you. ..... .....

g I'll have the breast of duck, please. ..... .....

h Pink in the middle, please. ..... .....

i Well, actually, it's a local speciality. ..... .....

j No, I insist, this is on me. ..... .....

**7** **4.5** Now listen to the dialogue and check your answers.

**8** Work in groups of three: host, guest, and waiter. On the menu are the dishes you identified in **4**. Now role-play the meal in the restaurant.

# Case study

## Greenglade soft drinks

1 Study these advertisements for the same product in two different local markets. What differences do you notice and how could you explain them?

1 Look at the business tip. What roles within a company would need to be involved when preparing a product for a particular market?

2 How important is it to get the correct marketing mix when adapting a product to a local market?

### The Marketing Mix

**The Four Ps**

**Product** What are its characteristics; its brand name; its packaging?

**Price** How much will customers pay?

**Place** Where and how will it be sold?

**Promotion** How is the customer going to know about the product?

2 Read the information about the British company Greenglade and its current UK advertising campaign. Then list the reasons why you think the company may have decided to advertise the product Three Feathers in this way.

Greenglade is a British company based in Britain, which produces soft drinks based on a syrup made from concentrated apple and pear juice. All its fruit is grown in traditional English orchards. Its most successful product is Three Feathers, a bitter-sweet fizzy drink. In Britain, Greenglade produces and packages its own drinks at its plant. These are distributed by Greenglade's own distinctive lorries. A third of its production is delivered directly to hotels and retail outlets. The rest is delivered to a nationwide network of distributors.

Its recent advertising campaign is based around characters from the story of Robin Hood and set in the forest. All the characters are dressed in green, apart from Maid Marion who wears a blue dress. They all use the 'thumbs up' sign to show their enjoyment of the drink. The main scene shows them all enjoying Three Feathers, as they eat wild boar roasted on a spit. They are surrounded by large hunting dogs. The product's slogan is 'Three Feathers kills Thirst'.

3 Greenglade would now like to start exporting to other markets. It has identified Caronesia, a group of islands in the middle of the Pacific, as a potential market. Look at the statistics and buying habits of the islanders and decide whether Caronesia would be a good market for Greenglade.

| Caronesia | |
|---|---|
| Population: | 3,000,000 |
| Demographic trends: | 1% population growth rate. High percentage of young people leaving to obtain an education / non-agricultural work on the nearby mainland. |
| Climate: | Tropical, hot and humid. |
| Language: | English is used as the language of business; Caronesian is the official indigenous language. |
| Locally-grown products: | Cocunuts, bananas, mangoes, sugarcane. |
| Exchange rate | 1 British pound = 50 Caronesian dollars |

**Buying habits**

Most shopping is carried out by the male population. Large cash-and-carry discount warehouses are popular. Cans, or bottles of drink are sold in cases of 24. Otherwise people shop in small, local, family-run supermarkets. Many of these have fridges for selling cans or bottles of drink individually or in packs of six. The fridges are often supplied by soft drinks companies to store and sell their products exclusively, although the shopkeepers rarely respect this agreement.

A key problem for Greenglade would be to provide sufficient incentive to shopkeepers to stock a new product. Soft drinks are popular and the population has the income to spend on them. It is however, a fairly price-sensitive market and it would be difficult to introduce a 'premium' product which could sell for more.

Most families keep a stock of drinks for visitors. Consumers generally prefer to purchase them in glass bottles rather than in aluminium cans. Crates of empty bottles are often exchanged for full crates at the family-run supermarkets. Because of this, distribution is a headache and very labour-intensive. It is usually performed by delivery men in small vans or pick-up trucks. Large lorries are unsuitable except for delivery to coastal resorts and hotels. Family connections are important and a lot of contacts are via large extended families and networks.

**4** Read the cultural information about Caronesia. Why would the existing UK advertisement be inappropriate?

**5** Work in groups. Discuss the following questions and then decide on the appropriate marketing mix for Three Feathers in Caronesia.

1 How can Greenglade test the market and the potential popularity of the drink, before making an important financial commitment?

2 What changes, if any, should Greenglade make to the product?

3 Should Greenglade be responsible for its own bottling?

4 How should the drink be packaged and presented?

5 Can you think of any ways that distribution could be simplified?

6 Would this be better performed by someone local?

7 Where should the drink be sold?

8 Should it be sold at a premium price, or should it be priced competitively?

9 What incentives will encourage shopkeepers and distributors to stock the drink?

10 What special promotions could Greenglade use to make people try its drinks?

**6** Greenglade also plans to sell its products in your country. Repeat the stages in **3**, **4** and **5**, this time applying them to your own country.

*Culture is the software of the mind.*
**Geert Hofstede**, culture guru

# Cultural information

1 The number 3 is considered extremely unlucky. 4 and 7 are considered the luckiest numbers.

2 Dogs are considered unclean. Parrots and small monkeys are popular pets.

3 The colour of mourning is blue.

4 Orange is considered a lucky colour, while green is associated with sickness.

5 *'Thirst'* sounds like a commonly-used Caronesian surname.

6 Caronesians admire all things modern. Their ambition is to live in a modern house or apartment with air-conditioning.

7 The older generation prefers sweeter, less fizzy drinks to the younger generation.

8 The 'thumbs-up' sign is considered obscene.

9 Caronesians still use old imperial measurements such as pints instead of litres.

45

# 5 Fitting in

## Talking business

1 Read this sex discrimination case which went to an employment tribunal. What does this incident tell you about the culture of the organization in which Mrs Owen worked?

The Professional Golf Association was found guilty of sexual discrimination against a female employee ordered to change into a skirt or a dress after turning up for work dressed in a trouser suit. Judy Owen, 39, resigned from her job as training manager at the PGA's headquarters after being told that 'women don't wear trousers at the PGA'. An industrial tribunal found that the association had discriminated against Mrs Owen by applying standards of dress to women which did not apply equally to men.

2 How important are dress codes at work? How much freedom should employees have in the way they dress?

3 Should dress codes include aspects of personal appearance other than dress, such as hair and beards, weight, and body art like tattoos and body piercing?

## Listening

### Questions of culture

1 Intercultural management experts Fons Trompenaars and Charles Hampden Turner have identified four distinct organizational cultures. Read the descriptions and decide:

1 in which culture(s) personal relationships are very important.
2 which culture has the strictest hierarchy.
3 which culture has the least formal organization.
4 which culture regularly sets employees different goals and objectives.

**THE FAMILY CULTURE:**

Highly personal with close face-to-face relationships, but also hierarchical. The leader is the caring father.

**THE EIFFEL TOWER CULTURE:**

Has a steep hierarchy, broad at the base and narrow at the top. Impersonal. Authority comes from a person's role and position in the hierarchy.

**THE GUIDED MISSILE CULTURE:**

Egalitarian and oriented to tasks typically undertaken by teams or project groups. Impersonal.

**THE INCUBATOR CULTURE:**

The organization serves as an incubator for self-expression and self-fulfilment. Personal and egalitarian with almost no structure at all. Often a strong emotional commitment to the work.

**2** [5.1] Four people speak about their companies.

  1 Listen and decide which culture from **1** is described in each passage.

  2 Turn to the tapescript on page 156 and underline the expressions that let you know.

**3** Match 1–6 to a–f to form complete sentences.

  1 This firm is extremely *hierarchical*; … ......

  2 We're very *familiar* and *informal* here; … ......

  3 He pretends to be *egalitarian*, … ......

  4 They're rather *conservative* and *paternalistic*, … ......

  5 Relationships were so *impersonal* and *unfriendly*;… ......

  6 My old boss was very *authoritarian*; … ......

  a … but they do take good care of their staff.

  b … he expected complete obedience from his staff.

  c … I felt I didn't exist as a human being.

  d … each level has its specific powers and responsibilities.

  e … everybody uses first names.

  f … but it's he who makes the decisions.

**4** Decide which adjectives in italics in **3**:

  1 suggest a small or large power difference between people.

  2 belong to which organizational culture.

**5** Which culture would appeal to you most?

**6** Look at the diagram below which maps the results of research into organizations in many different countries.

  1 See if your country is represented. According to the diagram, which company culture dominates in your country? Do you agree?

  2 If your country is not represented, where do you think it should be placed?

  3 How could such a matrix be useful either in the workplace or for someone applying for a job?

**7** Discuss these questions in groups.

  – Do people become like the kind of company they join, or are they attracted to the company because of their personality?

  – What happens to people who find themselves in the wrong culture?

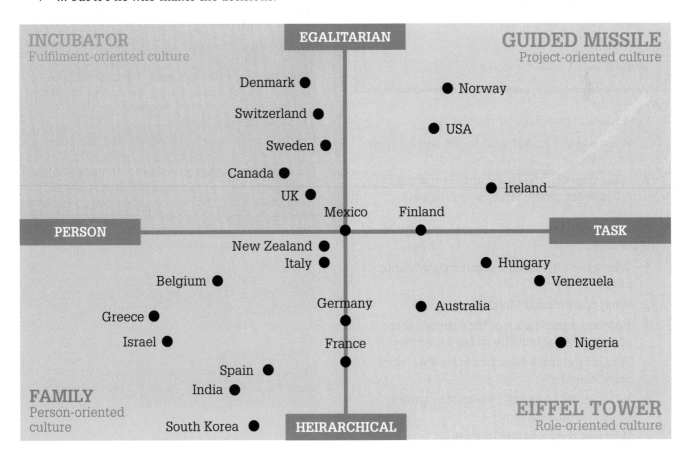

# Reading

## Follow your values

1  This statue, called 'The Gift of Sight', stands in the headquarters of the American pharmaceutical company Merck & Co., Inc. Why do you think Merck is proud to display it?

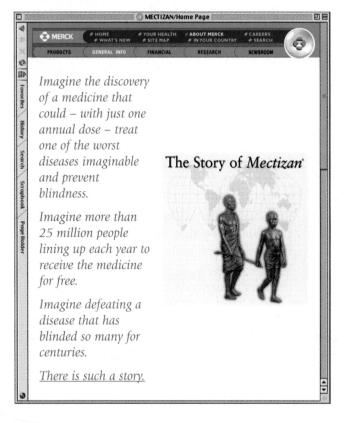

*Imagine the discovery of a medicine that could – with just one annual dose – treat one of the worst diseases imaginable and prevent blindness.*

*Imagine more than 25 million people lining up each year to receive the medicine for free.*

*Imagine defeating a disease that has blinded so many for centuries.*

*There is such a story.*

**The Story of *Mectizan***

2  Read the first paragraph of the text.

  1  What was the background to the development of the drug?

  2  What does this tell us about the importance of research for pharmaceutical companies?

3  Read the rest of the text which explains how Merck proceeded.

  1  Why wasn't Mectizan a commercially viable product?

  2  What dilemma did Merck face?

  3  How could the launch of the drug affect the pharmaceutical industry in the longer term?

  4  Why do you think Merck failed to find 'third party' funding?

  5  How did the company's philosophy guide it towards a final decision?

  6  Why was their decision 'historic'?

In 1975 Merck researchers, while evaluating soil samples for possible therapeutic value, began research on a molecule that proved to be extremely effective against parasites in many animals. It was later realized that this molecule (ivermectin) could be adapted to prevent river blindness, a terrible human disease, affecting 18 million people in the developing world with a further 126 million at risk. Merck eventually succeeded in developing an effective medicine called Mectizan. The drug underwent many clinical trials and was finally cleared for use 7 years later.

During the late 1980s, as clinical trials were proving the breakthrough nature of Mectizan, a debate was taking place at Merck.

- What price – if any – should the company charge for Mectizan? The company's dilemma was that the people who could benefit from this medicine were also the least able to pay for it.

- If the company donated the medicine, would it create an expectation that future medicines for diseases in the developing world would be donated? Would this philanthropic act prove, in the long run, to be a disincentive for research against tropical diseases?

- In addition to manufacturing and administrative costs, what risks would Merck face if Mectizan caused unexpected adverse reactions?

In vain Merck investigated third party payment options such as the World Health Organization and the US Agency for International development. But in the face of limited health budgets and competing health priorities no legislation was passed. Meanwhile people continued to suffer from river blindness.

In the end the company's decision would be based on one simple yet profound belief expressed by George W. Merck, the company's president from 1925–1950, who said, 'Medicine is for the people. It is not for the profits. The profits follow, and if we have remembered that, they have never failed to appear.' In the same speech Mr Merck said, 'How can we bring the best of medicine to each and every person? We cannot rest until the way has been found with our help to bring our finest achievements to everyone.' Today, these words form the foundation of Merck's values. They define what the company does and why it does it. In 1987 Roy Vagelos, then Merck's chairman and CEO, made the historic announcement in Washington DC, that the company would donate Mectizan for the treatment of river blindness to all who need it for as long as needed.

4 Now read about another drug called Vaniqa. How different is this from the Mectizan story?

> Vaniqa is a life-saving drug for victims of sleeping sickness. The company which developed it saw little profit in the drug and so gave the patent to the WHO (World Health Organization). Médicins Sans Frontières, the French-based aid charity, tried to find a manufacturer, but twenty-four companies turned it down as not being commercially viable. To the charity's anger, Vaniqa has now been re-formulated into a profitable cosmetic hair remover. It has been launched in America and advertised in *Cosmopolitan*.

5 Read the quotation below and discuss the questions.

– How far do you agree with Friedman?

– How do you think Merck's shareholders and employees felt at the decision to donate Mectizan?

– What effect do you think a strong sense of mission has on the people who work in an organization?

– How reasonable is it to expect the pharmaceutical industry to behave differently from any other business?

*"There is one and only one social responsibility of business – to use its resources and engage in activities designed to increase its profits…"*

**Milton Friedman**, American economist

## Language study

### could, would, should

1 *Could*, *would* and *should* are three of the most commonly used modal auxiliary verbs. Their meaning changes according to the context of the sentence. Which sentence using *could*:

a describes a general ability in the past?

b is a request for permission?

c expresses a theoretical possibility?

1 *Could* I leave ten minutes earlier today?

2 A skilled worker *could* make two pairs a day.

3 We *could* send it by courier, I suppose.

2 Which sentence using *would*:

a indicates the future in the past?

b describes a habitual activity in the past?

c is a polite request?

1 *Would* you send this brochure to our Frankfurt office?

2 We decided we *would* submit our revised proposals as soon as possible.

3 In the past, they *would* work from dawn to dusk.

3 Which sentence using *should*:

a expresses the best course of action in someone's opinion?

b says that something is morally correct?

c says that something is expected to happen in the normal course of events?

1 Your delivery is on its way. It *should* arrive just after lunch.

2 We *should* leave now if we want to get there on time.

3 Multinational companies *should* pay producers a fair price for their coffee.

Ⓖ Grammar guide, page 145

4 Complete the sentences by choosing between the forms in italics.

1 Fifty years ago people *would / should* use traditional cures and remedies.

2 I really think you *should / would* reconsider our offer.

3 *Would / should* you help me carry these boxes upstairs?

4 As long as we keep up the hard work, we *should / would* be on schedule for the end of the month.

5 We *could / would* organize a meeting with managers from our overseas branches, but it may be difficult to find a suitable date.

6 I'm sorry, we had no idea that it *could / would* cause such a scandal.

7 *Would / Could* I borrow your notebook this weekend?

## Language in use

### Obligation and necessity

1 **5.2** Gavin Wilson is starting a new job. A colleague, Judith Parker, is showing him around his new workplace. Listen to their conversation and make notes about the following *dos* and *don'ts*.

|  | do | don't |
|---|---|---|
| dress |  |  |
| name tags |  |  |
| the research and development section |  |  |
| smoking |  |  |
| telephoning |  |  |

2 How different are the rules between Gavin's old and new workplace?

3 Decide which forms in sentences a–f below are used to:

1 express a strong prohibition.

2 describe general duties or obligations.

3 describe an important requirement or obligation.

4 say something was done even though it was unnecessary.

5 talk about a regulation that is not always respected.

6 say someone didn't do something because it wasn't necessary.

a I *had to* wear a jacket and tie in my last job.

b You *needn't have* spent your money.

c You've *really got to* wear your ID tag.

d I *didn't need to* do that in my old job.

e You *mustn't ever* bring anyone in without permission.

f You're *supposed to* use the pay phones.

4 Re-arrange the words to form sentences using *make*, *let* and *allow*.

1 to – not – you're – allowed – on – the – smoke – premises

2 from – won't – they – even – workstations – so –us – let – phone – our

3 made – were – we – tighten – up – security – to – on

5 Turn to the tapescript on page 157 and find two other expressions with a similar meaning to *supposed to*.

6 **5.3** Listen to situations 1–6 and respond accordingly.

### Pronunciation: connected speech

1 **5.4** Listen to four sentences from Gavin and Judith's conversation again. Can you hear all the words clearly?

2 Underline the sounds which 'disappear' at the ends of words, as in the example.

1 I had to wear a jacket and tie in my last job.

2 You're supposed to use the pay phones.

3 I didn't need to do that in my last job.

4 You're not allowed to smoke on the premises.

3 Can you think of an explanation for when these sounds disappear?

4 Read the following sentences aloud, then mark the sounds which disappear when they are spoken fluently.

1 You mustn't ever bring anyone in without permission.

2 It's smart casual, I suppose.

3 I even bought a suit for the interview.

4 You're expected to challenge anyone who isn't wearing one.

5 **5.5** Listen to these sentences again to check.

# Speaking

## The rules

1 Complete the following questionnaire. What rules would you like to have in the company you work for?

2 Now work in pairs and compare your completed questionnaires.

– What do you learn about each other?

– Would you like to work for the same kind of company as your partner?

---

**1 Forms of address**

a ☐ People at all levels use first names.

b ☐ People at the same level use first names but have to address the boss by title and surname / family name.

c ☐ Everyone addresses each other with their title and surname / family name.

**2 Working space**

a ☐ Everyone has his or her own office.

b ☐ People have their own workstations or cubicles in an open-plan area.

c ☐ People are expected to 'hot-desk' and take whatever working space is available at the time.

**3 Dress codes**

a ☐ Men wear smart jackets and ties, and women wear skirts and blouses.

b ☐ As *a*, with a 'dress down Friday', when employees dress smartly but casually before the weekend.

c ☐ People wear what they want, when they want.

**4 Personal use of telephones and the Internet**

a ☐ Telephones and the Internet are for work-related use only.

b ☐ Employees should record any personal calls they make and will be charged monthly at a given rate.

c ☐ Employees may use telephones and the Internet for personal use as long as this privilege is not abused.

**5 Parking**

a ☐ Managers have their own reserved parking spaces.

b ☐ Parking is on a 'first-come-first-served' basis.

c ☐ Parking is allocated according to individual needs and the circumstances of all employees.

**6 Timekeeping**

a ☐ People are trusted to manage their own time honestly.

b ☐ Everyone has to clock in and out, or sign a book.

c ☐ As *b*, but managers are not expected to do this.

**7 Overtime**

a ☐ Any overtime is unpaid.

b ☐ Overtime is paid at an hourly rate.

c ☐ The employer encourages the employees to leave the premises on time and overtime is not encouraged.

**8 Accepting gifts from grateful customers or suppliers**

a ☐ Any gifts are shared equally amongst all staff.

b ☐ There is a complete ban on accepting any kind of gift or favour.

c ☐ Staff can accept personal gifts up to the value of €70.

---

3 Work in two groups. Group A, your company has strict rules. Group B, yours is more relaxed. Create a set of rules for your company, using ideas from the questionnaire, along with your own ideas.

4 Now form pairs, one from each group. Student A, you are going to work in Student B's company. Student B, explain the rules and regulations. Student A, react as appropriate, comparing the new rules with those of your old company.

# Writing

## A memo to all staff

1 In your country how common is it for people to smoke at work? Is smoking allowed in restaurants, theatres, cinemas, and on public transport?

2 **5.6** Simon Jones and Andrea Fox are discussing the smoking policy in the company where they both work. Listen and answer the following questions.

  1 What is the background to the smoking ban?
  2 How many staff agreed with it?
  3 Who do they suspect is breaking the rules?
  4 What solution do they come up with?
  5 What will happen to staff who continue to break the rules?

3 Expressions 1–6 all appear in the listening passage. Now match them to their written equivalents A–F below.

  1 I'm really fed up, ... ·····
  2 We've got this no-smoking policy but nobody seems to respect it. ·····
  3 The other day I noticed that ... ·····
  4 People who don't respect the new rules will really have to go! ·····
  5 How will it affect our insurance? ·····
  6 ... make our no-smoking rules clear. ·····

A
> It has recently come to our notice that ...

B
> I am writing to express my concern about ...

C
> ... state that smoking is not permitted.

D
> There are a number of employees smoking on the premises despite the no-smoking policy.

E
> Failure to comply with the new regulation will lead to serious action.

F
> What implications does this have for our insurance?

4 Based on Simon and Andrea's conversation, write the memo to all members of staff. Write a short introductory paragraph and then use bullet points to make the memo clear and easy to read. Try to use some of the written expressions from **3**.

# In conversation

## Pet loves, pet hates

1 Which description of a TV programme below is:

  1 a soap opera? ·····
  2 reality TV? ·····
  3 a quiz show? ·····

2 How popular are these programme types in your country? Which is the most popular at the moment?

> **A** ·····
> Contestants have the chance to become very rich by answering a series of questions. Each correct answer means they can double the money they have already won. In Britain, they can win up to £1,000,000.

> **B** ·····
> A continuous story often with several episodes a week. The main characters are either ordinary working people, or else rich and glamorous. The story can continue for years or many decades.

**C** .....

Members of the public apply to take part in the programme. Those who are selected live together, away from other people, for a fixed period of time. They are given tasks to perform and cameras observe them so that viewers can see how they interact. Each week one person is evicted, and the last remaining person wins a prize.

3 **5.7** Listen to three friends discussing a TV programme.

1  What kind of programme is it?

2  Whose views are closest to your own?

4  Turn to the tapescript on page 158.

1  Find out where and how often these words or expressions occur.

| | | |
|---|---|---|
| basically | after all | to tell you the truth |
| anyway | the thing is | you know |
| mind you | | |

2  Which one is used to:

a  introduce a reason that shouldn't be forgotten? ...............

b  introduce the most important reason in a simple way? ...............

c  introduce a conclusion or final reason?
...............

d  gain time while you think of what to say next? ...............

e  introduce an alternative idea that you think of while speaking? ...............

f  change the subject or add some extra information? ...............

g  show the person you are talking to that you want to be frank and say exactly what you are thinking? ...............

5  We can often make what we say more emphatic by using the words *it* or *what*. Study tapescript **5.7** on page 158 and find out how Maggie expresses these ideas.

1  You watch them. ...............

2  Most of all, I hate the way they are forced to fight each other. ...............

6  Make these sentences more emphatic using *what* or *it*.

1  I love programmes about wild animals.
What ........................................................... .

2  In the end they arrested the strange-looking man in the white sweater.
It ........................................................... .

3  I was annoyed when they changed the time of the news.
What ........................................................... .

4  The faulty brakes caused the accident.
It ........................................................... .

7  In groups, think of examples from your own country of quiz shows, soap operas and reality TV.

1  Describe these programmes to members of your group who have never seen them.

2  What do you like and dislike about these programmes?

8  Now discuss your opinions on examples of other forms of entertainment. Consider the following:

–  music

–  books

–  theatre

–  cinema.

# Case study

## Frost's

1 Read the information about Frost's. How many steps are there between customers showing initial interest and a sale?

> In the early 1990s Malcolm Frost identified the growing trend of people working from home. He set up Frost's Offices specializing in building space-saving offices in people's homes.
>
> Frost's has no showrooms and instead relies on advertisements in national newspapers and magazines to generate business. Potential customers who reply to an advertisement are telephoned by a specialized telesales agency which then tries to set up meetings with a sales representative. A salesperson then visits the client's home to help design the office and to close the sale. Most of these visits are carried out in the evenings and at weekends.
>
> Last year, Frost went into semi-retirement and appointed Sally Rose as the company's new managing director. He is still the firm's owner and key decisions require his approval.

FROST'S FURNITURE

2 Three years before he retired, Malcolm Frost introduced a number of important changes. Read the information concerning these changes below.

   1 What do you think were his reasons for making these changes?

   2 What effects do you think these changes have had since they were introduced?

> Frost introduced a new reward system which he copied from his biggest competitor. This was to stop his best salespeople from being headhunted by competitors. The sales force moved from a guaranteed basic salary plus commission to commission only. Commission rates have been increased greatly and successful salespeople can earn much more than ever before.
>
> Sales staff used to work in teams of five seated around a large table. Each group had an administrator who allocated the responses to the magazine and newspaper advertisements. Individual salespeople made their own appointments with potential clients. It was common for a monthly prize to be given to the table with the best sales figures for the previous month and there was a lot of friendly rivalry between the tables. Now the replies are dealt with by a telesales agency which generates considerably more appointments than salespeople ever did.
>
> In an attempt to cut overheads and make the firm more efficient, most of the sales administrators and back-up staff have been dismissed. Salespeople now handle their own paperwork and invoicing, and work out their own routes for visiting customers. Instead of working round tables, salespeople are now expected to 'hot-desk'. This means they find a spare phone and cubicle wherever they can when they arrive at work. Frost believed that the table system encouraged his sales force to spend too much time at the office and not enough time out selling.

3 **5.8** Members of Frost's have reacted differently to the changes. Listen to what five employees have to say about their present working lives and match the comments (A–E) to the profiles (1–5).

1

Toby aged 31:
3 years with the firm.

-----

2

Sally Rose aged 38:
12 years with the firm.
1 year as managing director.

-----

3

Raymond aged 43:
10 years with the firm.

-----

4

Jenny aged 25:
18 months with the firm.

-----

5

Paula aged 40:
8 years with the firm.
Sales Manager.

-----

4 Are the effects of the changes similar to the ones you predicted in 2?

5 Listen again and decide who:

1 seems to care most about the newer members of the sales team. ................

2 feels very insecure with the new pay structure. ................

3 has little sympathy for the salespeople's feelings. ................

4 is considering leaving the firm. ................

5 is unhappy about how much time people are taking off work. ................

6 Work in three groups. Group A should focus on the reward system, Group B on staff confidence and morale, and Group C on administration and paperwork at Frost's.

Group A, your information is below. Group B, turn to File 10 on page 129. Group C, turn to File 16 on page 131.

1 Identify the problems Frost's faces.

2 Suggest possible solutions. You will need to consider the following questions.
– How practical and easy are the solutions to implement?
– What would be the cost?
– How acceptable would they be to staff?

**Group A**

1 What effect do you think the reward system is having on staff performance?

2 How can the requirements of the highly successful salespeople, and those who are less successful, be accommodated?

3 What winning formula could you come up with?

4 What ways can you think of for motivating and rewarding the sales team? Consider the following suggestions.
– Maintain the system of commissions only with no basic salary.
– Return to basic salary plus commission, and reduce the commission rates.
– Introduce a proper salary structure with bonuses for high-performing salespeople, but no commissions.

7 Now form new groups with one person from each group. Each group should put together a presentation for Sally Rose and Malcolm Frost with suggested solutions to the company's problems. Be ready to revise some of your ideas!

# 6 Supply and demand

## Talking business

1 How far do you think everything has a fair price? Read the questionnaire and decide how you would react. Compare your answers with a partner.

2 Are there any goods or services which should have a fixed price and which should not depend on the laws of supply and demand?

1 You haven't been able to get a ticket for your favourite team's most important match of the season. Tickets usually cost €50. An hour before the match a ticket tout says that he can sell you a ticket for €200. Do you:

  a  ☐  pay and think, 'It's a once in a lifetime opportunity'?

  b  ☐  refuse to pay and miss the match?

  c  ☐  wait until the match is about to begin, and offer him €25?

2 There is a petrol shortage in your country. Your car is nearly empty when you arrive at a filling station which still has some petrol. You notice that the owner has doubled his usual prices. Do you:

  a  ☐  pay and think, 'That's life'?

  b  ☐  fill up your car and tell him that you will only pay the normal rate?

  c  ☐  pay and say you'll never use his filling station again?

3 A soft drinks company has introduced a new vending machine which increases the price of a can of drink the hotter it gets. It's a hot day and you are extremely thirsty. Do you:

  a  ☐  buy the drink anyway?

  b  ☐  stay thirsty and refuse to buy the drink?

  c  ☐  wait for the temperature to drop?

## Listening

### The price is right

1 Read the business tip about price elasticity of demand. What goods can you think of whose prices are particularly elastic, or inelastic?

> **Price elasticity of demand**
>
> Price elasticity describes how sensitive the demand for a product is to a change in its price. If a small change in price causes a large change in demand then we can say that demand is elastic.
>
> The demand for everyday products such as washing powder tends to be highly elastic. A small drop in price can stimulate a large increase in demand, whereas a small increase in price can stimulate a large fall in demand. By contrast, demand for exclusive, or luxury products tends to be less price sensitive.

2  `6.1`  Tara Williamson is an economist who is being interviewed by Jay Thomas about setting prices. Listen to part A and answer the questions.

1 How did she feel about the actions of the petrol station owner from the point of view of:

  a  an ordinary citizen?

  b  an economist?

2 Which economic principle does she claim her story illustrates?

3 What were the short-term benefits, and long-term consequence of the owner's actions?

3  In part B Tara talks about pricing policy. Listen and find out:

1  what unhappy experience Jay had recently.

2  how Tara explains what happened to Jay.

3  what pricing strategy is used by many companies.

4  In the final part of the interview, Tara and Jay discuss the price-fixing powers of manufacturers and retailers. Listen to part C and decide if statements 1–8 are true (*T*) or false (*F*).

1  Big brands often leave prices to the discretion of retailers. ......

2  Discounted prices damage some brands. ......

3  Supermarkets buy luxury brands on the black market. ......

4  The same goods are offered at different prices in different markets around the world. ......

5  Brands simply accept the supermarkets' action. ......

6  Supermarkets will re-sell luxury brands at a loss. ......

7  Loss leaders attract customers to stores. ......

8  Supermarket chains try to maintain the same prices as their competitors. ......

5  Many verbs are used with the noun *price* to form strong collocations when talking about pricing. Replace the words in italics in 1–8 with the correct form of one of the verbs from the box.

| set | fix | fetch | match |
|-----|-----|-------|-------|
| charge | double | raise | dictate |

1  Everything is really expensive in that shop; they are always *increasing* the prices.

2  He *asked me to pay* a high price to repair my car.

3  She said she would *equal* the price if I could find it cheaper elsewhere.

4  If you *put* your prices too high, then people simply won't be interested.

5  He knows everybody will buy his goods, so he is able to *control* the prices.

6  The clock *got* a surprisingly good price at the auction.

7  It is considered unfair for competing shop-keepers *to secretly agree on* their prices.

8  This restaurant has become so expensive; since last month their prices have almost *increased by two*.

6  Many other words frequently occur with the word *price*. Combine words from the box with the word *price*. In which of the combinations is *price* the first word? Which word is used twice?

| half | range | retail |
|------|-------|--------|
| list | war | full |
| asking | predatory | ~~cut~~ |

7  Now match the words or expressions you formed in 6 to definitions 1–10, as in the example.

1  sold at a reduced price *cut-price*

2  an unfair and exploitative price ...............

3  the price the seller wants ...............

4  the official, written price ...............

5  a battle between retailers who reduce the price ...............

6  spread of prices ...............

7  50% of the usual price ...............

8  the price with no reduction at all ...............

9  the piece of paper with the seller's official prices ...............

10  the price at which shops generally sell something ...............

8  Work in pairs. Discuss how you would explain concepts 1–6 to someone with little understanding of business. Think of clear examples to illustrate each concept.

1  the grey market

2  skimming the market

3  price elasticity of demand

4  a loss leader

5  predatory pricing

6  breaking even

# Reading

## Big oil faces pump protest

**1** How many different steps are there from getting the oil out of the ground to putting fuel in your car? Who makes money at each stage?

**2** You are going to read an article about fuel retailers in Britain. Before reading, look at the background information below, and complete it with words from the box.

| | | |
|---|---|---|
| refineries | tankers | crude |
| taxes | wholesalers | pump |
| franchised | retailers | |

Recently in Britain, lorry drivers, frustrated by huge rises in fuel costs, blockaded oil **1**..... , preventing oil- **2**..... from leaving their depots. The protest arose because of increases in the price of **3**..... oil, along with increases in government fuel **4**...... Fuel **5**..... at filling stations across Britain quickly ran out of fuel. The petrol companies were tempted to recover some of their losses by increasing **6**..... prices at their own, **7**..... petrol stations. The government discouraged them however, which meant the fuel **8**..... needed to find another way to recover some of their losses.

**3** Now read the text and answer the questions.

1 How did the petrol wholesalers originally want to regain money lost during the fuel protest?

2 What action did they eventually take, and why?

3 How has this affected independent retailers?

4 What is Garage Watch and what does it hope to achieve?

5 Who does Garage Watch appear to blame most?

**4** Read the article again and complete statements 1–3.

1 Independent retailers .................. the same prices for fuel as company franchisees.

  a no longer pay

  b still pay

  c have never paid

2 Independent retailers are .................. .

  a choosing to become franchisees.

  b planning to protest through official channels.

  c raising prices at their pumps.

3 According to the Petrol Retailers Association, the British government .................. .

  a has sent the problem elsewhere.

  b was right to interfere.

  c will suffer the consequences of its actions.

A group of more than 1,500 independent petrol retailers are launching an assault on the government over what they see as the unfair wholesale prices being charged by oil giants. The Garage Watch campaigners are accusing the giants of predatory pricing and have condemned the Government for encouraging it. They are considering legal action to bring prices down.

Britain has around 3,500 petrol retailers, but they have been going out of business at the rate of two a day since the petrol crisis last autumn. Operators blame the creation of a two-level wholesale price structure for this situation. According to Garage Watch, oil companies including BP, Shell and Esso, want to raise pump prices at their franchised petrol stations to compensate for revenue which was lost during the refinery blockades, but were dissuaded from doing this by the Government and instead raised wholesale prices.

Independent petrol stations have always bought their fuel from one of the majors but have been able to compete with franchises so long as everyone is charged the same price for fuel. Now that this is no longer the case, many are unable to survive, says Garage Watch. Independent retailer Mark Bradshaw, one of the leaders of the campaign, said, 'Nobody in the industry can remember there ever being two-tier pricing before, and it is destroying us. What we want is the right to buy at a competitive price.'

Mr Bradshaw's campaign has gained widespread support and he is preparing to take the matter to the Office of Fair Trading. In a letter laying out its case, Garage Watch suggests that since the fuel crisis, the wholesale prices charged by oil majors are actually higher than the prices they charge at the pumps of their franchises. Garage Watch further accuses the Government of going for a short-term solution with the suppression of prices at the majors' garages. It highlights that where competition from independent retailers disappears, prices will rise. It argues that in areas where independents have closed, the majors have raised their prices.

A spokesman for the Petrol Retailers Association applied the following analysis, 'This situation is certainly the Government's fault. After the crisis it was looking politically disastrous. It looked good to stop the oil majors raising their pump prices, but it was ultimately the independents who had to bear the cost of them making that concession.'

*The Independent*

5 According to the article, how successful was the British government's intervention in the fuel crisis?

6 Should government ever interfere with the prices charged by private companies?

## Price control

**Commodity** A bulk product which is indistinguishable between producers, e.g. oil, cocoa, copper.

**Cartel** A group of suppliers who get together to control the supply or price of their product.

**Organization of Petroleum Exporting Countries** (OPEC) An agreement between most of the world's major oil-exporting countries that attempts to co-ordinate their policies and smooth out fluctuations in the oil market.

**Monopoly** A situation where a single producer has a sufficiently large share of a market to be able to control prices in that market. A monopoly implies the absence of competition.

7 Work in groups and discuss the following questions.
- Are the producers of commodities or their buyers in a stronger position?
- Who gains the most in 'added value' when these commodities have been processed?
- What right do producing countries have to control the supply of an essential commodity to the rest of the world?
- Are there any monopolies in your country? If so, do they exist on products such as tobacco; on utilities such as water or electricity; or on services such as transport?

*A monopoly is a terrible thing until you've got one.*

**Rupert Murdoch**, Australian-born US publisher and media entrepreneur

# Language study

## Transitive or intransitive?

1 Transitive verbs take a direct object. Intransitive verbs take either an indirect object or no object. Some verbs may be used transitively or intransitively. In sentences 1–4, which verb(s) are:
- transitive?
- intransitive?
- able to be used transitively or intransitively?

1 The following analysis *applies*.
2 Where competition *disappears*, prices will rise.
3 They *applied* the following analysis.
4 They have *condemned* the government.

(g) Grammar guide, page 150

2 Complete the two sentences by choosing between the words in italics.
1 The oil tanker *lost / disappeared* in the storm.
2 The first oil shock *died / killed* a lot of infant industries.

3 Which sentence can be made passive? What does this tell you about transitive and intransitive verbs?

4 Match verbs 1–3 to their definitions a–c.
1 raise .....
2 arise .....
3 rise .....

a to increase or move upwards
b to appear, or occur as a subject for discussion
c to increase the amount or level of something, or to introduce something for discussion

5 Which of the verb(s) in 4 is / are transitive?

6 Complete 1–5 using a form of *rise*, *raise* or *arise*.
1 Worries about the increase in the price of raw materials were ............... at the meeting.
2 The following year's harvest was poor and prices ............... once again.
3 Some problems have ............... with the contract.
4 Do you think we will be able to ............... the extra capital?
5 Unemployment has ............... to an all-time high.

7 Find further examples of transitive and intransitive verbs from the text you have read.

59

## Language in use

### Participating in meetings

1  Certain expressions are commonly used at different stages in meetings. Complete sentences 1–12 with endings a–l.

1  So to re-cap, .... _____
2  Can I just finish off ... _____
3  Wouldn't it be a good idea to ... _____
4  We haven't heard from ... _____
5  It's an interesting point, but ... _____
6  I'd just like to say ... _____
7  Do you mind ... _____
8  Could you just run through that again, ... _____
9  Does anyone have anything ... _____
10  So what you're suggesting ... _____
11  To return to ... _____
12  The point I'm trying ... _____

a  ... you yet, Chantal.
b  ... further to add?
c  ... we all feel that transport costs have risen too high.
d  ... is waiting until next month before making a final decision.
e  ... to make is, if we don't act now, it will be too late.
f  ... my earlier point, I still think we should reject their proposal.
g  ... I'm not sure how relevant it is to our discussion.
h  .... that I think we should keep the schedule in mind.
i  ... if I say something here?
j  ... what I was saying?
k  ... contact the supplier again?
l  ... as I'm still not quite clear.

2  **6.2**  Listen and check your answers.

3  Decide which expressions from 1 and 2 could be useful for the following functions. Some of the expressions may be used for more than one function.

1  contributing
2  asking for contributions
3  making a suggestion
4  asking for clarification
5  clarifying
6  continuing despite interruptions
7  keeping the meeting on the right track
8  summarizing and concluding

4  Team leaders have many different functions.

1  What do you think the role of a team leader might be in meetings?
2  Which of the expressions from 1 and 2 might a team leader use?

### Pronunciation: word stress

1  Some two-syllable words may be used as nouns or verbs. In some cases the stress changes, for example: *increase* (noun);  *increase* (verb)

2  **6.3**  Study the list of words which can be both nouns and verbs. Underline the part of the word which is stressed in each case. Then listen and check your answers.

| | nouns | verbs |
|---|---|---|
| 1 | refund | refund |
| 2 | welcome | welcome |
| 3 | report | report |
| 4 | contract | contract |
| 5 | support | support |
| 6 | invoice | invoice |
| 7 | project | project |
| 8 | transport | transport |
| 9 | research | research |
| 10 | progress | progress |

3  Which verbs and nouns from 2 are pronounced in the same way?

4  Which words from 2 change their meaning according to the way they are pronounced?

5  You are the leader of a sales team. Write a short speech introducing a new team member. Include as many of the words in 2 as you can. Then read it aloud to other members of your group.

# Speaking

## Team players

1 Sometimes candidates for jobs are rejected because they are not 'team players'. What exactly do you think this means? How important do you think it is to be a team player?

2 The following key roles have been identified for effective teams. Which role would suit your character best?

### Key roles within teams

**Team leader** Finds new team members and develops the team working spirit.

**Critic** Guardian and analyst of the team's long-term effectiveness.

**Implementer** Ensures the momentum and smooth-running of the team's actions.

**External contact** Looks after the team's external relationships.

**Co-ordinator** Pulls together the work of the team as a whole into a cohesive plan.

**Ideas person** Sustains and encourages the team's innovative vitality and energy.

**Inspector** Ensures that high standards are sought and maintained.

3 Read the extract below from the *Essential Manager's Manual* and then discuss the questions in pairs.

- In your opinion, to what extent should you adapt when you take on a new role in a company?
- How easy do you think it is to find a job which suits your individual character?
- Which roles from the business tip do you think share similar characteristics?

> Try to match roles to personality rather than attempting to shoehorn the personality into the role. It is not necessary for each person to perform only one function. If the team has only a small number of members, doubling or trebling up the roles is fine – as long as all the needs of the team are truly covered and the members feel comfortable with their roles.

4 Work in groups of four. You are members of the quality control team at Harper's Cameras. You are going to hold a meeting to discuss a problem with breakages and losses. When you are ready, hold your meeting. You can invent and improvise as much as you wish.

**Student A:** you are the team leader / external contact. Turn to File 29 on page 135.

**Student B:** you are the critic / inspector. Turn to File 17 on page 131.

**Student C:** you are the co-ordinator / implementer. Turn to File 38 on page 138.

**Student D:** you are the ideas person. Turn to File 9 on page 129.

5 Which role was prominent in the meeting? How did this affect the outcome?

# Writing

## Describing movements and trends

1 Study the verbs in the box. Which ones mean:

1 to rise?

2 to fall?

3 to stay the same?

4 to change frequently or suddenly?

| | | |
|---|---|---|
| peak | hold | drop |
| rise | plummet | soar |
| jump | fluctuate | remain steady |
| increase | surge | level off |
| creep up | decrease | fall back |
| slump | collapse | strengthen |
| weaken | tumble | rally |

*[handwritten annotations: fiyat talep, artan, büyük, düşüş; soar→hızla yükselmek; surge→fiyatların satışların aniden yükselmesi; tumble→düşmek; rally→düştükten sonra fiyatları arttırmak, fiyatların artması]*

2 Which of these verbs:

1 can also be used as nouns?

2 suggest a large change?

3 Which of the adjectives in the box suggests a small change and which suggest a large change?

| | | |
|---|---|---|
| dramatic | slight | steady |
| sharp | steep | |

4 What differences do you notice between the following sentences?

1 There was a *dramatic rise* in the price of crude oil.

2 The price of crude oil *rose dramatically*.

5 Continue the second sentence so that it means the same as the first sentence, as in the example.

1 The cost of crude oil rose slightly.

There was a slight *rise in the cost of crude oil*.

2 There was a dramatic collapse of the property market last year.

The property market ............... .

3 Fuel prices have climbed steeply over the past six months.

There has been a ............... .

6 The verbs in 1 can be followed by a prepositional time phrase to provide more detail about the movement or trend. Continue the sentences as in the example.

1 Demand fell *in the first six months of the year*.

2 The share price plummeted ............... .

3 Internet use soared ............... .

4 After initial heavy selling, the share price remained steady ............... .

7 Read the two market reports about Stomex Communications.

1 In what kind of newspaper do you think they each appear?

2 What differences in style and language do you notice?

3 What metaphor runs through the second article?

## FLUCTUATION IN STOMEX SHARES

STOMEX COMMUNICATIONS WAS IN DIFFICULTY for the second time this year following its delivery of a second profit warning to shareholders. Selling by investment houses saw shares fall sharply to 80p, their lowest level for six years. This is in marked contrast to just eighteen months ago, when they more than doubled, following the announcement of Stomex's new wide-band phone. CEO Günther Meier blamed the saturation of the mobile phone market for the firm's declining fortunes. He remained confident, however, that Stomex's competitive edge would allow it to return to profitability once excess capacity had been taken out of the market, and the public saw the advantages of the new technology. Shares rose slightly to 90p at the end of trading. Meier's position is, however, less certain as he meets troubled board members at a hastily-scheduled meeting next week.

## SHARKS GATHER AT STOMEX

Stomex Communications is heading towards the rocks again after announcing its second profit's S.O.S. this year. Panic selling saw the shares slump to 80p, their lowest price for six years, as city investment firms abandoned ship. It's hard to believe that just eighteen months ago, Stomex was riding the crest of a wave with shares soaring to £6.80 following the news of the Navigator wide-band phone. CEO Günther Meier points the finger at the over-capacity in the market but remains confident that Stomex will weather the storm. He maintains that as soon as the public sees the potential of the new technology, the firm will be back on course. Shares went up slightly, but there is trouble ahead for captain Meier as the sharks gather for next week's emergency board meeting.

8 Study the graph and fact file which gives market information about GFV, a pharmaceutical company. Use the information to write a paragraph for:

1 a popular Sunday newspaper.

2 a serious City newspaper.

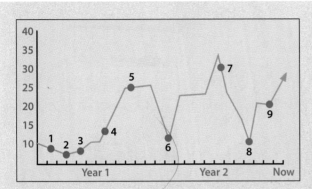

1 Company issues a profit warning.

2 CEO Wilfred O'Leary resigns.

3 CEO Cheri Carbone appointed. Whizz kid. Good track record. Ex-head of research at JKL Chemicals recently acquired by GFV. Carbone is a keen tennis player. 38 years old. American of Italian origin. Shares recover slightly.

4 JKL launches a new anti-ageing cream.

5 Animal rights protests outside GFV laboratories in Hertfordshire. Poor publicity leads to fall in share value.

6 Carbone announces takeover of HTY a cutting-edge biotechnology company. Shares rise to all-time high.

7 Scare over allergic reaction to anti-ageing cream.

8 Carbone announces complete recall and runs TV commercials. Confidence restored in GFV. Price recovers.

9 JKL invents safe tanning pill. Shares go up again.

# In conversation

## Shopping

1 Match sentences 1–10 with responses a–j. Who do you think is speaking in each case?

1 What size are you? .....

2 Do you think it goes with this shirt? .....

3 Could I try it on? .....

4 Would you like it gift-wrapped? .....

5 Do you need any help? .....

6 How would you like to pay, madam? .....

7 They don't fit; they're much too tight. .....

8 What do you think of the green one? .....

9 Do you have any more in stock? .....

10 Do you have this in any other colour? .....

a I'm afraid we only have what's on display.

b The colour really suits you.

c I'm sure they'll stretch.

d Yes please, I'm looking for a walkman.

e Of course, the changing room's through there.

f Well actually, the patterns really clash.

g No, but we're expecting an order next week.

h Yes please, it's for a present.

i Forty-two; I think it's size twelve over here.

j Is VISA all right?

2 **6.4** Listen to the recording and check your answers.

3 Which exchanges are to do with buying clothes?

4 **6.5** Luke Carpenter is from Boston. He has been to Cracow in Poland on business. He has a spare hour and wants to buy some gifts for his family. His colleague Caroline Zamoyski has taken him to the famous cloth hall in the centre of town. Listen and note down what he buys for:

1 his son.

2 his wife.

3 his daughter.

5 Listen again. What extra information does Caroline give about each of the items on sale?

6 Imagine that you are looking after a guest or colleague from overseas. They have asked you to help them choose some small gifts to take back to their country. Work in groups and consider the following questions.

– Where would you take a visitor?

– What would you tell them about the place? You might want to consider local history, or famous shops.

– What would you recommend as gifts and souvenirs? Think of traditional hand-made goods, local delicacies, models of famous buildings, T-shirts, scarves, etc.

7 Work in pairs and role-play your situation.

# Case study

## The Caxton Reader

1 Read the introduction about Virfen and the Caxton Reader.

   1 What is special about the Caxton Reader?

   2 What kind of consumer do you think it will appeal to?

Virfen is a Cambridge-based company which has built a strong reputation from producing up-market palm computers and personal organizers. It has recently developed the Caxton Reader, an electronic book used to view books, newspapers and magazines directly off the Internet using its powerful modem. Unlike its rivals, the Reader's tough, flexible screen folds in two, just like a real book. Virfen sells direct to its customers via mail order and the Internet.

## Costs

**Fixed costs** Business costs which do not vary with the amount of work produced, e.g. rent and salaries.

**Variable costs** The costs of producing something, which will vary with the amount produced, e.g. raw materials.

**Break-even point** The point where a business covers its costs and starts to become profitable. It is expressed as the number of units a business has to sell before making a zero profit. We can calculate this by dividing fixed costs by the selling price minus variable costs.

$$\frac{\text{fixed costs}}{\text{selling price} - \text{variable cost}} = \text{number of units}$$

**example**

$$\frac{\text{fixed costs} = €1000}{\text{selling price (€20 per unit)} - \text{variable costs (€10 per unit)}}$$

$$\text{break-even point} = \frac{1000}{10} = 100 \text{ units}$$

**Economies of scale** Savings which are the result of producing goods in large numbers. When goods are mass-produced, the unit price drops because fixed costs are spread over a large number of units. This is because each unit has to contribute less to paying the fixed costs.

2 Study document A below. Using the information in the business tip, calculate how many units of the Caxton Reader Virfen will have to sell to break even if it is priced at:

1 €150.

2 €300.

 **A**

### PRODUCTION AND COSTS

- All the components for Virfen's products are produced in the Far East. The products are assembled at Virfen's factory in Ireland and sent directly to customers.

- Virfen has already spent €1.5 million on research and development costs.

- It will cost a further €500,000 to set up its assembly line, which will enable Virfen to produce 500 units a day.

- The variable cost of each unit is €50 including labour and shipping.

3 Read document B and discuss in groups:

  1 how the Caxton is different from existing competitors.

  2 what present and future 'dangers' it faces.

## MAIN COMPETITORS

The two biggest existing competitors are the Lector and the Paston Voyager. Both models have a paperback-sized rigid screen.

**The Lector** – The first reader of its kind in the market. Heavier and less strong than the Caxton Reader. Current price is €250. Has been on the market for 3 years.

**The Paston Voyager** – same weight as the Caxton Reader. Can accept 'book cards' which can download complete books onto the Voyager's screen. Slow download time. Current price is €200. Has been on the market for 18 months.

You are certain that other manufacturers are developing similar products.

## TARGET GROUPS

**Group 1**
Business travellers. Academics who want access to foreign libraries and who need to download information. Consumers in the first group are the principal users of other Virfen products. Early adopters in groups 1 and 2 are prepared to pay up to €300.

**Group 2**
Large middle ground market.
Professionals / Commuters working in big cities who have plenty of reading time. University and high school students. To successfully penetrate this group, the price would have to be around €150.

**Group 3**
Potential mass market. General public. Occasional users. Consumers in group 3 are prepared to pay €100.

**Group 4**
Users in weak currency export markets, e.g. Southland.

4 Read documents C and D. In your groups discuss the following questions.

  – Which groups should Virfen target in its first year of production?

  – How much should they charge for the Caxton Reader?

5 Virfen is considering whether to sell the Reader in Southland, a non-EU market with a weak currency. Consumers in Southland could only pay €60. Could Virfen make a worthwhile profit if fixed costs were covered by sales in other markets? What dangers could Virfen face?

6 Managers from Virfen's marketing and finance departments are meeting to decide pricing and marketing strategy for the Reader. Work in groups of three. Student A, turn to File 15 on page 131. Student B, turn to File 27 on page 134. Student C, turn to File 36 on page 137. You may also add any of your own opinions.

  1 Which market(s) should Virfen target in the first year of the Caxton Reader's life cycle?

  2 Should a 'skimming' pricing policy be used for the initial launch period?

  3 Should the product be exported to Southland?

## PROJECTED FIRST YEAR SALES

Projected first year sales, domestic and overseas according to price.

| Price in euros | Projected sales |
| --- | --- |
| €300 | 10,000 |
| €200 | 15,000 |
| €150 | 30,000 |
| €100 | 76,000 |
| €75 | 120,000 |

# 7 Games people play

## Talking business

1 Look at these two layouts of parliamentary chambers. Which is more likely to encourage confrontation or agreement?

2 Which venue is the best place for doing business?
- a golf course
- a dinner party
- around a negotiating table

*British Parliament*

*European Parliament*

## Listening

### Deal makers

Eric Perrot is an area sales manager of a Belgian company which sells chips and potato-based products. Eric negotiates supply contracts with many of the biggest food retailers in Europe.

1 **7.1** Listen to part A of the interview in which Eric talks about the key to a successful negotiation and summarize what he says about:
- being prepared
- price
- winning or losing a negotiation
- short- and long-term aims.

2 Listen to part B and answer the questions.
1 According to Eric, what qualities should a good negotiator have?
2 How important is the ability to be persuasive?
3 What two types of customer does he discuss?
4 Which type is more difficult to deal with, and why?
5 What techniques does he use with each type?
6 How controlled does he stay?

3 In part C, Eric gives an example of two deals he made.
1 What concession did the buyer in the first deal want? What was Eric's reaction?
2 Why does Eric believe that you should never give something for nothing?
3 What went wrong in the second deal and what did he do?

**4** Negotiators are sometimes described as Red or Blue stylists.

1 Read the information. Which description fits Eric best?

2 What do you think happens when Red and Blue stylists meet?

---

**Negotiating styles**

**Red stylists:**

– see each negotiation as a separate contest.

– believe you win by dominating your opponent.

– enjoy manipulative tricks and bluffs.

– want something for nothing.

**Blue stylists:**

– regard negotiations in the longer-term.

– succeed through co-operation.

– address each party's interests.

– will only trade something for something.

---

**5** The following comments were made during negotiations. Which colour stylist is more likely to have made them? Label sentences 1–5 R (Red stylist) or B (Blue stylist).

1 'This is a once-only offer; take it or leave it.' .....

2 'We're happy to discuss a discount if we can work something out.' .....

3 'I want you to agree to this now, as a sign of your good faith.' .....

4 'I can fully understand that you don't want to leave yourself vulnerable to price rises.' .....

5 'How do you think we can best work together in the future?' .....

**6** Complete the gaps in each sentence to make a word which will fit the context, as in the example.

1 He will do anything to avoid a confrontation.

2 I found his reasons extremely pers................. .

3 The union has made an important conc................. on overtime pay.

4 Management says that the issue is not nego................. .

5 I'm sure we can reach a comp................. if both sides are prepared to give and take.

6 We are ready to listen to your revised prop................. .

**7** Decide which of the words in italics best completes the sentences.

1 After hours of discussion we finally managed to *overcome / come over* our differences.

2 They *undertook / overtook* to supply us components for three years.

3 We were satisfied with the *income / outcome* of the talks.

4 Louise Warren has *taken over / overtaken* as head of the negotiating team.

5 She *came over / overcame* as being extremely nervous.

6 She talked me *into / out of* signing the contract even though she knew I really wanted to go ahead.

7 I managed to beat them *up / down* from $60 a ton to $55.

8 You can't expect to *get out of / through to* the contract as easily as that.

**8** Collocations are words which frequently occur together to form useful expressions.

1 Match verbs from box A to nouns from box B to form collocations. Some words can be used more than once.

| A | B |
|---|---|
| make | a concession |
| settle | a deal |
| gain | business |
| reach | the initiative |
| do | the transition |
| build | a rapport |
| lose | your temper |
| take | a compromise |
| close | an insight |
| | a difference |
| | face |
| | an agreement |

2 How many of these collocations can you find in the tapescript on page 159?

*Any business arrangement that is not profitable to the other fellow will in the end prove unprofitable for you.*

**BC Forbes**, publisher

# Reading

## The negotiators

1 How possible do you think it is for both sides in a negotiation to feel happy with the outcome? How can a good range of negotiating techniques help?

2 You are going to read two stories about different negotiations. Work in two groups. The first group should read text A below and complete column A of the table. The other group should read text B in File 12 on page 130 and complete column B.

|  | A | B |
|---|---|---|
| People involved |  |  |
| Object of negotiation |  |  |
| Obstacle |  |  |
| Formal / informal |  |  |
| Level of experience of negotiators |  |  |
| Techniques used |  |  |
| Direct / indirect style of negotiation |  |  |
| How an agreement was reached |  |  |
| Winner / loser of the negotiation |  |  |

3 Find a partner from the other group and exchange information to complete the second column.

  1 What piece of wisdom did the narrator learn about the negotiation in each case?

  2 How important was the setting?

**A**

A Swiss entrepreneur once asked me to help set up a golf game outside Paris with a top French government official. My Swiss friend had sold merchandise to the government, but was deadlocked on some major issues. He thought that if he could get the official outside his official environment, the negotiations might improve. So he enlisted my help. I brought along a golf client whom the official admired, which made the outing special.

It was an interesting round of golf, largely because both the French official and my Swiss friend played abysmally. As the day wore on, their poor play seemed to bond them. 'Transaction golf' has a special protocol. If you bring up business at all, you have to be very subtle. It's understood, not spoken. But by the tenth hole, the two men were having such a bad day that they were ready to talk about anything but golf. My Swiss friend handled this beautifully, assembling his argument with a sound bite or two on every remaining hole. By the time we reached the clubhouse, the two men had ironed out all their differences and scribbled their agreement on a cocktail napkin.

I'll never know if it was the beauty of the day that made them so agreeable or their poor play that brought them together. But I do know that getting people out of the usual business setting and placing them in a congenial environment for four or five hours will improve almost any negotiation.

If you press the issue, you'll find that most people don't want to spend their time haggling with the other side. It's not that they don't like negotiating. They like the friendly competition, the manoeuvring, the development of a strategy and its execution. But more than anything, they like reaching an agreement.

I'm sure that's what's going on when people brag about the deals they've negotiated over casual drinks or a meal or a round of golf. When they come back to the office brandishing the cocktail napkin on which the deal terms are scribbled, I often think they're more pleased about how they negotiated an agreement than what the terms actually are. The cocktail napkin is a testament to their negotiating skill. Actually, it's a testament to negotiating in a quasi-social setting. It's proof of the wisdom of getting away from the 'negotiating table'.

*Mark H McCormack on Negotiating*

## Language study

### Conditional forms

**1** Match the examples of conditional sentences (a–e) with definitions of their use (1–5).

1 an unreal condition and result entirely in the past ......

2 an unreal past event with an unreal present result ......

3 an action in the present with a predictable result in the future ......

4 a tentative proposal which does not assume acceptance ......

5 a general truth or fact ......

a If you press the issue, you'll find that most people don't want to haggle.

b If you bring up business at all, you have to be very subtle.

c If you paid cash, I could work out a discount.

d If I'd been her, I'd have paid the money.

e If I'd had the same determination, I'd be as rich and famous today.

**2** Decide which sentence is an example of the following conditional forms:

1 zero ......

2 first ......

3 second ......

4 third ......

5 mixed ......

*g* **Grammar guide, page 141**

**3** What does *'d* replace in sentences d and e in **1**?

**4** The following sentences contain contracted forms. What is the full form of each?

1 I*'d've* gone to the conference if I*'d* known you*'d* be there.

2 I*'m* sure you *wouldn't've* offered him the job if you*'d* known how unreliable he*'d* be.

**5** Look at these sentences.

a Do it now, *otherwise* I'll have to let the other guy have it.

b *Unless* you have this gift, you will never win the big points.

1 In context, which word means *if you don't,* and which word means *or else?*

2 Which word introduces a consequence, and which word introduces a condition?

**6** *Provided that* ... and *on condition that* ... are used when the speaker wishes to impose a strong condition. In which sentence (a–e) in **1** can we substitute *if* with these alternatives?

**7** Complete these sentences by changing the verbs in brackets into an appropriate conditional form.

1 How much ............... (pay), Martin, if you ............... (be) in my shoes?

2 If we ............... (sign) now, she ............... (give) 25% discount. Let's do it before she changes her mind.

3 What ............... (say) if I ............... (pay) you some buyer's commission as an incentive?

4 Unless they ............... (agree) to an extra thirty days credit, I ............... (not go ahead) with the order.

5 I ............... (take delivery) provided you ............... (replace) the damaged goods.

6 We have lost a good customer. They ............... (renew) the contract if we ............... (not be) so greedy.

7 If you ............... (not agree) to their ridiculous conditions, we ............... (not be) in this awful situation now.

8 It's generally accepted that if you ............... (want to succeed) in life, you ............... (have to work) hard.

## Language in use

### Customer complaints

1 The following sentences are part of a customer complaint on the telephone.

  1 Put them in the correct order. What question do you think is being answered in each case?

    a Yes please, it's about a waterproof jacket I bought last year. ........

    b Thank you for your help. ........

    c Could you put me through to Customer Services please? ........

    d I washed it according to the instructions on the label and now it's leaking. ........

    e I bought it in your branch but I don't live in the area. Can I return it to my local branch? ........

    f I realize it's no longer under guarantee but I don't think a quality item should wear out so quickly. ........

  2 **7.2** Listen and check your answers.

2 Customers' calls are often directed to call centres where they are dealt with by strangers.

  1 How different is this from a face-to-face discussion?

  2 What extra problems in communication can this create?

3 Match 1–6 to a–f to form complete sentences.

  1 I can fully appreciate ... .....

  2 Do you happen ... .....

  3 I'm just ... .....

  4 If you'd like ... .....

  5 I'll ... .....

  6 I do apologize ... .....

  a accessing your details on my screen.

  b credit your account straight away.

  c your frustration, Mr Miller.

  d for any inconvenience you've suffered, Mr Hall.

  e to bear with me a moment.

  f to have your reference number?

4 **7.3** Listen and check your answers.

5 Now match the sentences to their functions a–f.

  a promising action .....

  b explaining what you're doing .....

  c asking for information .....

  d saying sorry .....

  e giving a polite order .....

  f sympathizing .....

6 Now say the same sentences less formally, as in the example.

*Do you happen to have your reference number?* (formal)
*Have you got your reference number?* (less formal)

7 **7.4** Listen and check your answers.

### Pronunciation: sentence stress

1 In spoken English the key words in a sentence are stressed more than the others, as in the example.

I can **fully appreciate** your **frustration**, Mr **Miller**.

  1 Turn to tapescript **7.3** on page 160 and underline the stressed words in the other sentences.

  2 **7.3** Listen again and check. Then repeat the sentences following the stress pattern.

2 Stressing different words in a sentence can change its meaning.

  1 Read the sentences below aloud, stressing the words in italics.

    a I'll send the order by *courier* on Thursday.

    b I'll send the order by courier on *Thursday*.

    c *I'll* send the order by courier on Thursday.

  2 In which sentence does the speaker mean:
    – before the end of the week
    – not by post
    – I'll do it personally?

3 **7.5** Listen to the same sentence spoken four times. Each sentence answers a different question. Match questions 1–4 to the answers you hear.

  1 When do you have to settle the invoice? ........

  2 Was it a firm offer? ........

  3 Did he offer you 30%? ........

  4 Who offered you a discount? ........

# Speaking

## Keeping your cool

**1** Study these rules of how to deal with difficult customers.

1 How realistic do you think they are?

2 How possible is it to follow them at all times?

**2** 🔊 **7.6** Listen to the telephone conversation.

1 Which rules does the call handler break?

2 How would a professional call handler have dealt with the call?

3 Work in pairs and role-play the call using the expressions you have learnt.

**3** Think of a situation when you have had to complain about something by phone. With a partner, act out one or more of these situations. Take turns to be the customer and the call handler. Follow the flowchart. Here are some examples to help you.

– The customer received the wrong goods.

– The customer was overcharged for something.

– The customer made an appointment with somebody who arrived late.

### Dealing with customers and their complaints

1 Allow angry customers to express their feelings without interrupting them.

2 Try not to take their complaints and criticisms personally.

3 Never argue with a customer.

4 Look or sound concerned. Show that you are listening.

5 Sympathize without accepting liability.

6 Never show your irritation or lose your temper.

**4** Use the expressions from the 'Language in use' section to create mini-dialogues for the following situations. Take it in turns to be the caller and the call handler.

1 The caller has been waiting all day for a service engineer to come to repair her cooker.

2 The customer is calling about a book which was ordered last month and which still hasn't been received.

3 The caller has telephoned a company with an enquiry, but has not yet managed to speak to the right person.

> ❝Never underestimate the power of the irate customer.❞
> Anon

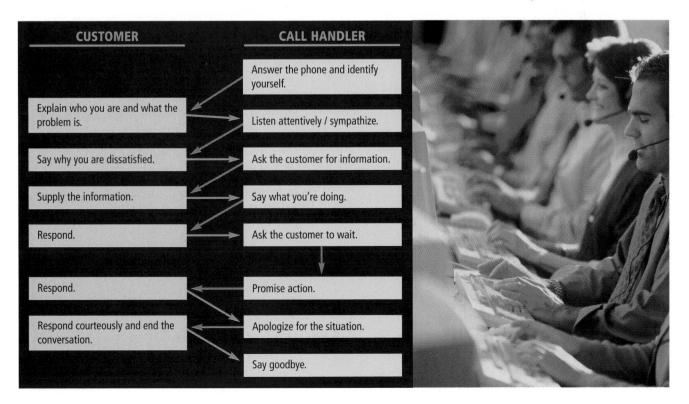

| CUSTOMER | CALL HANDLER |
|---|---|
| | Answer the phone and identify yourself. |
| Explain who you are and what the problem is. | Listen attentively / sympathize. |
| Say why you are dissatisfied. | Ask the customer for information. |
| Supply the information. | Say what you're doing. |
| Respond. | Ask the customer to wait. |
| Respond. | Promise action. |
| Respond courteously and end the conversation. | Apologize for the situation. |
| | Say goodbye. |

# Writing

## Handling customer complaints

**1** Lori Greene, the customer services manager of Scandipine, has received a letter of complaint from Mrs Davina Manners, a customer with a physical disability. Read reply A. What do you think was the cause of Mrs Manners' complaint?

**2** Read reply B and compare it with reply A. Which reply would you have preferred to receive if you were Mrs Manners?

**3** Discuss these questions with a partner.

1 Which letter contains an unconditional apology?

2 Which letter is warmer? Which is more official?

3 In which letter does the writer appear more defensive?

**4** Some people say that a complaint is 'an opportunity in disguise'. What do they mean by this? Which of the two letters turns the original complaint into an opportunity?

**A**

**Scandipine** | Head Office
Trafford Business Park
Manchester M17 AF

Telephone 0161-459-2371

Dear Mrs Manners

Thank you for your letter in which you outline your dissatisfaction with your treatment at our store three weeks ago. I appreciate your displeasure with the treatment you feel you received. I have discussed this matter with the individuals concerned who claim that no discourtesy was intended. Nevertheless, I have recommended that they undergo a period of retraining.

You will understand that in common with other large stores, Saturday is our busiest day of the week which makes it difficult to with special requests. In addition, we had to cope with a staff shor on that particular day. We are very sorry if you were upset by your reception but I think that you will agree these were exceptional circumstances. We regularly receive customers with disabilities ar within reason, do what we can to help. To my knowledge this is t first time something of this nature has ever occurred. However, t absolutely certain of avoiding any future misunderstanding, we strongly urge you to call customer services two or three days pr any future visit to arrange an 'accompanied tour'. I would advise make any arrangements as early as possible to avoid any possibl similar difficulty arising. Please find enclosed a voucher for €20 which can be exchanged against goods at any of our stores.

Yours sincerely

A Skinner

pp Lori Greene

Customer Services Manager

**B**

**Scandipine** | Head Office
Trafford Business Park
Manchester M17 AF

Telephone 0161-459-2371

Dear Mrs Manners

I was extremely concerned to receive your letter and have looked into the matter very closely. I fully share your displeasure and dissatisfaction with the treatment you received. I hope you will accept my sincerest apologies on behalf of Scandipine. I have discussed this matter with the individuals concerned. While this is no excuse, the young woman who greeted you so discourteously was a trainee who would normally not have been working alone. Saturday is our busiest day of the week and we were understaffed on that day. I would like to assure you that we take customer care very seriously and ensure that our staff are fully trained.

We regularly receive customers with disabilities and do our very best to assist them. However, to be absolutely certain of avoiding any future difficulty at the store, I have enclosed my personal card. Do not hesitate to ring me the next time you are planning a visit to our store, so that I can ensure that there will be someone available to accompany you. The earlier you are able to do this, the more certain I will be of having someone on hand. I hope you will accept as a token of our goodwill the enclosed voucher for €100 which can be exchanged against goods at any of our stores. Once again, I hope you will accept my most sincere apologies for this unfortunate incident.

I look forward to meeting you in person the next time you visit us.

With very best wishes

Yours sincerely

Lori Greene

Lori Greene

Customer Services Manager

**5** Choose one of the situations below and write a letter to the manager, expressing your anger. When you have finished, 'post' it to another member of the class, who will write a suitable reply.

1 You are a regular customer at Minty's CD store. However, when a friend gave you a CD as a gift, you discovered that you already had it. Even though the CD had been purchased at the store, you didn't have the receipt. When you tried to exchange it for something else, the shop assistant treated you with suspicion, and refused to make an exchange or give you credit.

2 To celebrate your birthday you went to an over-25s club where you were asked to prove your age before they let you in. Unfortunately, you didn't have any ID with you. You feel you were treated rudely by the people at the door and unnecessarily humiliated in front of your friends.

# In conversation

## Having your say

**1** **7.7** It can be hard to join in a conversation because one person is speaking without pausing. Listen to situations 1–6 and complete the table with:

- the topic they are discussing
- the expressions (a–f) which the second speaker uses to take a turn.

| Situation | Topic | Expression |
|---|---|---|
| 1 | | |
| 2 | | |
| 3 | | |
| 4 | | |
| 5 | | |
| 6 | | |

a That reminds me of the time ...

b Now, as I was saying ...

c I'll never forget the time ...

d I know what you mean, I ...

e Really! There was this book I read / film I saw / programme I heard ...

f Well, I don't know much about X, but I'm really into Y ...

**2** Work in groups of three or four and look at the list of topics.

1 Choose five you would like to discuss and write down two or three ideas for each topic. Do not show the other members of your group.

> pets
> law and order
> the weather
> a frightening experience
> sport
> a funny thing that happened to you
> your worst journey
> earliest memories
> family life
> problems in the city
> the government
> a favourite book / film / TV programme
> an embarrassing experience
> the day you lost something important
> a romantic meeting

2 In your groups, decide who is going to start talking. When you see an opportunity, use one of the turn-taking expressions to take control of the conversation and perhaps change the topic.

# Case study

## Troubleshooter

**1** Study the idioms and expressions in the box.

1 Match them to their definitions (a–h).

> to hit a stumbling block
> give (someone) an inch and (they'll) take a mile
> to play people off against each other
> to be at loggerheads
> to split the difference
> to have someone over a barrel
> I'll scratch your back if you scratch mine
> a bone of contention

a to agree to meet halfway between the asking price and the price which is offered ........................

b to encounter a problem which can prevent you from making progress ........................

c expression used when you agree to do someone a favour, provided they do one for you in return ........................

d an important topic of disagreement ........................

e to put two rivals in competition so that you can gain benefits ........................

f to argue and fail to agree about something ........................

g expression used when a person tries to get even more than what is offered ........................

h to put someone in a helpless position ........................

2 7.8 Listen to situations 1–8 using these expressions and check your answers.

**2** Six months ago, Wakely Ltd in England was acquired by an American conglomerate Stonebridge Inc. As a result, various issues have arisen which have caused tension at its main plant. There are three main grievances. Read them and identify the cause of the grievance in each case.

**Grievance one**
In order to improve its export opportunities, the company has decided to invest heavily in language training for sales and marketing staff. Most of the courses take place during work time. Blue-collar workers resent this, as they feel that they are being unfairly treated. Even though language tuition is available, they have to do it in their lunch breaks or after work. Some junior white-collar workers and secretarial staff have also been offered language tuition in work time.

**Grievance two**
The management has decided to substantially reduce the subsidy paid to the factory's sports and social club. The company traditionally supports the firm's rugby and soccer teams, pays for the team bus, and subsidizes the bar. Stonebridge's Vice-President Sam Walker, who does not drink alcohol, says the company should not promote or subsidize bad habits. Golfing weekends and management training trips to luxury hotels are offered to executives within the firm.

**Grievance three**
Workers are upset by the behaviour of an American technical manager who has been responsible for the installation of new equipment and staff training. They find her very aggressive. She has had to work closely with experienced technicians who feel that she does not value their skills and experience. She is at least twenty years younger than many of the men she is expected to supervise. Staff have little confidence in her and would like her to be replaced by someone older and easier to get on with.

**3** Work in groups of three. Student A is a union representative. Your information is in File 13 on page 130. Student B is a member of senior management and should turn to File 3 on page 126. Student C is an independent troubleshooter.

Each side should spend ten minutes preparing its case, deciding which issues are the most important and which it is prepared to negotiate. Study the documents opposite. Decide which ones will help you support your position in the discussion which will follow. The troubleshooter should anticipate likely arguments, and think of ways to solve each of the grievances which will do as little harm as possible to the factory's prospects.

**A**

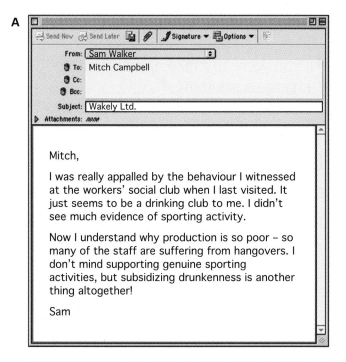

Send Now   Send Later    [icons]  Signature ▾  Options ▾

From: Sam Walker
To: Mitch Campbell
Cc:
Bcc:
Subject: Wakely Ltd.
Attachments: *none*

Mitch,

I was really appalled by the behaviour I witnessed at the workers' social club when I last visited. It just seems to be a drinking club to me. I didn't see much evidence of sporting activity.

Now I understand why production is so poor – so many of the staff are suffering from hangovers. I don't mind supporting genuine sporting activities, but subsidizing drunkenness is another thing altogether!

Sam

**B**

### Wakely Ltd.
#### Claim form for Staff UK expenses

**Name:** Graham Shepherd
**Department:** Marketing
**Claim period:** 14–16 March

| Date | Details of Expense | Sub-totals £ |
|---|---|---|
| | **Accommodation** | |
| 14.3–15.3 | Golfing hospitality weekend for suppliers: | |
| | 6 double rooms @ £140 x 2 nights | 840.00 |
| | Bar bill and telephone | 418.30 |
| | | **1258.30** |
| | **Business entertaining** | |
| 14.3–16.3 | Dinner Friday, lunch & dinner Saturday, lunch Sunday x 12 people (details attached) | 1116.25 |
| 15.3–16.3 | Golf tuition and equipment hire | 628.62 |
| | | **1744.87** |
| | **Travel** | |
| 14.3–16.3 | Petrol: 200 miles @ £0.20 | 40.00 |
| 15.3 | 3 taxis to restaurant and back to hotel | 30.00 |
| | | 70.00 |
| | **TOTAL CLAIM** | **£ 3073.17** |

#### CLAIM FORM MUST BE ACCOMPANIED BY RECEIPTS

| Payee's signature | Authorizing signature |
|---|---|
| G Shepherd | M Campbell |

**C**

Dear Mitch,

I am writing to you with regards to the training programme which was set up four months ago, and for which I have been responsible since my arrival at the plant. I am rather concerned by the attitudes of some of the technicians who I have been supervising on the programme, as I am under the impression that they fail to recognize the value of the training which is being offered. Apart from poor discipline with regards to punctuality and attendance, and sexist comments to myself as a female manager, there seems to be general resistance to learning something new. This is the first time in my career that I have encountered such a lack of motivation from staff. It is important that these employees be made to recognize the tremendous opportunity they are being given to keep up their level of skills in a competitive field. Action needs to be taken now to prevent the negative behaviour of a handful of male technicians affecting the morale of the other employees. I remain personally convinced as to the value of this training programme, and I hope I may have your full support on this matter.

Steffi

Stephanie Kennedy

**D**

##### INVOICE

**Grove's Coach Hire**
30-seat coach hire to return match against Walstron Wanderers football club. £260.00 inc. VAT

**E**

**Article 23.9** The Stonebridge organization pledges itself to follow a policy of equality for all employees and suppliers irrespective of sex, religion or race. Any breach of discipline will be dealt with under section 76.8. See disciplinary procedures.

**F**

# Stonebridge

Here at Stonebridge you'll find that everything possible will be done to enrich the lives of employees. Whether this involves learning a relevant new skill, or preparing you for professional examinations, Stonebridge will be there to back you up. The organization has a long history of sponsoring staff members to undertake full- or part-time training and ......

**4** When you are ready, hold your meeting. Incorporate as many of the negotiating expressions as you can.

You can either negotiate each issue separately or where appropriate treat them as a package with one or more other issues. Each side can call two breaks from negotiation to talk with its partners.

# 8 Survival of the fittest

## Talking business

1 Sometimes, inventions have an impact on society far greater than the purpose for which they were created.

  1 Look at these inventions and decide how they have changed the way people live and do things.

  2 Why do you think they have been named 'killer applications'?

2 Read about *The Times* newspaper.

  1 What does it show about our ability to resist technological change?

  2 Can you think of any similar examples from your own country?

  3 In what ways might change affect the lives of individuals? What measures should governments take to help those affected by change?

*The Times*, Britain's most famous newspaper, was first published in 1785. In 1814, it pioneered new technology which used steam-driven presses to print 1100 sheets an hour. These presses were installed secretly because the owners were afraid of machine-breakers. Over the next 170 years, it developed its reputation as a quality broadsheet. In 1978 a strike by print union members kept *The Times* out of circulation for nearly a year. In 1986 the paper's new owner moved to a new computerized plant. This change in technology meant that machines could be operated by members of the electricians' union, and print union members were made redundant. There were demonstrations and picketing by the print unions, but in the end the new technology was adopted throughout the newspaper industry.

> *If you want to make enemies, try to change something.*
> **Woodrow Wilson**, American President (1913–21)

## Listening

### Change master

1 What do you understand by the term *management consultant*? Discuss the following questions in pairs.

  – Why do you think companies might call in management consultants to advise them?

  – What experience and personal qualities do you think people might need to be successful consultants?

2 **8.1** Before he retired, Bill Watts used to work for top management consultants McKinsey.

  1 Listen to part A and note down the reasons he gives for firms calling in a consultant.

  2 How closely do they match the ones you gave in **1**?

  3 What examples does Bill mention of practical advice given by management consultants?

3 Listen to part B and answer these questions.

  1 How old was Bill when he started as a consultant for McKinsey?

  2 How did he feel when he went into a new company?

  3 Why did he feel confident about his abilities?

  4 How was he regarded by the staff of the organization he visited?

  5 How involved were clients in the consultation process?

4 In part C, Bill discusses the company's 'up-or-out' policy for its staff. What do you think this means?

  1 Listen and make notes about the long-term prospects for consultants at McKinsey.

  2 What reasons does Bill give for management consultancy being a high-pressured job?

  3 What are some of its compensations?

5 Based on what you have heard, how tempted would you be by a career as a management consultant?

**6** Complete sentences 1–7 using an appropriate form of the word in brackets. Then turn to the tapescript on page 161 to check your answers.

1 They improved their .................. (compete) by calling in a firm of management consultants.

2 Departmental .................. (rival) has damaged the firm's reputation.

3 I admire her high level of .................. (profession).

4 The CEO should focus on .................. (strategy) issues, not day-to-day management.

5 The firm changed its .................. (recruit) policy to hire people from ethnic minorities.

6 I thought some of their .................. (recommend) were totally unrealistic.

7 We managed to uncover some important market .................. (intelligent).

**7** McKinsey is an international company. What industries in your country can you think of which could benefit from the advice of a consultancy such as McKinsey?

## Language study

### The gerund and the infinitive

**1** Look at these sentences. In which one is the first verb followed by the infinitive?

1 I want to ask you something.

2 She keeps asking me to help her.

**2** Now look at the verbs in the box.

1 Which are followed by a verb in the infinitive, and which are followed by the gerund?

2 Create five sentences about yourself using a selection of these verbs.

| | | |
|---|---|---|
| avoid | hope | enjoy |
| finish | be interested in | manage |
| agree | plan | refuse |
| suggest | look forward to | tend |

**3** Some verbs can take the gerund or the infinitive. How does the meaning change according to the form used in 1–6?

1 Stop *to think / thinking* about strategy ... ......

2 I didn't remember *to bring* / I don't remember *bringing* the report; ... ......

3 I tried *to speak / speaking* to the boss ... ......

4 I like *to take / taking* the 7.43 train ... ......

5 We meant *to inform* / It meant *informing* her ... ......

6 She went on *to work / working* for our competitor ... ......

**4** Using the appropriate verb form, match the beginnings of sentences from **3** with their endings a–f.

a ... and she didn't like what she heard.

b ... can you make me another copy?

c ... but he wasn't interested in what I had to say.

d ... when she left the firm.

e ... because I always get a seat.

f ... and find some new customers.

**5** The *-ing* form has other uses. Look at the sentences a–c and say in which one the *-ing* form is used as:

1 an adjective. ......

2 a present tense. ......

3 the gerund. ......

a I'm *working* on an interesting project at the moment.

b How long is the *working* day in your country?

c *Working* late every day isn't good for you.

**6** Turn to tapescript [8.1] on page 161. Identify the gerund and infinitive forms and say why they are used.

(g) Grammar guide, page 144

**7** Use the verbs in brackets to tell each other about:

- your routines and preferences (like)
- early memories (remember)
- instructions and orders (remember)
- a problem you wanted to solve and the different things you did to solve it (try)
- something you did that you feel sad about (regret)
- bad news you have to give (regret)
- your business or educational career to date (stop, go on).

# Reading

## Coming together

**1** Complete sentences 1–5 with their endings a–e.

1 The decision to *acquire* a microchip-manufacturing company ... .....

2 The two rival companies decided to *merge* ... .....

3 The CEO is fighting a hostile *takeover* ... .....

4 We made a £10 m pound *bid* ... .....

5 Nokia *diversified* ... .....

a ... should guarantee future supplies of essential components.

b ... for our competitor.

c ... to protect themselves against the market leader.

d ... into telecommunications at the right moment.

e ... by encouraging shareholders not to sell.

**2** Match the words in italics in **1** with the definitions below.

1 an offer

2 to purchase

3 move into a different activity in order to be more competitive or to reduce a risk

4 to join together

5 a move to gain control of a company by acquiring a majority of shares

**3** Read the business tip about different types of merger. Which are illustrated in **1**?

**4** You are going to read about the merger between Daimler-Benz and the American car manufacturer Chrysler.

1 What do you think the advantages of this merger might have been?

2 Can you think of any problems which might have arisen?

**5** Read the first two paragraphs of the article. According to consultancy KPMG's research about mergers:

1 how many are successful?

2 what effect do they have on the value of a company?

3 what are two key reasons for their failure?

**6** Read the rest of the article. Who believes:

1 that mergers fail because of:

   a the way the two companies are combined?

   b differences in culture?

   c unrealistic expectations about the future success of the new company?

2 that companies merge essentially:

   a from fear of competitors?

   b to ensure their survival in a global marketplace?

**7** Read the text again and answer the questions.

1 Why is the writer so surprised at the money spent on mergers?

2 What motivated Daimler-Benz to merge with Chrysler?

3 What were the direct consequences of the culture clash?

4 How important are individual personalities in mergers?

5 Why has the BP Amoco merger succeeded where others have failed?

---

### Types of merger

**Horizontal**

Two companies making the same product combine. Aims:

– to reduce competition and increase market share

– to gain access to new markets

– to acquire additional plants and equipment

– to achieve synergy and economies of scale.

**Vertical**

A company either acquires or merges with another company in an immediately-related stage of production and distribution. This may be a supplier or immediate customer. Aims:

– to guarantee the supply and cost of raw materials and components

– to be closer to the consumer, by cutting out the wholesaler for example, and dealing directly with the retail trade.

**Diversification**

A company acquires another company in an entirely different sphere. Aim:

– to move into a sector which promises greater growth or profits.

# MERGER MOST FOUL

**Mega-mergers are the celebrity weddings of the corporate world, and all too often the shareholders are left heartbroken.**

Last week another marriage appeared to be in trouble when Daimler-Chrysler announced thousands of job cuts. Will it join the 83% of corporate tie-ups that end in failure? According to work by consultancy KPMG they should have known it was unlikely they would be able to deliver on their promises.

It found that 83% of mergers failed to produce any benefits for shareholders and more than half actually destroyed value. The seeds of a merger's destruction are often sown before it is even completed, with management too optimistic about prospects for the enlarged group and too confident they can overcome cultural barriers. Both accusations can be made at the £25 billion merger of US car group Chrysler with German giant Daimler-Benz.

John Thorp, head of finance and accounting at the European Business School in London said, 'There was a total clash of cultures and they were not good at communicating their strategy.' The clashes led to many of the US executives quitting after cashing in millions of share options. More damaging to shareholders were over-confident financial targets that were not met and which resulted in a steady decline in the share price. The result is that the company is now worth less than Daimler-Benz alone was worth before the deal. Jobs are being cut and there are rumours of a takeover bid.

Investment strategist James Montier said that over-optimism by management was a major reason why merged companies failed to perform well. John Kelly, UK head of KPMG's Merger and Acquisition Integration said, 'About 75% of mergers failed because of the ways the companies were integrated.'

Daimler-Chrysler enjoyed about six months of improved share price before the problems started. This is common for mergers where shareholders give companies a short breathing space to prove themselves. With the evidence so strong against mergers succeeding, it is astounding that last year, corporations worldwide spent more than £2 billion on mergers and acquisitions.

If everyone knows the marriage is doomed why do they have the nuptials? According to Thorp, 'It is about survival. Businesses cannot afford to be static these days. In the car industry, for example, economies of scale are vital as is access to an increased number of markets. Daimler-Benz believed its link with Chrysler would allow it to sell more Mercedes in the US.' KPMG's Kelly said, 'The key strategic rationale at the moment for mergers is "What happens if we don't?".' A lot of mergers are defensive in nature. He added that companies are worried that if they do not get together for mutual protection, they would either be taken over or lose customers to more powerful rivals.

A less justifiable reason is management egos and the endless desire of advisers to earn fees. KPMG is about to publish research following its initial study of 700 cross-border deals. It will show that the 17% of mergers it had found had succeeded did so spectacularly and shares in the new groups began to outperform the stock market and their peers. Montier says, 'Successful mergers tend to be between companies with similar businesses that can produce ongoing cost efficiencies rather than one-off savings.' One glowing example has been BP. Its share price has gone from strength to strength following its merger with US rival Amoco two years ago. Though successes are rare, the few that prosper prove that not all corporate celebrity marriages are doomed at the altar.

*Financial Mail on Sunday*

8 The writer uses idiomatic language throughout the text.

1 Find examples of words and expressions which are related to marriage. Why do you think the writer uses this metaphor?

2 Take a word from box A and combine it with a word from box B to form collocations.

| **A** | | | |
|---|---|---|---|
| cost | share | job | stock |
| investment | financial | share | takeover |

| **B** | | | |
|---|---|---|---|
| options | cuts | target | market |
| price | efficiency | strategy | bid |

9 Make a few notes under each heading to summarize the article.

- reasons for mergers
- problems with mergers
- types of merger

10 Now use the notes to present a brief summary answering these questions.

- What problems can occur with mergers?
- If the risks are so great, why do companies merge?

## Language in use

### Making presentations

1 Max Wilkes is a management consultant. Read his introduction to a presentation and find out how he:

1 states his aims.

2 tells his audience about the different stages of the presentation.

3 thanks the audience for their co-operation.

'Good morning everybody. As you know, I'm here today to present our findings and share our suggestions with you. First of all I'll outline the firm's current position and talk you through the evidence. Next, I will propose some immediate steps it should take. Finally, we shall put forward some recommendations for the longer term and discuss the alternatives. However, before I begin, on behalf of the entire team, I'd like to thank you all for your openness and co-operation. We all appreciate how difficult it is to be under the microscope.'

2 Match introductory phrases 1–10 to endings a–j.

1 Let's take a look at … ......

2 If you'd like to open … ......

3 As you can see, … ......

4 I'd like to draw your attention … ......

5 Right, I'm going to begin by … ......

6 So what can we … ......

7 I'd like to hand you over … ......

8 Sylvie will be talking you … ......

9 This brings me to the other key issue, … ......

10 Finally, I shall attempt to outline … ......

a … this pie chart reveals two other worrying features.

b … running through our main findings.

c … the evidence, shall we?

d … through our short-term recommendations.

e … a longer-term strategy for growth.

f … namely, the company's image.

g … learn from all of this?

h … to the following market intelligence.

i … the report at page 4.

j … to my colleague, Sylvie Grey.

3 **8.2** Listen and check your answers.

4 Which introductory expressions does Max use to:

1 direct his audience?

2 inform the audience of his plans?

3 signal a move to a new stage of the presentation?

### Pronunciation: linking between words

1 **8.3** In spoken English, a word beginning or ending in a vowel sound is generally linked with the word which follows or precedes it. Listen to Max's introduction and note how he links his words. Where does he:

1 link the final consonant sound of a first word with the opening vowel sound of a following word?

2 use a linking /j/ (as in *yes*) between two vowels?

3 use a linking /w/ sound between two vowels?

4 use a linking /r/ by pronouncing the normally 'silent r' before a vowel sound?

2 Now read the introduction aloud using all the appropriate links.

3 Look at the sentences you made in Language in use 2. Mark where you think the linked sounds will be.

4 **8.2** Listen again and check.

# Speaking

## The way ahead

1 Electrical appliances such as coffee-makers are popular consumer goods.

   1 How has their range and design changed over the last fifteen to twenty years?

   2 What has happened to their price and quality?

2 Chivers has produced high-quality coffee-makers since its foundation in 1963. However, in recent years sales have fallen dramatically. You are management consultants who have carried out a study for Chivers.

   1 You are going to make a presentation using the notes and graphs below. Work in groups of three or four. Study the notes and label the graphs and diagrams.

   2 Based on the notes, brainstorm possible options for Chivers and the recommendations you would make.

   3 Turn to File 14 on page 131. Compare the options and recommendations there to the ones you suggested. Are there any major differences?

3 Use the notes and any of your own ideas to prepare a presentation to Chivers' senior management.

   – Decide who will give the different sections of the presentation, including the introduction.

   – Use the expressions from the 'Language in use' section.

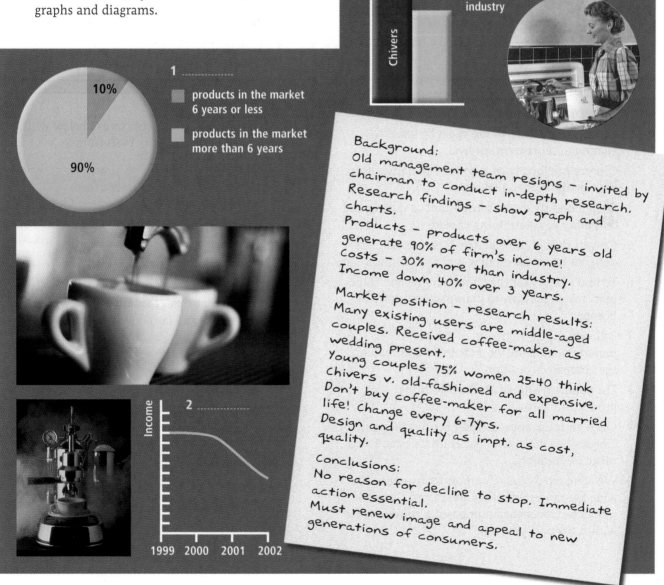

1 ............
- products in the market 6 years or less
- products in the market more than 6 years

10%

90%

Cost

3 ............

Average across industry

Chivers

Income

2 ............

1999  2000  2001  2002

Background:
Old management team resigns – invited by chairman to conduct in-depth research. Research findings – show graph and charts.
Products – products over 6 years old generate 90% of firm's income! Costs – 30% more than industry. Income down 40% over 3 years.

Market position – research results:
Many existing users are middle-aged couples. Received coffee-maker as wedding present.
Young couples 75% women 25-40 think Chivers v. old-fashioned and expensive. Don't buy coffee-maker for all married life! Change every 6-7yrs. Design and quality as impt. as cost, quality.

Conclusions:
No reason for decline to stop. Immediate action essential.
Must renew image and appeal to new generations of consumers.

# Writing

## Writing a report

1 Reports must be clearly signposted. Study the layout of a typical report.

1 Insert the headings a–f using the words from the box below.

2 How is the information presented logically under each heading?

3 What kind of information would you expect to find under each heading in a management consultant's report?

options
title
background
recommendations and conclusions
results
research

2 Decide under which headings of the report extracts 1–10 could belong.

1 Chivers' coffee-makers are perceived as old-fashioned and expensive by 75% women between 25–40.

2 Clearly, immediate action must be taken to guarantee short-term survival.

3 Chivers has long been a household name for its high-quality coffee-makers.

4 Design and style are as important as quality and durability in determining choice.

5 Chivers should immediately hire a world-class designer to produce a new range of products.

6 To find a buyer for the Chivers name and trade mark, or a company to manufacture under licence.

7 Following the resignation of the old management team, we were invited to evaluate the company's position.

8 The company should consider locating production abroad.

9 Once an innovative and pioneering company, Chivers has relied too heavily on its established range of products.

10 We conducted research among consumers of a wide age range. Some had purchased Chivers' products. Others had purchased a coffee-maker within the past year.

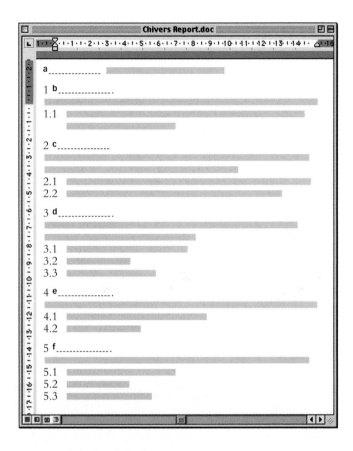

```
Chivers Report.doc
a _____    ████████    █████████
1 b _____
  ██████████████████████████████
  1.1  ████████████████████
2 c _____
  ████████████████████████████████
  2.1  ████████████
  2.2  ████████
3 d _____
  ████████████████████████
  3.1  ████████████████
  3.2  ████████
  3.3  ██████████
4 e _____
  ████████████████████████████████
  4.1  ████████████████████
  4.2  ██████████
5 f _____
  ████████████████████████████████
  5.1  ████████████████
  5.2  ██████████
  5.3  ██████████████
```

3 Match the spoken comments in a–c below with their written equivalents in 1–10 from 2.

a 'When the old management team resigned, they asked us to take a look at the company.'

b 'Three quarters of women in the 25–40 age bracket think that Chivers' coffee-makers are old fashioned and expensive.'

c 'It's obvious that we have to act straight away if the company is going to survive.'

**4** Read the business tip. How are the notes illustrated in the examples you studied in **2**?

---

### The language of reports

Formal reports do the following:

– often use the passive voice instead of the active.

> e.g. *The report was sent.* (rather than: *We sent the report.*)

– introduce options using the infinitive.

> e.g. *Short-term objectives*
> – *to increase our customer base*
> – *to maintain profitability*

– may begin sentences with an adverbial phrase.

> e.g. *As a result, the decision to introduce variable pricing was taken.*
> (rather than: *So we decided to introduce variable pricing.*)

– favour nouns over verbs.

> e.g. *We made a discovery of great interest.*
> (rather than: *We discovered something very interesting.*)

– tend to use more formal vocabulary.

> e.g. *undertake* (rather than *agree*); *retail outlet* (rather than *shop*)

---

**5** What do you think was actually said in 4, 9 and 10 of **2**?

**6** Based on the notes and presentation you gave in the 'Speaking' section, complete the rest of the report.

# In conversation

## Conversational gambits

**1** Study five techniques that can help you in conversation. Then work in pairs and practise reading the exchanges aloud.

---

1 Respond with a short question and ask for more detail.
A: *Her daughter is a doctor.*
B: *Oh is she? Where does she work?*

---

2 Echo the end of sentences and add a comment to show your interest.
A: *I'm a stockbroker.*
B: *A stockbroker! That must be an exciting job!*

---

3 Use 'tell me...' questions to show that you are really interested.
A: *So tell me. What's it like working here?*
B: *Well, It's ok I suppose.*

---

4 Show interest and surprise with *really / goodness me* + (*how* + adjective / *what* + noun)
A: *Do you see that woman over there? Well, she's the new marketing director.*
B: *Really! How interesting.*
or:
*Goodness me! What a change from Mr. Grayson.*

---

5 Reply with a comment which shows you sympathize with the speaker.
A: *I was stuck in a terrible traffic jam.*
B: *Poor you! The roads are terrible, aren't they?*

---

**2** 🔊 **8.4** Listen to five more exchanges. Which technique from **1** is used in each case?

a .....    c .....    e .....

b .....    d .....

**3** You are at a party where you are meeting some people for the first time. Start up conversations with each other using the techniques above.

# Case study

## Caught in the net

1 What is e-commerce?

  1 What impact do you think the invention of the Internet and e-commerce will have on retail?

  2 Find out how many people in the class have ordered something on-line. How satisfied were they with the experience?

  3 What are the advantages of buying books and CDs over the Internet?

2 Read about Bibliofile and decide if these statements are true (*T*) or false (*F*). Support your choices with evidence from the text.

  1 Bibliofile has a chain of high street shops. ......

  2 Its magazine has reviews from publishers. ......

  3 The threat from e-commerce has been an unexpected shock. ......

  4 Bibliofile has gradually invested more in the Internet. ......

  5 The website has already attracted new customers to Bibliofile. ......

  6 Despite everything, magazine subscriptions have continued to grow. ......

Bibliofile is a mail order bookseller which faces growing pressure from on-line booksellers. Bibliofile was founded in 1986 by Rona Kenton and is still run by her. Since its foundation, it has produced a well-regarded and beautifully produced magazine / catalogue called the *Bibliofile Quarterly*. This contains reviews of new books written by independent reviewers and is sent to subscribers. Rona Kenton realized that the Internet would pose a threat several years ago, but chose not to act. She didn't see how she could finance her own website and wanted to see what her competitors did first. Now, however, she is afraid that she has done too little too late. Over the past three years £185,000 has been invested in new IT systems. Kenton's daughter-in-law is in charge of the development programme. This year a further £90,000 is being spent to develop an interactive website and secure ordering system. Subscriptions to the magazine have fallen each year. It peaked five years ago and has fallen to 47,000 subscribers. This subscription income is very important for the company. It needs to generate enough business to pay for the enormous costs of producing and maintaining the website.

3 As a class discuss these questions.

  – How optimistic do you feel about the future of Bibliofile?

  – What positive steps has it taken to improve its position?

4 Read what management expert and writer Michael Porter has to say about the nature of competition. How does Bibliofile's example support or disprove what he says?

In any industry, whether it is domestic or international or produces a product or service, the rules of competition are embodied in five competitive forces:
– the entry of new competitors
– the threat of substitutes
– the bargaining power of buyers
– the bargaining power of suppliers
– the rivalry among existing competitors.

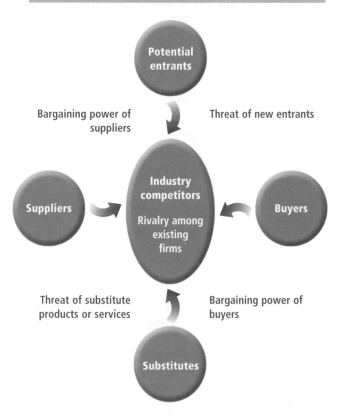

5 Bibliofile has now called you in as consultants to give advice on how the company can move forward. You have spoken to some of the people who work at Bibliofile. Look at their comments opposite. Which ones seem to you to be:

  – realistic?

  – unrealistic?

  – sensible and workable?

'I feel certain that our customers appreciate the Bibliofile magazine, and will continue to order books from us. There's still a place for mail order booksellers, even in the days of the Internet.'

'We can't possibly compete with the big on-line booksellers. We should become a niche bookseller. Maybe concentrate on academic books, that sort of thing, where price doesn't matter so much.'

'Our biggest mistake was not reacting early enough. It's Rona Kenton's fault. We told her things were changing but she just stuck her head in the sand. We'll never catch up our rivals now.'

'The days of mail order bookselling from printed catalogues are dead. We either need to go for e-commerce in a big way or close down before we lose any more money.'

'Bibliofile needs to stop being a generalist company and concentrate on a niche market such as cookery, gardening or novels, and establish a brand that stands for better and personalized service.'

'The biggest mistake was when Kenton asked her daughter-in-law to design the website. I say we should call in the professionals! We need to make our website different. We need to have book experts available online and add a forum where customers can chat with writers and other book lovers.'

'We've just been pouring money down the drain on this website. Either we need to invest a fortune or not bother at all. But Lucy, Rona Kenton's daughter-in-law is just a useless amateur and our livelihoods depend on her.'

'I'm sure we can get subscribers back if we make our magazine more attractive. We offer a fantastic service, and people love our reviews. Book lovers do not buy just on price.'

6 Work in groups. Based on the background information and employees' comments, suggest a strategy which will help Bibliofile survive both in the short- and longer- term.

7 Present your findings as a team to the members of your class.

# 9 Fair exchanges

## Talking business

1 Nowadays, people are more mobile than at any other time in history. Read the information below. Should the New Zealand government be worried?

> One million New Zealanders, about one in five of the population, live abroad. Half a million live in Australia, and a further 200,000 in England. There are even 3,000 New Zealanders in the US state of Utah. Many of these expatriates are highly-educated and are at the cutting edge of new technologies and academic research. They are attracted by better salaries and opportunities on offer elsewhere.

2 The 'brain drain' is a common phenomenon around the world. What other countries do you know which are affected?

3 What industrial fields do you think are most likely to be affected?

4 Can the movement of people with special skills towards countries which offer better employment prospects be considered as a fair exchange?

## Listening

### Fair exchanges

1 At what point in the following transactions should payment be made?

1 paying for goods in a supermarket
2 buying a car or a house
3 paying course fees
4 paying for a service such as building work
5 exporting goods from one country to another

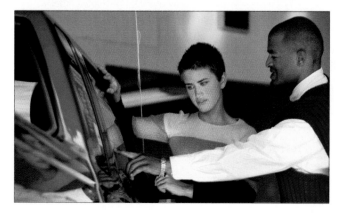

2 [9.1] Sheena Savage deals with export documentation and finance for a British company. Listen to part A and answer the questions.

1 What basic problem exists between exporters and overseas buyers?
2 What is the best solution?
3 Why is it attractive to both parties?

3 In part B, Sheena describes the process of obtaining and applying a letter of credit to a transaction. Listen and complete the notes summarizing the passage.

> The letter of credit is set up by **1**............... who pays all the fees. It is called a documentary letter of credit because it has to be accompanied by documents such as **2**............... and **3**............... . The letter of credit will specify conditions such as **4**............... . Transportation and finding a carrier are organized by the **5**............... . There is a lot of correspondence between banks, but in the end the exporter is paid when **6**............... . The buyer gets the goods by going to the port with **7**............... .

### Export documentation

**Bill of lading** A document that shows details of goods being transported. It is a receipt from the carrier to the sender. It entitles the receiver to collect the goods on arrival.

**Letter of credit** A letter from one bank to another bank, by which a third party, usually a customer, is able to obtain money.

**Documentary letter of credit** A letter of credit to which the exporter adds a number of other documents, such as a bill of lading and an insurance certificate, to obtain payment.

4 In part C, Sheena discusses pricing goods for export.

1 Before you listen, suggest what advantages and disadvantages there are of pricing goods for export in:
   - your own currency
   - the currency of your foreign markets.

2 Now listen to part C. What points does Sheena make about the dangers of pricing goods in a foreign currency?

3 How does she suggest that importers protect themselves against fluctuations in exchange rates?

## Language study

### Forms of the passive

1 Read sentences a–c below and decide which definition of use 1–3 best describes each sentence.

1 the agent (the person performing the action) is unknown

2 we are more interested in what happens to someone than who does it

3 the agent (the person performing the action) is assumed

a There's no guarantee the goods will be sent. ......

b My mobile phone has been stolen. ......

c Michael has been sacked for stealing from the bank. ......

2 Now study these further examples of different uses of the passive from the listening passage. Decide why the passive form is used in each case.

1 Both sides *are made to* think carefully.

2 Essentially, it adds a bank's promise to the buyer's promise that the seller *will be paid*.

3 What kind of documents have to *be supplied*?

3 Turn to tapescript 9.1 on page 162. Find other examples of the passive used with:

1 a future form.

2 a perfect form.

3 modals.

4 We use the causative when we have not carried out an action personally, but we wish to claim credit and responsibility for the result of that action. What differences in structure do you notice in sentences 1–3?

1 The buyer *sets up* a letter of credit.

2 The buyer *has* a letter of credit *set up*.

3 A letter of credit *is set up*.

5 Look at the sentences in 4 again.

1 In which sentence is the process more important than the person who carries it out?

2 In which sentence does the buyer personally carry out the transaction?

3 Which sentence tells us that the buyer delegates the task?

6 What everyday services do you pay for? Is there anything you do for yourself which you think other people may pay for?

7 Look at sentences 1–7. In each case, continue the second sentence with a passive or causative form, so that it is similar in meaning to the first sentence.

1 We have processed your request for a letter of credit.
   Your request ............................................................. .

2 We are doing everything to speed up your order.
   Everything is ............................................................. .

3 Someone had moved the documents from my desk.
   The documents ............................................................. .

4 Someone stole the goods while they were in transit.
   The goods ............................................................. .

5 I use a freight forwarder to deal with my exports.
   I have ............................................................. .

6 They lifted the cargo from the hold with a crane.
   The cargo ............................................................. .

7 Someone should find a way of making it more efficient.
   A way ............................................................. .

8 It is often a question of style as to whether we use the active or passive form. Decide if you would be more likely to use the active or passive when talking about the following activities.

1 telling someone how to use a cash machine

2 explaining how a cash machine works

3 giving directions to someone who is lost

4 teaching someone how to use a machine

5 describing a production process

6 giving the history of a famous company and its founder

9 Work in pairs. Choose one or two of the activities in 8 and discuss them with your partner.

# Reading

## Trade and technology

1 Why do you think oriental spices were so special in medieval Europe?

2 Study the background information below. How can you explain the large difference between the price of pepper in Asia and its cost to European consumers?

> Towards the end of the 15th century, pepper cost 1 gram of silver per kilogram in India or South East Asia. By the time it reached Alexandria its price was 10 grams, and in Venice, 14 grams. European consumers regularly paid 25 grams for each kilogram.

3 Before you read the text, check you understand the meaning of the adjectives in the box.

> tangible   perishable        negligible
> lucrative   virtual (two meanings)

4 Read the text, then complete paragraphs A–E in the text with their initial sentences 1–5.

  1 Vessels have become bigger and safer making voyages less hazardous. ......

  2 Despite this growth in e-commerce, the Internet has facilitated, rather than replaced, the old economy. ......

  3 In the Middle Ages, oriental spices such as pepper and cloves were the centre of a highly lucrative trade. ......

  4 In addition to maritime trade, overland routes have also been important. ......

  5 Indeed, throughout history, the evolution of trade has depended on the discovery or creation of new trading routes. ......

5 The following are answers to questions about the text. Now make the questions.

  1 From Indonesia.

  2 Because they wanted to avoid the Italian monopoly of Mediterranean trade.

  3 They cut the length of voyages.

  4 Not at all, they consider it quite normal.

  5 It could take weeks.

  6 Because they cost so little to transport.

  7 From China to Byzantium.

  8 Not usually. No direct contact existed between the original seller and the end consumer.

**A** ............... From the Spice Islands of Indonesia, they were shipped around the coast of India to the upper limits of the Persian gulf or Red Sea. From there they travelled overland by caravan to Mediterranean ports such as Alexandria. Italian merchants, who had a virtual monopoly of Mediterranean trade, carried them to other markets. In 1497 the Portuguese navigator Vasco da Gama discovered a less costly sea route to the east by following the African coast round the Cape of Good Hope. Thereafter merchant vessels followed the Cape route and were able to bring spices and silk to Europe more cheaply than before.

**B** ............... Great engineering projects like the Suez and Panama canals greatly reduced sailing times. Breakthroughs in transport and dockside technology, and the development of a commercial infrastructure have also played a vital role. Specially adapted vessels can transport perishable goods around the world cheaply. Nowadays, British families think nothing of a Sunday lunch of New Zealand lamb and green beans – airlifted from Kenya – with a 'New World' wine .

**C** ............... A modern petrol tanker could swallow a fleet of sailing ships in its hold. And until fifty years ago, vessels spent weeks in port being unloaded. Containers have changed all this. Giant cranes can empty a container ship in hours. Transportation costs per unit are now so negligible that big brands can have their goods made in lower-cost economies. And doing business internationally

9 No, it just helps it to work better.

10 Because you can't actually see or touch it.

is far less uncertain than it once was. Developments in international banking and marine insurance, mean that voyages can be financed and underwritten more smoothly.

**D** .............. Historically, none is more famous than the Silk Road which stretched from the far side of China to Byzantium. For much of its 4000 miles, what could be carried by camel determined what was traded. Nowadays, the term 'Silk Road' is used as a metaphor to describe the far reach of the Internet. Yet there is a key difference: hardly anyone travelled the length of its ancient namesake. Instead goods were relayed from station to station, each merchant taking his profit. By contrast, this new, virtual Silk Road allows direct contact between supplier and customer and dramatically reduces transaction time and cost.

**E** .............. This may explain the backlash experienced by many dot.coms. Tangible goods still need to travel to the customer. Nevertheless, the digital Silk Road has been instrumental in the development of a virtual or 'weightless' economy. Unlike the transportation of tangible products, banking services, education, and data processing can be transported invisibly over the Net. This has seen activity boom in previously unlikely areas. In India, Bangalore's progress has been outstanding. It has rapidly become India's silicon state and could overtake Silicon Valley as the world's leading software provider – another example of a new route changing how, and with whom, we do business.

**6** Find the words in the text which match the definitions.

1 a general name for any ship that floats on the sea: *v*...............

2 a large metal box used to transport goods: *c*...............

3 a machine used for lifting: *c*...............

4 the place on a ship where cargo is often stored: *h*...............

5 a line of camels travelling across the desert: *c*...............

**7** Complete each gap with a word to combine with the word in italics to form another word.

1 Our project has been .............. *written* by two of the largest insurance companies in the world.

2 The hippy trail went.............. *land* to Afghanistan.

3 There has been an important .............. *through* in negotiations.

4 The company has produced .............. *standing* profits for three years running.

5 Since the crash there has been a .............. *lash* affecting high-tech companies.

---

**Trade organizations and agreements**

**Association of South East Asian Nations** (ASEAN) Formed in 1967 by Indonesia, Malaysia, the Philippines, Thailand and Singapore. Brunei, Laos, and Vietnam have since joined.

**European Union** (EU) An economic and political association of certain European countries as a unit with internal free trade and common external tariffs. It was created on 1 November 1993, when the Maastricht Treaty came into force.

**North American Free Trade Agreement** (NAFTA) An agreement between Canada, the United States, and Mexico that aims to remove tariffs and other barriers to trade between the three countries.

---

**8** Discuss the following questions in groups.

– What contribution have international organizations such as the WTO had on the ease and volume of world trade?

– What advantages now exist for members of a free trade area such as the EU?

– Containers have been described as the eighth wonder of the business world. How justified do you think this is? In groups decide what, for you, would be the first seven wonders.

## Language in use

### Guiding visitors and describing a process

1 Read the information about silk. Is there anything that you find surprising?

> **Did you know ...?**
>
> Silk comes from the cocoons of silkworms.
>
> Each cocoon contains up to a kilometre of fine thread.
>
> The exportation of silkworm eggs from China used to be punishable by death.
>
> Around 7,000 cocoons are needed to produce one kilo of raw silk.
>
> Coloured silk is so bright because it can absorb up to seven times its weight in dye.
>
> Silk was once worth its weight in gold.

2 A group of visitors is visiting a factory which weaves textiles from silk. Complete the guide's introduction by joining the beginnings of sentences 1–5 with endings a–e.

1 On behalf of Xu Silks, ... ......
2 My name is Mei and ... ......
3 As you can see, ... ......
4 Now, before we begin our tour, ... ......
5 If you'd like to gather round the display, ... ......

a ... we're standing in the Information Centre.
b ... I'd like to tell you a little about the history of silk and its production.
c ... I'd like to welcome you to our factory.
d ... I'm going to be your guide today.
e ... I'll tell you about the silkworms which produce it.

3 **9.2** Listen to the introduction and check your answers.

4 Which expressions does Mei use to:
1 welcome the visitors?
2 introduce herself?
3 refer to where the group is situated?
4 state the objectives of the visit?
5 ask people to come closer?

5 **9.3** Mei describes how finished silk is produced. Listen and re-arrange sentences a–h to put the process in the correct order.

a Next, each cocoon is carefully examined. Only those which are perfect are chosen. ......
b After a month, the worms are large enough to weave a cocoon of fine thread. ......
c Then each cocoon is carefully unwound and spun into thread. ......
d Finally, the thread is ready to be dyed or woven into material. ......
e First of all, silk moths lay hundreds of thousands of eggs which hatch into worms. ......
f After that, the cocoons are brought to a smoking chamber where the worms are painlessly destroyed. ......
g Afterwards, they are thoroughly washed to remove the glue which holds them together. ......
h Once they have woven their cocoons, the silkworms go to sleep. ......

6 Listen again and check your answers. What verb forms are used to describe the process?

7 Which expressions are used to highlight the different stages of the process?

### Pronunciation: *ough*

1 The spelling -*ough* has many different pronunciations. For example, *cough* rhymes with *off*, and *plough* rhymes with *now*.

1 Look at the words in the box from the listening passage. How are they pronounced?

> enough      thoroughly      brought

2 **9.3** Listen to Mei again to check your pronunciation.

3 Think of words which rhyme with these different pronunciations.

2 Brainstorm other words containing the spelling -*ough*. Form them into groups according to their pronunciation.

# Speaking

## Chocolate

1 Work in groups of three. You are going to describe a process and provide a guided tour for each other. Student A, read the 'Did you know?' notes below. Student B, study the photos. Student C, look at the flow diagram.

> **Did you know?**
>
> Mayans and Aztecs took beans from the cacao tree and made a drink they called 'xocolatl'.
>
> Chocolate was first noted by the Spanish explorer Hernando Cortez. He witnessed the Emperor Montezuma of Mexico drinking it.
>
> The first chocolate house was probably opened in 1657 by a Frenchman.
>
> Eating chocolate was introduced in 1674.
>
> Nowadays, world annual cocoa bean consumption is approximately 600,000 tons.
>
> Two thirds of world output comes from African countries. Most of the remainder comes from South America.

### PRODUCTION OF MILK CHOCOLATE

1 Cocoa beans are processed ▶ cocoa mass (contains 55% cocoa butter).

2 Fresh liquid cream milk + sugar + condensed milk cooked ▶ thick liquid.

3 Cocoa mass is added ▶ rich creamy chocolate.

4 Evaporated to produce milk chocolate 'crumb'.

5 The 'crumb' ▶ broken up by heavy rollers.

6 Mixed with additional cocoa butter (depending on consistency of chocolate needed), e.g. thick chocolate for bars, thinner chocolate for coverings and chocolate assortments.
In UK ▶ 5% of vegetable fat added (compensates for variations in cocoa butter).

2 Use the notes and visuals to create the presentation and tour.

**Student A:** You are greeting visitors at a chocolate factory. Welcome your visitors and tell them something about the history of chocolate.

**Student B:** Use the photos to present the first part of the process.

**Student C:** Using the flowchart, explain how chocolate liquor is used to produce milk chocolate.

3 When you are ready, give your presentation in your groups.

### CHOCOLATE PRODUCTION
### THE PROCESS

1 Cocoa beans come from the fruit of the cacao tree.

2 The beans are fermented and then dried.

3 Then they are cleaned, roasted, and shelled. They are now referred to as 'nibs'.

4 The 'nibs' are ground up and cocoa butter is released. Finely ground 'nibs' + cocoa butter = chocolate liquor (basis of different varieties of chocolate).

# Writing

## A poster presentation

1 Poster presentations are a common way of presenting information at conferences. Study the posters below.

  1 What are export credit guarantees for?

  2 What is the difference in layout and structure between the two posters?

  3 Work in groups and decide what a presenter would actually say when presenting the information. Use the expressions in the 'Language in use' section.

2 6.7% of the world population use the Internet today, but do we really understand how it works?

  1 Read the text opposite and find out.

  2 Work in groups and decide how you will transform the article into an eye-catching poster presentation.

   – How will you lay the poster out?

   – What diagrams could you use to bring the presentation to life and make the operation of the Internet clear to your audience?

   – How will you make it easier for a non-technical person to visualize the process?

   – How many stages will you include in your explanation of the process? What will these be?

---

### EXPORT CREDIT GUARANTEES

**WHAT ARE ECGs?**

• A way of providing finance for capital projects where there is a financial risk for exporters.

**WHAT KIND OF RISK DO THEY COVER AGAINST?**

• Financial risk: often resulting from political risk.

**WHO ISSUES ECGs?**

• The government of the exporting country.

**WHAT ARE THE ADVANTAGES TO BOTH SIDES?**

• Stimulate exports by reducing risks for exporters (government pays if borrower defaults).
• Extend the issuing country's influence by helping set up capital projects in poor countries.
• Allow underdeveloped countries to build capital projects essential for development.

**WHAT ARE THE RISKS?**

• Exporters expose own country to unacceptable risk.
• Importers buy unsuitable / inappropriate technology.
• Unfair competition with other exporting countries.

**WHAT KIND OF CAPITAL PROJECTS DO THEY FINANCE?**

• infrastructure projects:

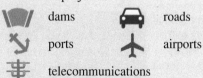

  dams    roads

  ports   airports

  telecommunications

**ARE ECGs SIMPLY A FORM OF AID?**

• NO! They are loans. A helping hand. Not a handout.

---

### HOW DO ECGs WORK?

EXPORTER AND RECIPIENT COUNTRY DISCUSS INFRASTRUCTURE NEEDS

EXPORTER ASSESSES PROJECT / FORMS CONSORTIUM WITH OTHER EXPORTERS AND INTERESTED PARTIES

CONSORTIUM APPROACHES GOVERNMENT

GOVERNMENT ASSESSES RISKS AND POTENTIAL BENEFITS

IF IT AGREES, IT SETS CONDITIONS FOR GUARANTEE AND PREMIUMS

MAY APPROACH OTHER AGENCIES
e.g. World Bank

FINANCE APPROVED

**How the Internet Works**

The thing that characterizes the Internet is how data is transferred from one computer to another. Did you ever wonder what magical things go on behind the scenes that result in a Web page being displayed on your screen seconds after you request it? How does the data get from one side of the world to the other? Here's what happens to a piece of data (e.g. a web page) when it is transferred over the Internet: It is broken up into a whole lot of same-sized pieces called 'packets'. A header is added to each packet that explains where it came from, where it should end up and how it fits in with the rest of the packets.

Each packet is sent from computer to computer until it finds its way to its destination. Each computer along the way decides where next to send the packet. This could depend on things like how busy the other computers are when the packet was received. The packets may not all take the same route.

At the destination, the packets are examined. If there are any packets missing or damaged, a message is sent asking for those packets to be resent. This continues until all the packets have been received intact. The packets are reassembled into their original form. Each computer connected up to the Internet has software called TCP/IP (Transmission Control Protocol/Internet Protocol) which is responsible for receiving, sending and checking packets. TCP/IP is the 'glue' of the Internet.

*UNITEC Institute of Technology*

# In conversation

## Describing events

1   **9.4**  It's Monday morning and colleagues are talking about their weekends. Listen to conversations A and B. Which events are described?

2   Study the tapescript on page 163 and underline the expressions which deal with beginnings and endings.

3   Sometimes we exaggerate to make an event or story more interesting. In sentences 1–4, replace the words in italics with phrases from the box.

| absolutely terrified | completely useless |
|---|---|
| incredibly tiny | absolute agony |

1   I was *very afraid* of him.
2   She was a *very small* woman.
3   I'm *not very good* at it.
4   It was *very painful*.

4   Match the adjectives in box A with their extreme alternatives in box B, as in the example. Some adjectives have more than one alternative.

**A**

| good | intelligent | big |
|---|---|---|
| bad | ill | cold |
| ~~hot~~ | interested | surprised |
| great | funny | surprising |

**B**

| enormous | hilarious | dreadful |
|---|---|---|
| awful | ghastly | wonderful |
| ~~boiling~~ | freezing | fascinated |
| amazing | marvellous | huge |
| incredible | brilliant | astonished |

5   Work in pairs. Take it in turns to describe an interesting or memorable event. Exaggerate as much as you like.

# Case study

## All manner of risk

1 Multinational companies are often faced with decisions about setting up branches or plants overseas.

- Do you know of any foreign companies which have set up in your country?
- What do you think might be the possible benefits of setting up in another country?
- What kind of risk would the company be running when taking the decision to set up overseas?
- What risks and benefits would there be for locally-employed people, and for employees from the parent company sent to work abroad?

2 Read the information about Kasada. What key decisions does it have to make?

### kasada

Kasada, a high-tech company based in Canada, produces personal organizers and hand-held computers. Components built abroad to its specifications are imported to Canada for final assembly. In the past two years it has experienced difficulty with late deliveries from suppliers. Competitors have also managed to imitate Kasada's latest designs. The company suspects leaks from at least one of its sub-contractors. It has made the decision to become vertically integrated and produce its designs and components in a more secure environment. For cost reasons, it is seriously considering building a new production plant abroad. This would also have the advantage of being closer to potentially new markets. Before it makes a final decision, it will have to weigh up the costs and benefits of the destinations which it has identified, and decide who from within its Montreal-based organization it could send.

3 Now look at the rest of the information about Kasada's current position.

1 What factors does Kasada need to take into consideration when deciding whether to build a larger or smaller facility?

2 What are the risks and benefits of options 1 and 2?

Kasada is confident its products will continue to do well, but are aware of the dangers posed by the competition and the health of the world economy. Its analysts believe that there is a 60% chance of a buoyant market and 40% chance of a downturn leading to recession over the next three years.

The company is considering two different production facilities. A larger facility will clearly give them the opportunity to expand production if the new range is successful, but could leave Kasada with high costs and over-capacity if the range fails to meet expectations. The smaller facility would find it difficult to satisfy a particularly high demand.

**Option 1: smaller plant**
A small plant would cost the company $24m to build. In a strong market it would generate a $3m profit, but in a weak one, a loss of $1m.

**Option 2: larger plant**
A large plant would cost $36m. In a good market, this could produce a profit of $5m in the first year. However, a downturn in business would produce a $3m loss.

4 Read the business tip and look at the statistics on Canada. What can you deduce about the cost of living and inflation in Canada?

| | Canada |
|---|---|
| Population (millions) | 30.6 |
| Human Development index | 93.5 |
| GDP per head $ | 20,750 |
| Economic Freedom index | 2.05 |
| Annual inflation % (1990–2000) | 2.0 |
| Cost of living (NY=100) | 76 |
| Unemployment rate average % (1990–99) | 9.6 |

5 Kasada has been considering a number of different locations for its new factory. It has made a preliminary selection of these countries:

| France | UK | Mexico |
|---|---|---|
| India | Singapore | China |

- Can you think of any obvious risks associated with each location?
- Why do you think these countries have been shortlisted?

6 Work in two groups. Each group will study a shortlist of three possible locations. Group A, turn to File 18 on page 132. Group B, turn to File 35 on page 137. Compare your statistics with those for Canada.

- What does each statistic tell somebody looking to locate a factory or company?
- What can you deduce from your statistics?

7 Work in your groups to select one country from the shortlist. Think about:

- the benefits and risks for a foreign company relocating overseas, which you identified in **1**.
- labour costs.
- access to the markets.
- the size of the plant as discussed in **4**.

8 Now work together with members from the other group to come up with a final decision on the location and size of the plant.

---

### Key indicators of economic activity

**GDP:** Gross Domestic Product. The sum of all output produced by economic activity within a country.

**Human Development index:** An indicator of the quality of life. Combines income levels with life expectancy and literacy / years of schooling. A score of 80 and over = high human development; 50–79 = medium; those scoring under 50 have a low level of human development.

**Economic Freedom index:** Ranks countries according to how much the government intervenes in the economy and thus restricts economic freedom. 1 = the most free; 5 = the least free.

**Inflation:** measured as a percentage increase in the price of consumer goods between two dates.

**Cost of living:** Looks at conditions for expatriates rather than citizens of the country. The index is based on typical urban prices an international executive and family will face abroad. The prices are for products of international comparable quality found in a supermarket or department store. New York city prices are used as the base, so United States=100.

---

9 Companies have to weigh up the risks before deciding to expand abroad. Employees who have the opportunity to work overseas also have serious personal decisions to make. Read the descriptions below of five employees whom Kasada is considering sending out to the new plant. They would be expected to sign a four-year contract.

1 What factors should these individuals consider before accepting a foreign posting?

2 To which of these people would you offer posts?

3 Which people are likely to turn down a job offer because of the consequences a move abroad could have on their families?

**Sheena McNamara 32**
After finishing her degree she worked for an aid organization for three years. Very competent, with a wonderful head for costs and figures. Bright and cheerful and good diplomatic skills. Divorced, single parent with a two-year-old daughter. She would be promoted on her potential rather than her experience.

**Regine Scott 28**
Brilliant software engineer and a key player in the development of the new product range. Quiet and a nervous traveller. Well respected by her immediate colleagues, she keeps her work and personal life strictly separate. This would be hard to maintain in a location where there is a narrow ex-patriate community.

**Jerry O'Shea 44**
Accomplished manager with experience of starting new operations from zero. Jerry could definitely get the job done. Extrovert but many consider that his straight-talking style lacks diplomacy. Lives in a comfortable house near Montreal. Two teenage children aged 17 and 13. The elder child will soon be beginning her pre-university studies. Wife active in local issues. They lived in the Middle East when the children were small.

**Dilip Rahman 25**
A junior member of Regine Scott's team. Brilliant engineer but young and with little experience of management. Parents Indian but considers himself more Canadian than Indian as he was brought up in Montreal. Speaks Hindi. Engaged to a Canadian girl of Indian origin. Going to work abroad would be a joint decision.

**Hesther Liu 35**
Production engineer and senior manager responsible for quality assurance and the setting up of two of the key production lines. Grew up in Singapore but studied at London University where she met her future husband, who has a successful dental practice in Montreal. They have two children aged 7 and 9.

10 How easy would it have been to take each of the decisions (location, size of the plant, and people) in isolation?

## Talking business

**1** Finding the right person for a job can be a long process. Rank these stages 1–7 to show the order in which they normally occur.

  a  Interested candidates send off a letter of application and CV. .....

  b  The employer makes a final decision and offers the job to one of the candidates. .....

  c  Candidates are selected for a first round of interviews. .....

  d  The employer writes a job description. .....

  e  The job is advertised in the media. .....

  f  A shortlist is prepared for a second round of interviews. .....

  g  The employer follows up references and check applicants' qualifications. .....

**2** Read the text about CV fraud.

  1  According to Steven Sayers, why is it so common?

  2  Why do you think Experian's service has become so popular with businesses?

  3  How dishonest is it for candidates to exaggerate on a CV? Is it 'just part of the game'?

Experian, a company specializing in checking CVs, completes between five and six hundred checks a week. Steven Sayers of Experian claims that 75% of CVs carry embellishments while 25% contain complete lies. 'The job market has become increasingly competitive,' said Mr Sayers. 'People will do anything to ensure that they get on shortlists. They think the CV is just a tool to get them inside – into an interview.' For about €80 Experian constructs a highly detailed picture of each applicant, investigating everything from date of birth and school records to specific projects undertaken at previous jobs.

*Independent on Sunday*

## Listening

### Just the job

**1** Look at this list of ways of finding a job or getting an interview. Do you have personal experience of any of them?

  1  careers and placement services
  2  family contacts
  3  networking and professional contacts
  4  responding to advertisements
  5  speculative applications made by approaching organizations directly
  6  being 'headhunted'

**2** **10.1** Listen to six people describing how they got their current job and match the methods from **1** to person A–F in the table below.

**3** **10.2** Now listen to the same people describing what they feel about their job and how they are rewarded, and complete the remaining columns in the table.

| Person | Method | How they feel about their job | How they are rewarded |
|---|---|---|---|
| A | | | |
| B | | | |
| C | | | |
| D | | | |
| E | | | |
| F | | | |

**4**  Read about the characteristics of successful people.

1  Which of these strengths do the people in the interviews demonstrate? Find evidence in the tapescript on page 164 to support your answers.

2  Which areas do you think you need to develop?

> Successful people tend to have the following strengths. They:
>
> 1  control events, rather than letting events control them.
> 2  set themselves clear goals.
> 3  know how to prioritize.
> 4  think of solutions that suit everyone.
> 5  are good listeners.
> 6  combine activities that work well together.
> 7  keep their skills up to date.

*The 7 Habits of Highly Effective People: Powerful Lessons in Personal Change* by Stephen R. Covey

**5**  What is the difference between the following?

1  a *demanding* job and a *challenging* job
2  a job which is *worthwhile* and one which is *rewarding*
3  a person who is *skilled* and one who is *talented*
4  a *dead-end* job and one with *prospects*
5  *the next rung on a ladder* and a *stepping stone*
6  *to pull strings for someone* and *to headhunt them*
7  a good *aptitude* and a bad *attitude*

**6**  The words in boxes A and B all commonly occur when talking about work.

1  Form collocations by joining a word from box A with one from box B, as in the example.

*brain + drain = brain drain*

| A | | |
|---|---|---|
| ~~brain~~ | skills | fringe |
| pension | company | pay |
| stock | annual | expense |
| career | basic | health |

| B | | |
|---|---|---|
| benefits | options | bonus |
| salary | ~~drain~~ | structure |
| scale | account | insurance |
| scheme | shortage | car |

2  Turn to the tapescript on page 164 to check your answers.

3  Which collocations deal with:

a  salary and conditions?
b  incentives and rewards?
c  losing / not having workers?

4  Which would you expect a future employer to provide?

**7**  Tell each other about the job of your dreams. What will you need to do to make this dream a reality?

**8**  Now read about the elevator test.

1  How difficult do you think it is?

> You have been called to the final interview for the job of your dreams. For years you have planned and prepared yourself for this moment. You are about to talk to the Managing Director who will make the final decision, when suddenly the phone rings. There is a crisis and she has to leave immediately but she asks you to take the lift with her. As the doors close she says, 'OK, I'm listening. Tell me why I should hire you.' The journey down takes just sixty seconds.

2  In groups, take it in turns to listen or say why you should be hired. Who would get the job in your group?

# Reading

## How loyal are you?

1 Read the text below and find out the connection between the two men.

1 How common is such loyalty?

2 How far does loyalty depend on getting something in return?

> Nicholas Ross, a helicopter pilot, has donated a kidney to save the life of his boss, billionaire businessman Kerry Packer. Mr Ross has worked for the tycoon for thirty years. He is so devoted to him he even calls him 'father'.

*Evening Standard*

2 Discuss the following questions.

- Which sectors of the economy suffer most from staff and skills shortages?
- What sort of organizations and businesses have a high turnover of staff?
- What methods and incentives could companies use to prevent staff from leaving?

3 Now read the article about incentives companies offer to keep their staff.

1 What is the reason for Arthur Andersen's gift to new recruits?

2 What has happened to employee loyalty?

3 What does Nick Page mean by *giving out universal benefits*?

4 Why is this no longer appropriate?

5 What does Microsoft do to keep its workforce happy? How successful has its policy been?

6 How do other companies try to make their employees feel at home?

7 According to Nick Page, what price does the employee pay for all these benefits?

8 How does the writer feel about attempts to make the workplace like a home or village?

So you think you get along well with your boss? Maybe they compliment you on a job well done or send you a birthday card, but what do they really *think* of you? Enough to remember you in their will? A wealthy couple recently did, leaving money to fifteen long-serving members of staff from the farm manager to the laundry lady. Whereas most employers might not go this far, there is evidence that an increasing number of firms are keen to *build up* a similar paternalistic culture of loyalty in order to attract or retain staff. One recent example of this came from management consultants Arthur Andersen who announced that they are to *hand out* £10,000 'golden hellos' to welcome all new graduate trainees. They claim that rather than wanting to trap them into a job for life, they were doing this because they wanted to help the recruits *pay off* their student debts.

Elsewhere, particularly in the City, companies are so desperate to *hang onto* staff that they will do almost anything. Increasingly, companies are trying hard to remind stressed-out workers that although they are working 12-hour days the boss really cares. According to personnel expert Nick Page the days of the wise loyal boss giving out universal benefits are dead. This disappeared during a period of high white collar unemployment when employees became disillusioned and more demanding. 'Now bosses are having to wake up to the fact that their staff are both individuals and customers. Companies are having to address the diversity of lifestyles among their workforce.' In a creative business with a young staff, for example, it's not appropriate only to offer childcare and pension plans. By contrast, many people in those types of firms *go for* pet insurance. Other companies offer grocery shopping and laundry services while one firm has *come up with* providing fresh underwear and free toothbrushes to staff when they *stay on* late.

'If you want to keep staff then you have to look after them,' says Hilda Barrett, group human resources manager at Microsoft. 'That's why we try and create a campus atmosphere at our office.' At their headquarters there is an area called 'the anarchy zone' where stressed-out workers can play pool, watch TV, play video games

**4**  We can often work out the meaning of a phrasal verb from its context. Find the verbs in box A in italics in the text and match them with the definitions in box B.

| A | | | |
|---|---|---|---|
| think of | hang onto | lay out | stay on |
| sort out | go for | hand out | build up |
| pay off | come up with | | |

| B | |
|---|---|
| choose | keep |
| to have an idea | finish repaying a debt |
| arrange / design | distribute |
| organize / solve a problem | develop and make grow |
| have an opinion about | remain at work after the usual leaving time |

**5**  Discuss the following questions in groups.

–  How far do you think it is possible for a business to be one big happy family?

–  In your country, how common is it for people to spend all of their working lives in the same company?

–  How often do you think you will change your career or place of work?

and read the latest magazines. Despite the fact that a writer recently called the firm's employees Micro*serfs*, the staff turnover is only 8%. 'We must be doing something right,' says Barrett.

But even though forward-looking firms are *sorting out* your shopping or laundry Nick Page believes 'the end result is that you may be working longer and longer hours with no overtime.' As we all spend more and more of our lives at work, many employers are attempting to restore the balance by making office life more like home, often with the boss in the role as substitute parent. Business development agency the Fourth Room, for example, has offices which are *laid out* like a house. Each morning the kitchen table is set for breakfast and a family lunch is held twice a week so people can sit down together. British Airways has designed its head office so that it looks like a corporate

village with its own high street and TV station. More worrying still, staff are no longer known as employees, but as residents.

*The Guardian*

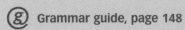

### Phrasal verbs

**1**  What is the difference in meaning of *turned up* in sentences 1 and 2?

1  He *turned up* the street.

2  He *turned up* late.

In which sentence is *turned up* a phrasal verb?

(g)  Grammar guide, page 148

**2**  There are four types of phrasal verbs.

1  Look at sentences a–d. Identify the mistake in each sentence and correct it.

2  What type of phrasal verb does each sentence include?

a  The value of shares was gone up.

b  The application form was sent back because he hadn't filled in it properly.

c  If we increase our sales force we'll be able to break the market into.

d  I look forward hearing from you to next week.

**3**  A single phrasal verb can also often have different meanings. Study sentences a and b below.

1  In which sentence does *take in* mean *understand*?

2  In which sentence does it mean *trick* or *deceive*?

a  She *took* them *in* with the lies in her CV.

b  I couldn't *take in* the instructions because they were too complicated.

**4**  Now identify the difference in meaning of each phrasal verb in the following pairs of sentences.

1  He *picked up* German on holiday.
Don't worry. Sales should *pick up* soon.

2  I can't *make* these sentences *out*. Can you ask them to send the fax again?
Even though it was her fault, she *made out* it was our mistake.

3  Let's *take* our jackets *off*, it's very hot in here.
The plane *took off* three hours late.

4  They have *put up* the price of oil again.
I'm coming to Paris, could you *put* me *up* for a couple of nights?

## Language in use

### Handling difficult questions

1 Expand the prompts to form full questions.

   1 *What – you – see – yourself* doing in five years time? ...........................................................................

   2 *How quickly – you learn* new skills?
    .............................................................................................

   3 *What – be – most important thing – you learn* from your placement last summer?
    .............................................................................................

   4 *you – rather – be* out and about, or office based? ...............................................................................

   5 *you think – could* tell us about your greatest weakness? ...................................................................

   6 *you tell us* what qualities you would bring to this job? ..........................................................................

   7 *I – like you – describe* a difficult situation you handled well. ..........................................................

   8 *you – mind – tell – us* how much you are currently earning? .........................................................

2 Study the questions in **1** again. How are questions 1–4 different in structure from 5–8?

3 **10.3** Listen to replies to the questions from **1**.

   1 Which reply a–h belongs to which question 1–8?

   2 What kind of jobs are the man and woman being interviewed for? Find evidence in the tapescript on page 164 to support your answers.

   3 Why wouldn't they be at all suitable for each other's job?

   4 How likely are their replies to impress the interviewer?

4 Listen again. How do the candidates win themselves some 'thinking time' before providing their answers?

### Pronunciation: /θ/ and /ð/

1 *th* can be pronounced /θ/ as in *thin*; or /ð/ as in *father*. What is the difference?

2 The words from the box below are all from the listening passage. Place them in the correct row according to the sound.

| think | rather | the | think |
|---|---|---|---|
| another | that | thorough | truth |
| methodical | thought | although | |

/θ/   ........................................................................

      ........................................................................

/ð/   ........................................................................

      ........................................................................

3 Listen to **10.3** once more and check your answers.

4 Underline the /θ/ and circle the /ð/ sounds in the following sentences and practise reading them aloud fluently.

   1 Although they thank you for a job well done or send you a birthday card, what do they really think of you?

   2 To tell you the truth, I think you should think through their offer as it's a worthwhile job with good prospects.

   3 Rather than cutting costs, some companies think there are advantages in offering perks such as health schemes.

   4 Have you had any further thoughts on those three documents for the meeting this Thursday?

   5 I think you'll agree, Mr Smith is thorough and methodical, and is therefore the right person for this job.

5 **10.4** Listen and check.

# Speaking

## Preparing for an interview

1 Match the interview methods 1–4 with the definitions (a–d).

1 one-to-one interview
2 panel interview
3 group interview
4 serial interview

a a group of candidates perform a task in front of a team of interviewers
b the candidate has a series of one-to-one interviews with different people
c the candidate is interviewed individually by one interviewer
d the candidate is questioned by several interviewers at the same time

2 Read what four people say about the interview they attended. In each case, what kind of interview did they have?

1 'Well, I went into this huge room and there they were, lined up behind an enormous table. All six of them. One just smiled, and kept nodding all the time, so I looked at her. The worst was this guy who stared out of the window when he wasn't doodling on my CV. Finally he looked at me and asked an impossible question. My mouth went dry immediately and my mind went blank.'

2 'It didn't really feel like an interview at all. I went from office to office and spoke to loads of different people. I've never drunk so many cups of coffee in my life! Everyone was really friendly apart from one person in marketing. I've got no idea at all of what kind of impression I made.'

3 'She asked me to come in and we sat down around a coffee table. Then she fussed about with tea and biscuits and asked me a few questions. She seemed rather embarrassed by the whole thing. I think I had more experience of interviews than she did! Anyway, she offered me the job there and then and asked if I could start straight away.'

4 'You know, you want to do your best but you don't want to show off either. There were two people who were desperate to show that they had "leadership potential", so they bossed everyone else around. And all the others were trying their hardest to show that they were good team players. I thought it was a real circus and no good at all for judging people.'

3 Which method do you think:
   – is the most stressful for candidates?
   – gives the most accurate impression of a candidate?
   – is the most common in your country?

4 What kind of interview would be most suitable for selecting:

1 a personal assistant reporting to a number of managers in a medium-sized company?
2 a graphic designer for a newspaper or magazine?
3 a customer services manager dealing with lots of people in potentially difficult situations?

5 Work in three groups. Each group should prepare questions for candidates for one of the posts from 4.

6 Form new groups and take it in turns to ask each other your questions.

# Writing

## Jumping through hoops

**1** The following extracts form part of a cycle of correspondence. Read each extract and complete the tasks.

1 Complete the extract with prepositions.

> **A**
>
> Further **1**..... your application, we would like **2**..... invite you **3**..... attend an interview day **4**..... our assessment centre **5**..... 23 June. The day will begin **6**..... 9.45 **7**..... two one-hour aptitude and psychometric tests. **8**..... lunch there will be a group task which will be observed **9**..... members of our team. **10**..... some point in the day you will have the opportunity **11**..... discuss your application **12**..... a member **13**..... the Human Resources department. We should have finished **14**..... 17.45 **15**..... the latest.

2 Change the words in brackets into an appropriate form.

> **B**
>
> I have pleasure in informing you that your job **1**............... (apply) for the above post has been **2**............... (success). We would like to make you a provisional job offer **3**............... (depend) on the **4**............... (receive) of **5**............... (satisfy) references and original copies of your **6**............... (qualify). This is a permanent post subject to the **7**............... (complete) of our standard three-month trial period. This **8**............... (appoint) will be at scale three of our general **9**............... (manage) grade and the starting salary is currently £23,000 reviewed after six months. If you still wish to take up this offer, please sign and return the **10**............... (accept) letter to us by 18 September.

3 Change the verbs in brackets into the correct form.

> **C**
>
> I **1**............... (write) to express an interest in one of the posts of dot. com analyst which **2**............... (be advertised) in last week's edition of *Bizztalk*. I am a twenty-four-year-old computer sciences graduate with two years' work experience. I **3**............... (currently work) in a computer start-up. I **4**............... (search) for exactly this type of opportunity for a long time and I **5**............... (believe) that I **6**............... (have) the combination of the right academic background and experience for this post.

4 Identify the unnecessary words in the extract.

> **D**
>
> I am regret to inform you that on this occasion your application has not been a successful. A great deal of interest was shown in the posts which attracted an extremely strong field. We agreed that while you certainly have the necessary qualifications and enthusiasm, despite other candidates had more appropriate, practical, firsthand knowledge. We would like to thank you ourselves once again for expressing an interest in the our organization and would welcome any future application once you have gained a further experience.

5 Expand the extract using the prompts.

> **E**
>
> *Further – letter – accept – our offer – employment, please find enclosed two copies – your contract – confidentiality agreement. Read them both carefully – sign – return one copy – each. I – like – draw your attention – the non-competition clause – forms part – general conditions – employment. On – personal note, I very much – like – take this opportunity – welcome you – the company – look forward – work with you – future.*

**2** Now put the extracts in order. Which two outcomes are possible?

**3** Study this advertisment, and write a cycle of correspondence between Greta Koenig and a successful applicant.

> **The Beacon Organization** seeks enthusiastic people to manage their international summer camps for disadvantaged teenagers. Ideal candidates will have experience of working with young people. They should be sensitive to different cultures and expectations. They should speak good English and be ready to lead an international team of co-workers. They should be fit and active, and willing to participate in all aspects of the camp's sporting and cultural activities.
>
> **Write to Greta Koenig at PO Box 765.**

# In conversation

## Leaving messages

**1**  How do you feel when you have to leave a message on an answering machine or voicemail? What is the key to leaving a successful message?

**2**  `10.5`  HYS is an engineering company. Listen to the recorded message on their answering machine.

1  What information does HYS give the caller?

2  What information does HYS ask the caller to provide?

3  What does HYS promise to do?

**3**  `10.6`  It is Friday morning. Sabine Robert from HYS is playing back the message left on the answering machine.

1  Listen to the message and complete her message pad.

> **Telephone messages**
>
> Name:
> Company:
> Time:
> Contact number:
>
> Message:

2  Listen again. Complete the second column of the table below with the expressions Patrick uses.

|                      | Patrick | Sabine |
| -------------------- | ------- | ------ |
| introduce self       |         |        |
| state purpose of call |        |        |
| leave message        |         |        |

**4**  `10.7`  When Sabine calls Patrick back, he is away from his desk and he has activated his voicemail.

1  Re-arrange the jumbled sentences a–c to re-create his message.

a  *through – are – voicemail – to – Patrick – Donovan's – you.*

b  *contact – leave – a – your – please – number – the – giving – call – message – time – of – a – and.*

c  *my – I – do – best – hours – to – shall – return – working – call – within – your – four.*

2  Listen and check your answers.

**5**  `10.8`  Sabine Robert leaves a message for Patrick Donovan.

1  Listen and complete her message.

> Hello, Mr Donovan. This is Sabine Robert from HYS here returning your call **1**............... . This is simply **2**............... that your order was despatched **3**............... yesterday evening, and **4**............... with you before midday. **5**............... to contact me again, my mobile number is **6**............... . If I don't hear from you, I **7**............... the parts have arrived. Goodbye.

2  Complete the third column of the table in **3** with the expressions she uses.

**6**  Work in pairs. You are going to make several phone calls to each other. You are both busy people and are unable to answer the phone, so you will have to leave messages.

1  **Student A:** You work for Winchester Scaffolding. You are organizing a special staff dinner at your office to celebrate a successful year. You are going to ask Ace Caterers to take charge of everything.

**Student B:** You are from Ace Caterers. You will be asked to provide a meal and service for a company client at their offices.

2  Write the outgoing message for your own answering machine.

3  Student A, turn to File 19 on page 132. Student B, turn to File 32 on page 136. Follow the instructions there, taking it in turns to make and receive calls.

> **Leaving a message**
>
> – Work out before you call what you will say.
> – Identify yourself.
> – Give the time of the call.
> – Leave a clear and concise message.
> – Leave a contact number.

# Case study

## The right stuff

1 Work in two groups. Group A should discuss the differences between the pairs or groups of adjectives in box A. Group B do the same with box B. When you have finished, find a partner from the other group and exchange definitions.

**A**
1 conscientious, tenacious
2 efficient, methodical
3 charming, diplomatic
4 ruthless, tough
5 astute, intelligent, crafty
6 persuasive, articulate, self-confident

**B**
1 sensitive, sensible
2 assertive, aggressive
3 numerate, computer-literate
4 ambitious, dynamic
5 reliable, trustworthy, punctual
6 outgoing, volatile, easygoing

2 Which adjectives describe:
1 determination and desire to succeed?
2 reliability and working habits?

3 Which adjectives can have a negative connotation?

4 Choose the three most important adjectives for the following professions:
- a sales manager
- a personnel manager
- an accountant

5 Some people say that interviewers make up their minds about a candidate in the first thirty seconds. How true do you think this is?

6 Study the business tip about preparing for interviews, and how to behave during them.
1 Which advice do you think:
- the most useful?
- unnecessary or inappropriate?
2 What further tips would you add?

*Character is destiny.*
**Heraclitus**, Greek philosopher

## Preparing for an interview

### Before the interview

- No earrings or pony-tails for men.
- Have your hair cut and shave off beards.
- Visit the company beforehand to find out what the dress code is.
- Wear comfortable clothes.
- Carry a smart briefcase – never a plastic bag.
- Think of a couple of intelligent questions to ask.
- Avoid onions and garlic for forty-eight hours before the interview.
- Make sure you have a good night's sleep.

### During the interview

- Smile and shake hands with the interviewer(s).
- Look people in the eye.
- Appear modest and not over-confident.
- Sit with your hands on your lap.
- Don't fidget or fiddle with hair or jewellery.
- Don't cross your arms and legs.
- Keep both feet on the ground.
- Never ask about money at first interview.

7 Read the details about Drivers. What personal profile do you think would be most suitable for this post?

> Drivers, the sports equipment and sportswear company, is trying to recruit a salesperson to break into the golfing equipment market. It wants to recruit just one person to cover the clubs in the south of England and Scotland. The successful candidate would have to visit specialist sports suppliers and golf courses to sell its goods. They would have to spend up to six weeks a year away from home on short business trips within the sales area and a further two weeks a year in the US or at hospitality events.

8 The Human Resources Manager at Drivers has received four sets of details from the employment agency it used for its initial search. In groups of four or five, read the notes and decide which two people you would like to call for interview.

9 Now hold the interviews. Two of you are the candidates you have selected for interview. The others are the selection panel. Interviewers should spend five minutes thinking of questions they might like to ask. Candidates should predict the questions which are likely to be asked and may invent further personal details.

Name: Linda Stalker

Age: 33

**Marital status:** Divorced, two small children.

**Qualifications:** Diploma in Marketing.

**Experience:** 7 years working in fashion sales and insurance.

**Sales aptitude test:** 10 / 10

**Expected salary:** €60,000 plus help with school fees for children.

**Initial impressions from interview:** Self-confident and dynamic. Very well-presented. Says she loves sales. Claims she can sell anything. However, not very knowledgeable about sport in general or golf in particular.

**Notes:** Reservations about her family situation. Could she travel?

Name: Milton Brody

Age: 25

**Marital status:** Single.

**Qualifications:** BA and Teaching certificate.

**Experience:** 2 years teaching sports and gymnastics.

**Sales aptitude test:** 5 / 10

**Expected salary:** €60,000

**Initial impressions from interview:** Self-confident. Says that he could learn the techniques which would make him a better salesperson.

**Notes:** Feels that he would be able to exploit his reputation as a nationally-known athlete. Successful sportsman with medals. National level. Forced to withdraw because of knee injury. Says he knows what athletes want and can speak with confidence about our different ranges.

Name: Adrian Sterling

Age: 52

**Marital status:** Widowed, two grown-up children.

**Qualifications:** Left school at 18 after 'A' levels to join army.

**Experience:** Army officer for 10 years. Left with rank of Captain. 23 years of sales experience.

**Sales aptitude test:** 9 / 10

**Expected salary:** €75,000 plus commission and usual perks.

Initial impressions from interview: Active and dynamic. Likeable. Looks younger than 52. Would be able to bring clients with him. Keen tennis player.

**Notes:** On your instructions we approached Mr Sterling. Have heard on the grapevine that he does not get on well with the new sales manager of his existing company.

Name: Jolanda Scholes

Age: 24

**Marital status:** Married, no children.

**Qualifications:** BA Ancient history. MBA in export management.

**Experience:** 1 year in family import / export business.

Sales aptitude test: 7 / 10

**Expected salary:** €50,000 plus commission.

Initial impressions from interview: Pleasant and charming. Well-educated and softly spoken. Not really interested in a long-term career in sales. Not motivated by money.

**Notes:** Daughter of Findley Scholes, a professional golfer who won lots of competitions in the 1980s and 1990s. Plays golf herself and knows a lot about our equipment.

# 11 Look before you leap

## Talking business

1 Some people are happier working on their own, while others like to belong to some kind of organization. Where would you personally prefer to work?

- in a multinational company
- in a large national corporation
- in a state-run industry or service
- in a small company
- in a family firm
- as an entrepreneur running your own business

2 How easy or common do you think it is to move from one kind of organization to another?

## Listening

### Look before you leap

1 You are going to listen to an interview with Anthea Fowler who works for an organization called the Franchise Group. Before you listen, read the business tip below and discuss the questions.

- What kind of people do you think make successful franchise-holders?
- How many franchises can you think of in your country which operate in the fast food sector; the business services sector; and the car tyres / exhausts industry?

---

**Franchising**

A franchise is a contractual agreement in which one party (the franchiser) sells the right to market goods or services under its name to another party (the franchisee). McDonald's and Häagen-Dazs are examples of retail franchises.

The franchisee is usually given exclusive selling rights in a particular area.

---

2 [11.1] In part A, Anthea Fowler gives advice on becoming a franchisee. Listen and answer the questions.

1 According to Anthea, what are the advantages of taking on a franchise rather than starting an entirely new business?

2 Complete the following statistics.

a percentage of British businesses which are franchises ......

b number of people employed in franchises ......

c amount of business generated ......

3 Listen again and decide if statements 1–5 are true (T) or false (F).
Anthea believes that:

1 franchises are the perfect way to learn about a new business. ......

2 real entrepreneurs can make poor franchisees. ......

3 franchises require less work than other businesses. ......

4 franchises are good for older people. ......

5 previous experience is essential. ......

4 In part B Anthea discusses how franchisers make their money, and the advantages for franchisees.

1 According to Anthea, how much money should people be prepared to pay for a franchise?

2 What mistake of the interviewer's does Anthea correct?

3 Anthea describes how franchisers commonly help franchisees. Study the list, and tick the areas she mentions. Does she mention anything else?

- national advertising ......
- help with recruitment of staff ......
- brochures and promotional material ......
- competitive buying power ......
- management systems ......
- a logo you can use ......
- reputation ......
- assistance with finance ......

4 What big advantage does a franchise holder have over a nearby, independent competitor?

**5** In part C Anthea gives practical advice for choosing a franchise. Listen and answer the questions.

1 How should people go about finding a franchise which will suit them?

2 When looking for a franchise, what questions should you ask franchisers?

3 What should you do if the franchiser:

a recommends which franchisees you should talk to?

b tries to make you sign straight away?

**6** Turn to the tapescript on page 165. Find expressions with *and* which match definitions 1–7.

1 employing people and dismissing them
----------------

2 rapidly becoming successful ....................

3 having proven ability ....................

4 most importantly ....................

5 in general ....................

6 operating ....................

7 strict ....................

## Language study

### Adjective and adverb patterns

**1** What is the difference in grammar and meaning between the words in italics in pairs 1–3?

1 She works *hard*.
She *hardly* works.

2 He hasn't been *late*.
He hasn't been *lately*.

3 I *nearly* passed the exam.
The exam is getting *near*.

Ⓖ **Grammar guide, page 140**

**2** Find the adjectives and adverbs below in 🔲 11.1 on page 165. Now use them to create further sentences.

| | | | |
|---|---|---|---|
| actual | actually | real | really |
| eventual | eventually | short | shortly |

**3** What differences in structure and meaning do you notice in the pairs of sentences below?

1 The price change hasn't made *much* difference in demand.
The price change has made *hardly any* difference in demand.

2 This model is *far less* reliable *than* the old one.
This model *isn't quite as* reliable *as* the old one.

3 *It's the easiest* way of going into business for an inexperienced person.
*There's no easier* way of going into business for an inexperienced person.

4 *The longer* we stay in business *the less* profit we seem to make.
*Every extra* year we stay in business, we seem to make *less* profit.

**4** Continue the second sentence in 1–6 so that it is similar in meaning to the first one.

1 Setting up a franchise has fewer risks.
It's much less ----------------------------------

2 It's the best way of going into business for someone with limited experience.
There isn't ----------------------------------

3 They feel too old to set up a concept from zero.
They don't feel ----------------------------------

4 Entirely new businesses have a much worse chance of survival than franchises.
A franchise has a ----------------------------------

5 Fees increase with the size of the franchise.
The bigger ----------------------------------

6 You need to make a good and wise selection.
Select ----------------------------------

**5** Decide what you would say in these situations.

1 You are convinced that the best kind of advertising is by word of mouth.

2 You have interviewed a candidate for a job. Tell your colleague that in your opinion, the candidate lacks confidence.

3 You think that building new roads simply leads to worse traffic jams.

4 You had extra memory installed on your computer, but its performance has not improved. You are disappointed.

5 You want to sell last year's version of a software programme to a customer. The old version has fewer features but, in your view, it is easier to use.

# Reading

## Keeping it in the family

1  You are going to study two texts which examine different aspects of family business. Before reading, discuss the following questions.

  – What disadvantages exist for both family and non-family members working in a family firm?

  – What problems could you predict when a business is handed over to the second generation?

2  Read text A, which is about children joining their family business, and answer questions 1–6.

  1  Why didn't Satbir want to join the family business?

  2  Why did she eventually change her mind?

  3  How is Satbir's story different from her brother's?

  4  How do their experiences support what Ben Williams says?

  5  How does JW Lees & Co integrate family members into the firm?

  6  So far, how successful has the firm's policy been?

**A**

### To join or not to join?

Working in her father's manufacturing company during the school holidays and at weekends convinced Satbir Billen that she did not want to go into the family business. 'I enjoyed working there but I saw the hard work that was needed, the long, unsociable hours, the setbacks and the stress. I also saw the good things – but I had no illusions,' she explains.

After completing her degree, Satbir worked as a scientist, followed by a couple of years in public relations. Satbir's views have changed since working in PR. 'I realized that to be successful in your career, even if you're working for somebody else, you still have to work long hours and deal with stress. That's when I started to re-think my views about working for yourself: at least my father has reaped the rewards from being his own boss,' she adds.

'My brother, Jatinder, joined the family business straight from university, but decided to leave after two and a half years. He felt that because it was our father's company, he would never get the recognition he deserved. He went to work for another company for a year. However, he has now realized that working for himself is what he wants to do and he has started his own company. When my father retires he will see if he can try and run both companies,' she says. So according to Satbir, working outside the family business helps you decide whether it's right for you.

Ben Williams, a corporate psychologist agrees that it's rarely a good idea for graduates to go straight from university into the family business. He says that graduates who do, can expect 'resentment from other people in the business who feel that they don't have the experience or ability for the jobs they are doing.' Mr Williams advises graduates to work in the outside world before joining the family business so that they can 'learn how to fail and make mistakes. If graduates entering family businesses bring outside work experience, they have something to offer other than the fact they are related to the owner,' he explains.

This is supported by Simon Lees Jones, a surveyor who joined the family business, J W Lees & Co, a brewery, after working elsewhere for several years. 'My father and uncle have a policy that before any family member joins the business they have to have worked outside the business for at least five years,' he says. Simon is now property director, his brother is sales and marketing director, and his two cousins also work in the business. 'When I joined the family business, I had to do every job, including the menial ones like cleaning and delivery. This gave me a good all-round knowledge of the business and helped me to get to know everyone. The workers now respect our dedication to the business,' he explains.

*The Guardian*

3 Text B is about passing on the family business. According to the text, are statements 1–8 true (*T*) or false (*F*)?

1 Bogod feels ill-equipped for the job. ......

2 The printing business case was typical of father-to-son succession. ......

3 Daughters who take over the family business from their fathers approach it in the same way as sons do. ......

4 Succession issues should be discussed frankly as early as possible. ......

5 Passing on the business to the eldest child is the best course of action. ......

6 Murray believes that an outsider can be a good judge of what a firm needs. ......

7 A firm's board of directors can usually be expected to make a wise choice of successor. ......

8 It is better when a founder makes a clean break with the firm. ......

4 Complete the sentences with an appropriate form of one of the phrasal verbs in italics in text B.

1 At first she resisted ............... the family business but later she changed her mind.

2 He decided to ............... the family business to the oldest son.

3 They ............... over the inheritance, and haven't spoken to each other since.

4 We'll have to ............... who is going to succeed her sooner or later.

5 Give five pieces of advice about:

1 making family appointments work (Text A).

2 choosing a successor wisely (Text B).

6 Not all family firms are small. Some of the world's major companies are still owned or managed by second or third generations of the founding family. Can you think of any examples?

## B

# *When a founder steps down*

Handing over the family business often sets off a bitter feud. Tony Bogod, a family-firms consultant, regularly asks psychologists for help. 'Although I trained as an accountant, I now find myself working more with feelings than figures,' he says. 'I really need a leather couch in my office'. One owner-manager had *handed over* the running of his printing business to two sons. But the brothers fought furiously. Bogod says: 'One day the father phoned me up in tears, saying, "all I want is for them to be happy"'. This case follows a general trend for fathers who pass their businesses to sons. 'Father-son succession is much harder than father-daughter,' says Bogod. 'When a son *goes into* the business, it is about proving himself, being competitive, and wanting to make his father proud. But with a daughter, it is about support and wanting to be there for him.' Bogod believes that starting an early discussion about passing on the business is the key to a successful handover. Even though talking to parents about retirement is hard, you should start doing it ten years before they retire.

Barbara Murray, a family-business expert, believes that failing to talk is not the only pitfall. 'A common mistake that people make,' says Murray, 'is that when they are nervous about who is going to be the next leader they try to solve the problem very quickly without exploring it properly. So it's automatically the oldest son or the daughter with the business degree who gets the company. What they should really do is have an honest look at what the business needs, then find someone who is not directly involved in the firm. The outsider can say if the skills the business needs are in the offspring.'

Before making a final choice, owner-managers should consider another factor, says Andrew Godfrey of Grant Thornton, the accountant. 'You need to know what you want to do with your business before you select a successor. Until you know where the business is going, you don't know what kind of leader you need – is it a cost-cutting man or a marketing man?' Leaving the decision on succession to the board spells trouble says Godfrey. 'If you don't choose, you will end up with a committee. Rule by committee is disastrous. Nothing happens, you get a business vacuum and the firm drifts.' Many families *fall out* when the company founder stays on past retirement, says Godfrey. 'There has to be a plan about how the older generation is going to exit the business. To do this they need to have enough money outside the company to make themselves financially independent.'

But choosing a successor is just too hard for a lot of owner-managers. 'The classic mistake is the father who retires and just cannot tell his children who is going to be managing director. He says, "you can *sort* it *out* when I am dead". This will keep a lid on it while he is alive. But as soon as he dies, you can be sure that the family will have its own version of world war three.'

*The Guardian*

## Language in use

### Asking the right questions

1 Daisy Young and Simon Sharpe, two young entrepreneurs, are having a meeting with members of a venture capital organization. They want to obtain financial backing to bring their product to the market. What do you think the atmosphere of the meeting will be like?

2 **11.2** Now listen and complete some of the questions they were asked.

1 ............... your objectives for this meeting?

2 ............... leave your prototype with us?

3 ............... personally prepared to invest?

4 So ............... our help, ............... ?

5 ............... your sales forecast is too ambitious?

6 These figures are rather unrealistic, ...............?

7 You ............... carry out a feasibility study, ............... you?

8 ............... telling us who else you have approached?

9 ............... forgetting the competition?

10 ............... be better to manufacture abroad?

3 Decide which questions from **2**:

1 expect a yes / no answer.

2 are open-ended.

3 use question tags.

4 Which questions from **2**:

1 are indirect?

2 sound aggressive or challenging?

5 **11.3** Match the beginnings of the replies 1–10 to endings a–j. Then listen and check your answers.

1 Not at all, it's quite viable ... ......

2 I can assure you that they are ... ......

3 Naturally, so we feel confident that ... ......

4 I'm afraid their identity has to ... ......

5 If you don't mind, we'll ... ......

6 Unfortunately, we're not prepared to do that ... ......

7 Actually, we've already raised money ... ......

8 Obviously, we'd like to go away ... ......

9 Certainly, but we believe that other backers would ... ......

10 I'm glad you asked us that, but at this stage, ... ......

a ... we'd like to keep a close watch on quality.

b ... with your financial backing.

c ... based on detailed marketing research.

d ... before we've received a firm commitment.

e ... from our families and friends.

f ... remain confidential.

g ... we can meet these targets.

h ... welcome the opportunity to invest.

i ... discuss the competition later.

j ... given the uniqueness of the product.

6 **11.4** Now match the replies in **5** to the questions in **2**. Then listen and check your answers.

### Pronunciation: questions and tags

1 **11.5** Listen to questions 1–5 and mark each question ↗ or ↘ according to whether the voice goes up or down at the end.

1 What does your factory produce?

2 Does your factory produce components?

3 Doesn't your factory produce components?

4 It produces components, doesn't it?

5 It produces components, doesn't it?

2 Which questions expect the answer to be 'yes'?

3 In the following situations ask each other questions using an appropriate question type. Remember to use the correct intonation.

1 You have to catch a train to a nearby town but you do not know the train timetable.

2 You are going to lunch but do not have enough money. Borrow some from a colleague.

3 You are meeting a friend later to go to the cinema. You think the film starts at 19.30 but you are not sure.

4 You are working on a project which is behind schedule. Ask your partner to work late to help you catch up.

5 You have been invited to a party. You're sure it is tomorrow but want to confirm.

# Speaking

## Selling the dream

1 Would you like to start up your own business?
   - If so, in which sector? Why?
   - What factors would you need to consider?

2 Read the situation below.
   - What do you think of the Jubiolation concept?
   - Would it work in your country?
   - Would you risk your money in it?

During a holiday in the USA last year, some young business people were impressed by the number of juice bars which seem to have taken over from traditional coffee shops. On their return, they decided to bring this concept to the fashionable Covent Garden area of London and opened Jubiolation, a New York-style juice bar café. Jubiolation sells fruit- and milk-based drinks and sandwiches made exclusively from organically-produced ingredients. Now the founders of Jubiolation would like to expand, and open up further branches in other parts of London, and in Berlin and Copenhagen. They have decided to approach Hardman and Nailer, a venture capital organization, for financial backing.

3 Jubiolation have sent an initial business plan to Hardman and Nailer. Read the extracts below.

### Our concept
Our products are ethical.
They are good for consumers.
Our concept will help to encourage organic farming and help the environment. We promise customers a healthy and nourishing alternative to fast food such as hamburgers and fries.

### USPs and special service
Only totally-organic sandwich bar in London.
Affordable prices.
Text-message orders – great for people in a hurry.
Order your own sandwich on-line from a list of ingredients.
Delivery can be arranged at a small extra cost.
International choice of fillings.

### Experience
One of our partners used to work in financial services for a bank.
Another partner is a trained chef who has produced some amazing sandwich recipes.
The chef has also created some unique fruit-juice cocktails and milk-based drinks after months of experimentation.
Our team has youth and enthusiasm on its side.
Our small juice bar and sandwich shop has already become very successful in the fashionable Covent Garden area of London.

### Financial commitment and backing required
We have put all our savings into the first sandwich bar.
Friends and family have also invested a total of €120,000:
   - to rent and equip five juice and sandwich bars in commercial parts of London (x3), Berlin (1) and Copenhagen (1) .
   - to achieve economies of scale and bring down prices to the consumer.
   - to guarantee contracts with suppliers of organically-grown produce from suppliers.

We require a further €800,000. Half this sum buys a 20% share in the company. The remaining €400,000 will be paid back within four years.

4 Work in two groups with two or three students in each group. Group A, you are the founders of Jubiolation. Your job is to convince Hardman and Nailer to invest in your business. Turn to File 23 on page 133 for your information. Group B, you work for Hardman and Nailer. Your information is in File 24 on page 134.

5 When both groups are ready, hold your meeting.

# Writing

## Getting financial backing

**1** Inventions sometimes result from an unlikely combination of observations and ideas. Read the information and discuss the questions.

- How feasible do you think this invention is?
- How popular might it be?
- What problems could it face along the way?

Olga Phillips, an engineering graduate with a marketing MBA, and her friend Rudi Jacobson, who has a zoology PhD, have come up with an idea for a leisure activity they believe could challenge the popularity of skate-boarding and roller-blading. Rudi wrote his thesis on the kangaroo's ability to jump long distances. He and Olga have combined Rudi's research and Olga's engineering skills in the production of a special spring-loaded sports boot. This enables the ordinary person to make two-metre-long jumps. Whenever they have tested the invention in parks they have immediately attracted crowds of people, totally captivated by the concept. They have protected the invention, which they call 'Bounders', with international patents. Now, in common with many entrepreneurs, Olga and Rudi need to raise finance to take their invention to a more advanced stage and into mass production.

> ❚If you can dream it, you can do it.❚
> **Walt Disney**

**2** Olga and Rudi are writing to the venture capital organization, Hardman and Nailer. Reorganize the jumbled letter A–I according to steps 1–9 below.

1 Who we are and why we are writing.
2 The background to our idea. ......
3 How we have developed it. ......
4 Measure of our success so far. ......
5 Our next step. ......
6 Why we need your help. ......
7 What we could achieve together. ......
8 Enclosures. ......
9 Willingness to discuss the proposal further. ......

**A** *In this belief*, we have dedicated the past year to the development of a prototype boot. A crowd gathered around us as soon as we began testing it in Regent's Park last week.

**B** We would welcome the opportunity to see you in person and discuss our plans and requirements in further detail. In the meantime, we trust that you will respect the confidentiality of all aspects of our discussion.

**C** We believe that *your financial expertise*, combined with our keen understanding of the technology and mechanics involved, could bring *this dream* to fruition.

**D** We are two young inventors who are writing to you with a business investment opportunity we feel sure will be of interest. My partner and I are respectively an engineer and a zoologist who have developed a revolutionary leisure concept.

**E** Having proved that our invention can work, our ambition is now to bring it to a mass market.

**F** Enclosed is a preliminary business plan for your consideration.

**G** *This innovation* has resulted from a discussion in which we concluded that it would be possible to allow humans to replicate the kangaroo's jumping action through a pair of spring-loaded boots.

**H** *However*, we recognize that *doing so* will require the financial backing of an organization such as yours, which shares our vision and enthusiasm.

**I** *Their interest* demonstrates the boot's enormous appeal and potential.

**3** How did the words and phrases in italics help you to put the letter in order?

**4** To avoid repeating the same word too many times in a text, we can use a synonym or pronoun. How many different words are used to refer to the boots in the letter to Hardman and Nailer?

**5** Now look back at the 'Speaking' section. The founders of the Jubiolation juice bar would also have had to contact Hardman and Nailer before being granted an interview. Write the letter they would have sent.

# In conversation

## Telephoning

**1** Philip Hawkins recently met Juliet Winters at a franchise fair. He is now trying to call her to discuss a franchise opportunity. Put the telephone conversation below in the correct order, as in the example.

1 When would be a good time to speak to you? ......

2 Well, yes. It's regarding some literature she gave me about your franchise scheme. I have a few queries. ......

3 After lunch, shall we say between two and three? ......

4 Certainly, so if you'd just like to give me your details, I'll make sure that she returns your call as soon as she's available. ......

5 I see. And could I ask what it's in connection with, Mr Hawkins? ......

6 Yes, certainly. My name's Philip Hawkins, I spoke with Ms Winters at the franchise fair last week. ......

7 Good morning, could I speak to Juliet Winters, please? ..2..

8 Would you like to try again later, or would you rather she phoned you? ......

9 New Affiliates. Gemma Michael speaking. ..1..

10 Oh dear, what a pity. ......

11 May I ask who's calling, please? ......

12 I see. If you'd like to hold the line I'll see if she's available. Hello, Mr Hawkins, I'm terribly sorry, but I'm afraid she's with another client at the moment. ......

13 Perhaps it would be better if she rang me when she's free. ......

**2** 🖥 **11.6** Listen and check.

**3** 🖥 **11.7** Listen to the second conversation.

1 What is the reason for Jerry's call?

2 How is the tone of the second conversation different from the first?

**4** Study the tapescripts on page 166. Complete the table with words and expressions from the two conversations.

**5** Work in pairs. Student A turn to File 8 on page 129. Student B, turn to File 33 on page 136. Take it in turns to telephone each other.

|   |   | Conversation one | Conversation two |
|---|---|---|---|
| 1 | answering the phone | | |
| 2 | asking to speak to someone | | |
| 3 | asking who is telephoning | | |
| 4 | asking the reason for the call | | |
| 5 | asking the caller to wait | | |
| 6 | saying someone is busy | | |
| 7 | asking for the caller's details | | |
| 8 | promising to get the person to call back | | |

# Case study

## Up my street?

1 The *Global Entrepreneurship Monitor* compares entrepreneurial activity in twenty countries. Guess the results of its survey by completing the text below with the percentages from the box. Discuss your answers with a partner.

| 1% | 2% | 3% | 6% | 7% |
|----|----|----|----|----|
| 8% | 16% | 45% | 56% | |

GEM found that **1** ............... % of British adults have set up a business, equal with Italy. This is in contrast with France and Germany, where the figure is about **2** ............... %. However, this is much worse than the US, where **3** ............... % of adults have set up a business. The figure for Canada is **4** ............... % and for Israel, **5** ............... %. Only **6** ............... % of British people think there are good opportunities for starting a business in the next six months compared with **7** ............... % in the US. The Japanese, at **8** ............... %, are the least optimistic. Strangely enough, the failure rate for new businesses in all industrialized countries is around **9** ............... % within the first three years.

2 Turn to File 21 on page 133 to find out the results of the survey. Then discuss the following questions.

– Are there any results that you find surprising?

– What does this tell us about national attitudes towards risk-taking and failure?

– What could the government of your country do to encourage people to go into business on their own?

3 Read the text about Angela and Maurice Butler.

1 What has happened to both of them quite recently?

2 In theory, how much money would they have to put into a new business venture?

Angela and Maurice Butler, both 47, have both recently been made redundant from their jobs in the City of London. Angela was a human resources manager and Maurice was a computer services manager in the same firm. Together, their redundancy payments total £100,000. Fortunately, their home is paid for and their children are financially independent. They live in a large comfortable farmhouse and have several acres of land with two old barns in the countryside on the outskirts of London.

They have both been looking for jobs but have found that opportunities for 'used' executives in their late forties are scarce. They have decided that setting up their own business could provide the answer. They have both come to the conclusion that a franchise could be the best way of starting out again. Both are fit and active. Angela is a keen golfer and Maurice loves cooking and entertaining friends. At a recent franchise fair, their imagination was caught by two possible franchise opportunities, Top Hole and Puddings Galore.

4 Read the information about Top Hole golf ranges and the Puddings Galore franchise. Then discuss the following questions.

– How clearly defined do you think each of the concepts is?

– What unique selling points does each have?

– What potential customer groups do these franchise opportunities target?

– Which of these two opportunities would best suit Angela and Maurice?

**Puddings Galore**

As its name suggests, Puddings Galore is a café-franchise chain specializing in desserts. Each dessert is served as an individual giant portion which the average person cannot finish. The company's slogan is: 'A dessert that's a meal in itself'. An international range of desserts including Crème Brulée, Tiramisu, Pecan Pie, Bread and Butter Pudding, and Mississippi Mud Pie are sent ready-prepared by the mother company to be cooked in the franchisees' ovens. For £4.80, customers get the dessert of their choice plus a large cup of freshly-brewed Italian coffee. Customers eat their dessert standing up around large pillars or at the central bar. The Puddings Galore look is for brightly-lit premises, with stainless steel counters, mirrors and marble and chrome finishes.

### Top Hole

Top Hole builds on a popular concept from Japan, based on golf-firing ranges for long-range driving practice.

Players can turn up and practise their drives. These ranges are particularly popular in Japan where space is at a premium. Joining a proper golf club in the Tokyo area can cost around ¥3.5 million plus annual fees of a further several thousand. A round of golf often costs more than ¥17,000 per player. By contrast, an hour at one of the firing ranges costs just a few hundred Japanese yen. It is an excellent way of relaxing at the end of a hard day's work. Players drive from under a covered area, which protects them from bad weather, and practise their drives without having to bother picking up the balls afterwards. Joining Top Hole is a chance to get in at the beginning of a completely new franchise opportunity. The green belt area around London has been targeted as the best area for these franchises.

5 Angela and Maurice are now seriously considering taking up one of these franchise opportunities and have obtained initial details and rough costings. Work in pairs. Student A, look at the details for Top Hole below. Student B, turn to File 42 on page 139 for information about Puddings Galore.

Compare details with your partner. Which opportunity:

1 requires the bigger investment?
2 has the greatest potential?
3 has more chance of breaking even quickly?

6 Would you advise Angela and Maurice to go for one of these opportunities?

## Top Hole

| Franchise opportunities | Costs |
|---|---|
| • Four franchises are available for the green belt area around London. | • Franchise fee: £15,000 up-front joining fee for five years, plus 10% of turnover after the second year. |
| • Basic facilities would consist of a covered area for up to twenty players and a fenced 300 m range, as well as a small bar and club house. Barn conversions are popular in this part of the country. | • Clubs and balls: £3,000<br>• Markers and targets: £2,000<br>• Conversion of barns to changing room and clubhouse / shop: £160,000 |
| • Average golf clubs in this area cost around £1000 to join with an annual fee of £250. However, they usually offer a full course of eighteen holes and club-house facilities. Coaching is usually available from a professional. | • Fencing and construction of a covered firing range: £40,000<br>• Lighting (for night use): £6,000<br>• Players pay: £10.00 for an hour's driving practice. |
| • A lot of business people and executives live in the countryside around London, from where they commute to work. | |
| • British people tend to have more leisure time than the Japanese. | |

# 12 Reputations

## Talking business

1 Down through the ages, people have fought to preserve their names. Read this modern-day case of the misuse of people's names on the Internet.

- What do you understand by the term *cyber-squatter*?
- How far do you agree with the court's decision?
- How would you act to prevent somebody using your name?

> A Cambridge University cyber-squatter lost his battle with novelist Jeanette Winterson after it was ruled he had acted in 'bad faith'. Mark Hogarth had registered more than 130 novelists' domain names. He intended to sell the domain names back to the authors for a big profit. When Ms Winterson complained to the World Intellectual Property Association they upheld her complaint.

*The Telegraph*

2 Champagne growers prevent other sparkling wine manufacturers who use the champagne method from calling their product *champagne*. Can you think of any other products which have trademarked the name of the region where the product is originally produced?

3 Some products are so dominant that their names have entered the English language as a generic term. For example, *Hoover* is a brand of vacuum cleaner, and the verb *to hoover* has come to mean *to clean with a vacuum cleaner*.

- Can you think of any such terms in your own language?
- Can you see any reasons why manufacturers might object to this use of their name?

## Listening

### Cyber-libel

1 You are going to listen to an interview with Stella Moss, a lawyer, who discusses some of the legal problems involved with business use of the Internet, together with possible solutions.

1 During Stella's interview you will hear the words in the box below. Do you know what they all mean?

| cyber-space to download | a website virus | a hacker litigation |
|---|---|---|

2 Brainstorm some of the legal problems associated with the Internet which you think Stella may mention.

2 **12.1** Listen to part A and answer questions 1–4.

1 According to Stella, what do people believe about the law and the Internet?

2 What particular legal problem can hackers cause?

3 What are the four problems that a company's employees can cause?

4 Which of these problems does she suggest could be accidental or deliberate?

3 In part B, Stella discusses the issue of cyber-libel. What do you think cyber-libel might be? Listen to find out, and then decide if statements 1–7 are true (*T*) or false (*F*).

1 People put less thought into writing an e-mail than an ordinary letter. .....

2 E-mail messages tend to be less formal. .....

3 E-mail is an intimate form of correspondence. .....

4 Letters written on a firm's headed paper have more legal importance than e-mail messages. .....

5 Libel is only committed if a deliberate lie is told. .....

6 Cyber-libel occurs once the message leaves a company. .....

7 The financial consequences of libel are more serious in the USA than in the UK. .....

8 Slander is as serious an offence as libel. .....

**4** In part C, Stella discusses how businesses can protect themselves from the actions of their employees. Listen, and complete the notes.

1 Companies can try to protect themselves by
........................................................................... .

2 They also need to have a policy which says
........................................................................... .

3 As one of their conditions of employment, employees should sign .............................. .

4 However, the employer will also have to prove that ............................................... .

5 If anyone is caught using the Internet improperly they ..................................... .

6 If a company is involved in litigation, it may escape liability if ................................ .

**5** Look at these sentences from the tapescript and explain the difference between the words in italics.

1 Now if company B can prove that A had won the contract by *damaging* B's reputation, the consequences could be serious.

British courts tend to award comparatively small amounts in *damages* ...

2 It's still libel even if it's circulated within the company, but it's only likely to be recognized as such once it is read by the victims of the *libel*.

Well normally, a company is *liable* for any act carried out by its employees.

Someone accused of *slander* could simply deny having said anything offensive ...

## Language study

### Determiners

**1** Complete the text with the definite article *the*; the indefinite article *a / an*; or Ø (no article).

> Right, well, let's say there are two companies bidding for **1**..... contract, **2**..... same one. Now imagine there's **3**..... person in company A who sends **4**..... e-mail message to **5**..... colleague saying that if company B doesn't get **6**..... contract it is likely to go bankrupt. Now, let's say **7**..... colleague reads **8**..... message and passes it on to **9**..... outsiders. If **10**..... story is untrue or malicious there could be **11**..... case to answer.

**2** Turn to tapescript [12.1] on page 167 and check your answers.

**3** How did you decide which article to use?

(g) Grammar guide, page 142

**4** Complete 1–7 by underlining which choice is correct or the most likely.

1 There isn't *any / some* ink in the printer.

2 I've got *some / any* stuff about the court case you were interested in.

3 Could I have *any / some* help with this form, please?

4 There isn't *many / much* detail in this report, is there?

5 I'd appreciate *any / some* information at all on cyber-libel.

6 Would you like *some / any* help with these invoices?

7 *Much / many* people nowadays think the Internet is a law-free zone.

**5** Are there any sentences in **4** where either choice is possible? If so, does the meaning change?

**6** Using *any*, re-phrase sentences 1–3.

1 All new employees have to accept this as a condition of employment.

2 The policy will provide no protection at all unless it is properly policed.

3 There is very little real difference between the rules governing libel and slander.

**7** Discuss the difference in meaning in pairs of sentences 1–5.

1 Is there *any* toner in the photocopier?
Is there *some* toner in the photocopier?

2 There are *a few* steps it can take.
There are *few* steps it can take.

3 You have *a little* control over what others do.
You have *little* control over what others do.

4 I'd explain the policy to *each* employee.
I'd explain the policy to *every* employee.

5 *Your* lawyer will tell you I'm right.
*Any* lawyer will tell you I'm right.

# Reading

## See you in court

1 Match the words and expressions in italics in a–h in the sentences below to definitions 1–8.

1 lack of proper care or attention .....

2 the person / people accused in a legal case .....

3 making a legal claim against someone for causing harm in some way .....

4 the person / people bringing a court action against someone in a law court .....

5 unfairly invading someone's legal rights to do something .....

6 ideas or designs that have been created or invented by somebody .....

7 to state or claim something that has not yet been proved .....

8 when someone breaks the conditions of an agreement .....

– Hospitals are so afraid of dissatisfied patients and their families **a** *suing* them for **b** *negligence* that they have to take out insurance.

– They've copied our logo. We should take them to court for **c** *infringing* our trademark.

– They broke the terms of our agreement and are now **d** *in breach of* contract.

– The **e** *claimants* both **f** *allege* that the **g** *defendants* acted in bad faith by hiding the true state of the company before the takeover.

– Publishers of digital software and music find it hard to protect their **h** *intellectual property*.

2 You are going to read about four court cases A–D. Read the cases and decide in which case:

1 judges supported an earlier judgement. .....

2 false suggestions were made in a newspaper. .....

3 a company was held responsible for the activities of its customers. .....

4 judges disagree with suggestions made by a organization which examines the law. .....

5 someone was accused of not carrying out their duties properly. .....

6 the judgement may be harder to enforce in other countries. .....

7 the judgement was welcomed by a top lawyer. .....

8 someone was compensated for their hurt feelings. .....

9 a judgement was made based on examining a few examples of typical situations. .....

10 an agreement was made before all the facts had been presented. .....

**A**

FIVE Court of Appeal judges yesterday turned down a Law Commission recommendation that damages for some personal injury claims should be doubled. They insisted that any increase should be limited to a maximum of 33%.

The decision was welcomed by the National Health Service and insurers. Philip Havers, QC, for the NHS, which is not insured, said the service was under 'immense pressures' over negligence claims.

Insurers had said that premiums for drivers and employers could rise by 30% if awards rose by a third. The judges had been expected to endorse the recommendation by the Law Commission, the Government's official law reform body, which called for a 50–100% rise in payments to victims of work, road and medical accidents.

But after hearing eight test cases the panel said that such rises would cause an unbearable burden on insurance firms and have 'a significant effect on the over-stretched health service'.

Tom Jones, a solicitor in one of the cases, said after the ruling: 'What world are these judges living in? The Court of Appeal have sided with the insurance industry that in 1998 made a trading profit of £1.2 billion. We are not asking for crazy awards. We do not want the American system over here.'

**B**

DARYL HANNAH today accepted undisclosed libel damages over allegations that she flew home to Los Angeles for her dog's birthday when she should have been attending last-minute rehearsals for a play in London.

Her solicitor Simon Smith told a judge that the 'false and very embarrassing' allegations appeared in an article in *The Mirror* last October.

The truth was, he said, that a month before the play's opening, Miss Hannah travelled to Toronto with the play's director, Michael Radford, to promote a film in which they had both been involved.

Anna Coppola, counsel for MGN Ltd, told the judge: 'Through me the defendant offers its sincere apologies to the claimant for the distress and embarrassment caused by this article. It entirely accepts that the allegations are false.'

**C**

A BRITISH violin dealer has agreed to pay £3 million damages to the estate of a millionaire which sued him for benefiting from the sale of one of the world's finest collections of instruments.

Mr Biddulph agreed to the settlement after a few days of a hearing which had been expected to last at least six weeks. Negotiations for a deal began before lawyers for Mr Segelman's estate had finished outlining their case. His estate's most valuable asset was his collection of about 50 violins worth millions of pounds.

Mr Biddulph was asked by the executors to store the collection and prepare valuations. But Mr Segelman's solicitor and an executor of his will, became unhappy about Mr Biddulph's conduct and sued him in the High Court 'for breach of duty in acting as agent'. Mr Biddulph was accused of selling violins at below market rates for the benefit of other dealers and of selling instruments for more than reported to the executors and keeping the difference.

**D**

THE legal defeat for Napster, the music-sharing web-site, was predictably welcomed by the music industry this week, but it remains unclear how 'music piracy' on the Net will be stopped.

On Monday, a US Court of Appeal upheld a previous legal ruling that the website should no longer be allowed to let users share music tracks for free. Anyone with a computer and an Internet connection can access Napster and copy anything from the endless list of songs.

The court also judged that Napster was liable for copyright infringement by its users, leaving it open to be sued by record companies for billions of dollars.

Jonathan Cameron, head of media law at law firm Paisner, said: 'It is the right decision. If you undermine intellectual property, you undermine the whole system, be it revenue for record companies or a poor group of kids from a slum that want to make it big.' He admitted, however, that it would be difficult to stop services that set themselves up in countries where copyright law is less established.

*The Telegraph*

**3** Summarize cases A–D by filling in the gaps.

A Judges in the court of appeal refused to accept the Law Commission's recommendations because they believed that **1** ................... . However; one solicitor was deeply disappointed with the decision because **2** ................... .

B *The Mirror* newspaper wrongly claimed that Daryl Hannah had **3** ................... . In fact she had **4** ................... .

C Mr Segelman's solicitor sued Mr Biddulph because he had failed **5** ................... . In addition, Mr Biddulph was accused of having **6** ................... .

D The court's decision means that Napster won't be able **7** ................... . However, the ruling is unlikely to end the problem of **8** ................... . According to one lawyer, you need to respect intellectual property because **9** ................... .

**4** Discuss the following questions in groups.

– Which of the cases do you think was the most surprising and the least necessary?

– How far is it the role of the court to protect the interests of insurance companies?

– How far do you personally respect copyright and intellectual property?

**5** Read the quotation. Then discuss the questions.

– What effect do you think the large number of lawyers has on American society?

– Do we shape the law or does the law shape us?

"Does America really need 70 per cent of the world's lawyers?…Is it healthy for our economy to have 18 million lawsuits … annually?"

**Dan Quayle**, former US vice-President

## Language in use

### Clarifying

1 Many small businesses have to rent office space. What kind of difficulties do you think could arise between landlords and tenants over:

- rent?
- the lease?
- maintaining and cleaning the premises?

2 [12.2] Sally Brewer is a graphic designer. She is looking for new office premises and has been visiting offices with Alan Judd, a letting agent. Listen to part of their conversation and answer the questions.

1 What does she like about the premises?
2 What is one of her main concerns?
3 What is the misunderstanding and how is this resolved?
4 What are 'dilapidations' and whose responsibility are they?

3 Turn to the tapescript on page 167. Find the words and expressions Sally and Alan use to:

1 show they don't understand.
2 clarify something.
3 check / recap what has just been said.

4 Study the introductory phrases below and then think of a further phrase for each heading.

1 **Saying you don't understand**
I'm sorry you've lost me.
I'm afraid I don't quite follow you.

---

2 **Re-formulating and summarizing**
So what you're saying is ...
So if I've understood you correctly / rightly ...

---

3 **Offering to repeat something**
Let me clarify that for you ...
Shall I run through it again?

---

4 **Asking for clarification**
What exactly do you mean by .... ?
What's meant by the term ...?

---

5 **Saying there has been a misunderstanding**
As I understood it ...
I was led to believe that ...

---

5 [12.3] Listen to situations 1–5 and make an appropriate comment using one of the expressions from 4.

### Pronunciation: intonation and meaning

1 [12.4] By changing the intonation in a phrase or sentence, we can convey a different mood. Listen to sentences 1 and 2 and then choose the most suitable ending a or b. In which sentence does the speaker sound doubtful?

1 The building is quite well-situated ... ........
2 The building is quite well-situated ... ........
a ... it's in the middle of the business area.
b ... although it's still rather too far from the centre.

2 How does the change in intonation affect the meaning?

3 [12.5] Listen to the beginnings of sentences 1–5 and choose the most appropriate ending a or b.

1 It's fairly close to the station; ... ........
 a ... it's just a two-minute walk.
 b ... although it's still too far to walk.
2 The reception area is really nice, ... ........
 a ... but it's spoilt by a really awful carpet.
 b ... there are lots of lovely plants.
3 The meeting is important, ... ........
 a ... so please be there on time.
 b ... but I'm afraid I have to finish this report.
4 The lift is quite slow, ... ........
 a ... but it doesn't matter because we're on the first floor.
 b ... we could waste a lot of time going up and down.
5 It's up to you, ... ........
 a ... but I hope you'll take our views into consideration.
 b ... so let us know when you've made your decision.

4 [12.6] Now listen and check your answers.

# Speaking

## Getting it straight

1 Work in pairs. You are going to role-play two short meetings where you need to check and clarify information. Look back at the 'Language in use' section on page 120. Student A, your information is below. Student B, turn to File 43 on page 139.

2 Prepare your questions based on the information you have, and anticipate the questions your partner will have. Go over any points which still remain unclear. Then have your meetings. By the end, you should each have a clear understanding of all the information provided by your partner.

### Student A

1 You wish to rent some office space through a letting agency. Student B is the letting agent. You know the company is reputable, but you nevertheless want to be clear about all the terms and conditions of the contract. Check all the information you are given and ask for clarification.

You want to find out as much as possible about the following:

**Lease**: length of contract and the renewal terms.

Notice period: how far in advance you have to say you're leaving / are you told you have to leave.

**Rent**: current rate and possible future increases.

Cleaning: who is responsible?

**Car park**: you are likely to have a lot of visitors and this is a busy part of town.

**Maintenance and repairs**: who is responsible? For example, what happens if the lift breaks down or the building needs to be repaired?

2 You work for Sutcliffe's Cars. You take a telephone call from Student B, who wants to rent a car. Read the information carefully and answer the caller's questions. Be patient, and explain and clarify each piece of information.

**Type of vehicle**

You have the following available for the weekend:

- family saloon: a comfortable car for four people
- air-conditioned
- special weekend rate: €120 including 150 miles. (extra miles 1 per mile)
- €200 unlimited mileage

**Insurance**

Car hire includes:

- fully comprehensive insurance with windscreen cover
- excess of €200; hirer pays the first €200 of any damage
- hirer is responsible for minor damage such as small scratches, broken lights etc. However, an extra payment of €40 will insure against this.
- payment is by credit card
- up to two named drivers may drive. All drivers must be over 21 years old and have had a full driving licence for at least two years.

Pick-up 15.00–18.00 Friday evening in front of Sutcliffe's Cars

Return 8.30–10.00 Monday morning

All cars are supplied and should be returned with a full tank.

# Writing

## In someone else's shoes

1 Read the business tip. What are the advantages of bonds over shares or ordinary bank investment accounts?

### Bonds

When bank interest rates are low, savers often consider investing their money in shares. However, this usually means sacrificing the security offered by a bank for a certain level of risk. A middle path is to invest in bonds, where savers are required to invest in the longer term (often 3–5 years) but are guranteed their money back at the end of the term of the bond, plus profits according to how well the bonds have performed. Bonds generally outperform ordinary interest-bearing bank accounts, but many do less well than shares.

Dear Mrs Barry

Further to our conversation I have pleasure in enclosing a brochure with full details of Neptune bonds. I strongly *urge* you to study carefully the *small print* which makes up the agreement. You are bound to have heard of cases of people who have been seriously misled when purchasing an investment package. Therefore, it is essential that you are aware of both the benefits and *drawbacks* of this type of investment.

An obvious consideration is that your money will be tied up between three and five years. You are probably wondering what happens if you require emergency access to it. I would like to draw your attention to clause 23.6, which outlines the penalties you will *incur* if you *withdraw* your money before the *maturity* of the bond. Were I in your position, I should make doubly certain that I could leave the investment undisturbed until such a time.

I must also stress that the performance figures which are given are estimates based on past performance. I imagine you have considered investing in the stock market on your own account. I would *dissuade* you from this as, in my experience, few investors possess the expertise to manage their own portfolios. You will certainly be aware that there is no such thing as a risk-free investment. However, these bonds are managed by a team of among the most highly-regarded fund managers in the sector. Previous results confirm their *proven track record*, although the overall performance of the bond will depend upon the *prevailing* economic climate over the next few years.

I shall give you a few days to read and digest the enclosed information, and will be happy to answer any further *queries* you may have in the meantime.

Yours sincerely,

Stephanie Miller

2 Mrs Greta Barry relies on the income generated by her savings. She is worried about the drop in interest rates and has called her financial advisor, Stephanie Miller, for advice. Stephanie has sent her details of Neptune bonds. Read her accompanying letter and match the words in italics to the definitions 1–10 below.

1 details
2 questions
3 take out money
4 strongest at a specific time
5 the date when an investment becomes payable
6 discourage
7 encourage
8 disadvantages
9 confirmed experience
10 become liable to through your own actions

3 Stephanie has advised people like Mrs Barry before. She is aware of their preoccupations and able to anticipate their questions. How does she show she has put herself in Mrs Barry's shoes?

4 What introductory phrases does Stephanie use to deal with these possible queries?

1 But what about if I need to get hold of the money?

2 There's no such thing as a risk-free investment, is there?

3 I wonder if I could play the stock exchange on my own.

4 I don't want to end up like poor Mr Harris who was talked into putting his money into futures.

5 Stephanie uses a variety of expressions when giving advice. What expressions does she use when giving Mrs Barry these pieces of advice?

1 Look carefully at all terms and conditions of the contract.

2 Make sure that you can spare the money for the period of the bond.

3 Don't invest in the stock market on your own account.

4 Don't forget that the figures you've been given are simply predictions.

5 Look at clause 23.6.

6 Be aware of both the advantages and disadvantages of this type of investment.

6 Write a letter from a commercial property agent to a person who wishes to rent premises. In your letter, try to predict as many of the questions they are likely to ask as you can, and provide some firm but friendly advice.

# In conversation

## On the grapevine

1 In many organizations, gossip is exchanged by the coffee machine. What other places are important venues for trading gossip?

2 Match expressions 1–8 with definitions a–h.

1 a little bird told me .....

2 let the cat out of the bag .....

3 my lips are sealed .....

4 spill the beans .....

5 it's all hush-hush .....

6 I'm all ears .....

7 still waters run deep .....

8 I heard it on the grapevine .....

a I promise I won't tell anyone

b I found out informally

c tell a secret, often by accident

d I won't say who gave me the information

e appearances can be deceptive

f something is top secret

g tell the whole story

h I can't wait to hear what you're going to say

3 [12.7] Listen to three short conversations in which a piece of gossip is circulated. How does the gossip develop across the three conversations? Do you have any direct equivalents of these expressions in your language?

4 Which of the expressions in 2 are useful for:

– introducing gossip?

– asking someone to keep a secret?

– promising to keep a secret / keep quiet?

– reacting to gossip?

5 Work in groups of four or five. You all work within the same company. Think of a piece of gossip on one of these topics:

– the future of the company.

– a promotion or a sacking.

– a new member of staff.

– a secret relationship between two colleagues.

6 Using the flow chart as a guide, exchange gossip with a partner. Then change partners and pass on the piece of gossip you have heard with an interesting addition or change. Continue to exchange gossip with other members of the group until your original piece of gossip returns to you.

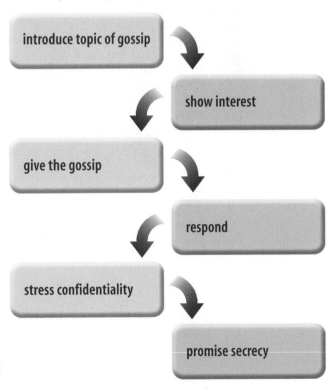

introduce topic of gossip

show interest

give the gossip

respond

stress confidentiality

promise secrecy

7 How did people's stories change as they passed from person to person?

# Case study

## Justice for all

1 Read the quotation. How far do you agree with Clarence Darrow?

> *There is no such thing as justice – in or out of court.*
>
> Clarence Darrow, lawyer

2 Work in groups and discuss cases A–D.

1 Decide who the plaintiff and the defendants are in each instance.

2 Brainstorm arguments for and against the plaintiffs in each of the four cases.

3 Make a decision based on the balance of your arguments. Decide who should win each of the cases.

4 Do you think it could be possible for the parties to reach an out of court settlement by coming to a compromise without the expense of going to court and the risk of losing the case?

### Case A: Hinton v Fanshawe Engineering

William Hinton, a 17-year-old apprentice, damaged the sight in one eye while operating a machine without wearing protective goggles. His parents are suing Fanshawe Engineering for negligence and for failing to supervise their son properly. Fanshawe, a local firm agreed to take on William as part of a government programme for young school leavers. However, because of the accident William will no longer be able to continue his training to become a precision instrument maker. His lawyers are claiming €1,000,000 in damages as compensation for future loss of earnings. William's foreman, Tony Bates told the judge 'You know, William had worked on the machine lots of times before. I must have told him fifty times to wear the goggles but he just never took any notice of me. He said they were uncomfortable. In the end, I let one of the other apprentices take them.'

### Case B: Wolf v Green

When Vince Green, an impresario, saw Brigitta Wolff's illusion and magic act in Munich he was so impressed that he immediately asked her to sign a contract to appear in eight English towns in the three weeks leading up to Christmas. For this he promised her €40,000 and Brigitta cancelled all her other engagements. However, one of the conditions was that Brigitta had to present herself at Vince's office in Soho, London ten days before the tour began. On the way to England Brigitta was involved in a minor car accident involving her van and equipment. She had to wait three days for the van to be repaired. She called him to tell him about her difficulty. However, when she arrived at Vince's office he told her that the tour was off because she had broken the terms of the contract. This suited Vince because bookings for the show had been poor and this seemed the perfect way to escape his obligations. A furious Brigitta immediately went to a British solicitor to see if she could claim the money she had been promised.

### Case C: Farinelli Fashions v Domus supermarkets

Farinelli Fashions produces world-famous designer clothes which are sold exclusively through boutiques and up-market department stores in the US, Japan and the European community. Their goods have a luxury up-market image reflected in their advertising and supported by their very high prices in these countries which are controlled by strict agreements between themselves and their retailers. Recently, however Domus, a big UK supermarket chain, has managed to obtain very large quantities of Farinelli jeans and sweatshirts on the so-called 'grey market' from wholesalers in less rich countries where Farinelli's price controls do not apply; or from the third world factories where the goods are produced.

'We want to give our customers good value for money and bring luxury goods within everybody's reach', claims Domus's managing director, Rory James. Paola Farinelli, the CEO of Farinelli does not agree. 'These imports are illegal and undermine the image of our products. These goods were only acquired in the first place by wholesalers in breach of their contracts with us or by our manufacturers illegally agreeing to make more of our lines in their factories.' Farinelli is taking Domus to court for unfair competition and wishes to make them withdraw their goods from their supermarkets.

### Case D: Salvo's Catering v Eventful Events

Eventful Events organizes functions such as receptions and entertainment for major companies. Last month it arranged with catering firm Salvo's to supply food and drink for the first night of an important exhibition of Oriental art in a fashionable London art gallery. After contacting several caterers, Eventful Events signed a contract to the value of €4,200 with Salvo's. The day before the launch, the caterer said that it had made a mistake with pricing the contract as the company had requested some very expensive items such as Japanese sushi and that the price was now €8,000. Jane Wilkinson the CEO of Eventful Events finally agreed to the new price and signed the contract under protest. However, when the invoice arrived she refused to pay it. Salvo's has taken Eventful Events and Jane Wilkinson to court to get its invoice paid in full and claims that Eventful Events acted in bad faith.

3 In English law judgements made by earlier courts are important. Where a precedent has been set, then it generally has to be followed. Turn to File 39 on page 138 and find out what happened in four similar cases. Discuss:
 - what you think of the courts' judgements in each case.
 - whether or not you would modify your judgement of the fictitious cases you discussed earlier as a result of what you have read.

4 Read the business tip.
 - Do you know what legal system operates in your country?
 - How might the law operate between different countries and what difficulties could you foresee?

#### Courts and the law

**European Court of Justice:** possesses the highest legal authority in the European Union.

**Case law / common law:** the law as established by the outcome of former cases. Case law is the basis of the legal system in the UK and the USA.

**Roman law:** the law code of the ancient Romans forming the basis of civil law of many countries today.

**Statute law:** the body of principles and laws laid down in statutes; i.e. written laws passed by legislative bodies.

# Information files

## 1 Unit 3
*page 33*

Use the information below to write a letter demanding payment.

> You supplied 200,000 blank CDs to Skunkx Records. It was an emergency order, so you supplied them straight away, on the promise that your invoice would be paid within ten working days. You have been working with the studio for the past three years and there has never been a problem. However, the invoice is now seriously overdue. You suspect that the company may be in financial difficulty. However, you supplied the goods in good faith and want your invoice to be paid. Otherwise, you will take your client to court to recover the debt, and will write to other suppliers of blank CDs warning them of Skunkx's bad payment history.

## 2 Unit 1
*page 12*

### AIDA

Advertisers often follow an AIDA model in their advertisements and sales literature.

**A:** Attention; the advertisement gets the reader's attention.

**I:** Interest; it develops the reader's interest.

**D:** Decision; it tries to encourage the reader to make a decision.

**A:** Action; finally the reader acts on his / her decision.

### USP

**Unique Selling Point / Proposition**
USPs are the key features of a product or service which set it apart from its rivals and make it different. Consumers will be attracted by the benefits offered by the USP.

## 3 Unit 7
*page 74*

You are a member of senior management. Read your information below and prepare your arguments. Then follow the instructions on page 75.

### Grievance one

Executives work longer hours than factory workers who work clear shifts and are paid overtime. Foreign languages are a necessary tool for the job of export sales and have nothing to do with taking foreign holidays. It is completely out of the question that blue-collar workers will be able to take language courses in work time. Secretarial staff may be required to answer the phone or deal with messages. A foreign language is an essential skill for them.

### Grievance two

There has been a lot of alcohol-related trouble recently at the social club. You see no reason why the company should continue subsidizing the bar. The golfing weekends are an essential part of cementing relations between important customers and suppliers and the sales and marketing staff. Most managers would rather spend time with their families instead of having to entertain visitors for work. They have to give up their weekends to do this. Other workers spend this time with their families. It is out of the question that these weekends should be made available to all workers.

### Grievance three

You have been appalled by the reaction to Steffi. You want an immediate change in the way the other staff treat her. She is a highly-qualified and competent manager and there is no question that you will replace her. You can understand her anger. Sexist comments have no place in a modern factory. Workers are fortunate that they have been given the opportunity to upgrade and improve their skills. This is a symbol of the company's commitment to its employees, so staff should be grateful not resentful. If people aren't capable of working with her and treating her with respect, then they should start looking for another job.

## 4 Unit 1 *page 15*

Present this extra information about 'Empire' to your partners, and say in which part of the matrix it belongs.

**Empire**
- An old, established product like 'Sherlock'.
- Slightly less successful.
- In danger of going out of fashion.

Suggestions: Research shows a version using different science fiction locations could be popular. We could consider producing a deluxe version.

## 5 Unit 2 *page 17*

1 You have decided to see a debt counsellor (Student B) because you are worried about your financial situation. Explain your situation using the notes below and listen to Student B's advice.

The company you work for has recently reduced the amount of overtime available. You depended on this to make ends meet as it added 25% to your salary.

- A year ago, you bought a TV, washing machine, and new furniture for your flat, all on hire purchase over three years. You have fallen behind with the payments and have received threatening letters from the finance company which set up the loan.
- You have a car which you use at weekends. You go to work on public transport.
- You don't know whether you should pay your rent, or utilities bills (phone, electricity, etc.).
- You have outstanding credit card bills of £2,000. You are paying 2% interest per month on these.
- You like to look well-dressed at work and have a charge card for a large department store. You pay 11% interest per month.
- You belong to a private gym which costs £50 a month.

2 You are an accountant for a business client (Student B) whose company is in severe financial difficulty. Listen to the problem and discuss:

- the current situation, possible solutions and ways of avoiding future problems
- ways of reducing overheads, e.g. losing staff; changing premises; selling company vehicles
- how to deal with the bank and your client's creditors
- ways of improving credit control in the future.

## 6 Unit 2 *page 19*

You are going to work with Student B to complete Fred Smith's story. Each of you has four stages in the story.

1 Decide the order of the complete story by describing your stages to each other.

2 When you have finished, retell the story in the past using a variety of past tense forms.

Ten years later, Fred has 20 planes. He wants money for investment.

Fred inherits £20,000 and buys a light aircraft at an auction.

ABC merges with XYZ.

Fred Smith leaves the airforce in 1985. He works in an office but dreams of flying again.

# 7 Unit 2 *page 25*

**15** The moment has passed. You never get organized and spend the next twenty years wondering what would have happened. *Go back to 1* and start again! *Disaster*

**16** With the business angel's money you expand rapidly. You can improve on your designs and invest in marketing. A top department store is interested in stocking your jewellery. However, it insists on exclusivity for the first two years.

You decide to take the store's offer and do not look for other opportunities. *Go to 9*.

You decide that you do not want to be tied to an exclusive contract. *Go to 21*.

**17** A fashion magazine writes an article about you and you are approached by small shops and private buyers and jewellery collectors. You have to decide whether to expand or consolidate.

You decide to raise awareness of your name by investing money in advertising on local radio. *Go to 27*.

You decide to keep your business small and produce expensive up-market items. *Go to 20*.

**18** The bank says you can't have a loan without a business plan which includes a budget, sales and cash-flow forecasts.

You produce a business plan you think the bank will accept. *Go to 11*.

You decide to approach your family and friends. *Go to 23*.

**19** By turning down this opportunity you have had your last chance. You simply run out of money and have to get a job with another jewellery firm. *Disaster*

**20** Your work is becoming better-known and you sell some expensive items to celebrities and film stars. You want to broaden your customer base.

You consolidate and open a tiny shop in le Marais, an exclusive area of Paris. *Go to 5*.

You invest heavily on a website and selling over the Internet. *Go to 24*.

**21** You have found two large potential customers. You only have the resources to supply one. Customer A insists on double discount but will pay in 30 days. Customer B is a chain of gift shops in mountain resorts. They offer to stock your jewellery on a sale or return basis. This means they will pay if they sell the goods or else they will return them to you. However, they promise to sell your jewellery at the full recommended price.

You choose customer A. *Go to 26*.

You choose customer B. *Go to 12*.

**21** Even though the factory's samples were good, its real production was of low quality. About 20% of the production is sub-standard.

You send the goods anyway and offer a substantial discount. *Go to 33*.

You send a part-shipment and promise to send the rest when it is ready. *Go to 34*.

You choose customer B. *Go to 12*.

**23** Unfortunately no one in your family is prepared to risk their money!

However, an uncle introduces you to a business 'angel' who is prepared to invest money in your business for a 25% share.

You accept the angel's offer and sign a legal agreement. *Go to 16*.

You decide to approach the bank again with a plan you think the bank will accept. *Go to 11*.

**24** Your website attracts hardly any business. You realize too late that people will only buy well-established brands over the Net. You become a victim of Net fraud and debts force you out of business. *Disaster*

**25** Your new range is a huge success. One of the world's foremost luxury labels offers to buy you out. You wonder if you can go even further on your own.

You decide to take the offer. *Go to 29*.

You stretch your brand to cover clothes and fragrances. *Go to 3*.

**26** Your new customer places big orders but, as you expected, your profit margin is quite low. Somehow you need to cut your costs.

You see some low-cost, high-quality samples from a Far Eastern jewellery manufacturer. You let them produce your designs for you. *Go to 22*.

You explain your position to your customer and try to negotiate a better deal for their next season's order. *Go to 7*.

**27** Your previous actions have cost you a lot of money and put the future of the company in danger. Now you need to re-think your operation completely. With a new business manager you choose between these options.

You start a jewellery-making franchise teaching manufacturing techniques and supplying materials to your franchisees. *Go to 31*.

You adapt your designs to cheaper dress jewellery and sell it through network marketing. *Go to 32*.

**28** The bank is horrified that you have wasted its money. It makes you liquidate all your assets to get its money back. *Disaster*

**29** The offer makes you rich and you decide to leave the rat race. You move to the South of France and become a member of the international scene. Sometimes when you see your designs advertised in expensive fashion magazines you wonder if you could have made it even bigger! *Triumph*

**30** You know nothing about operating shops in the USA or Russia. You are wiped out and lose everything.
**Disaster**

**31** You underestimate the difficulty of turning ordinary people into craftspeople capable of producing high-quality jewellery which sells well.

You persevere with the franchise and improve your training. **Go to 6**.

You abandon the franchise and look for new opportunities at the San Diego Jewellery Fair. **Go to 8**.

**32** he direct marketing concept is a brilliant success. Many women have been searching for bold well-produced dress jewellery at a reasonable price. You become rich and are the topic of many business magazine articles.
**Triumph**

**33** A bad move. The customer angrily rejects the entire consignment. You are unable to find another buyer and suffer a cash flow crisis. You cannot satisfy your creditors and go bankrupt.
**Disaster**

**34** The customer is not very happy but at least they accept you have acted honourably. However, you doubt whether they will place any further orders. You need to rescue your business fast!

You go to the San Diego Jewellery Fair in an attempt to make new contacts. **Go to 8**.

You decide to appoint a new business manager to help you investigate other business openings. **Go to 27**.

**35** The department store rejects your new designs as too avant-garde. Tired and fed up, you sell your business to another jewellery manufacturer.
**Disaster**

## 8 Unit 11 — page 113

1 You are Jo Kellogg. You are calling Mrs Sharpe, a human resources manager, about arranging a student placement. You are speaking to Mrs Sharpe's secretary. Mrs Sharpe can telephone you at any time between 9.30 and 12.00.

2 You are Danny Roper's brother or sister. Take a call from Andy Green, one of Danny's college friends. Tell Andy that Danny isn't there, but promise that he will phone later.

## 9 Unit 6 — page 61

The quality control team at Harper's Cameras have noticed a 10% increase in costs incurred through breakages. Members of the team are now meeting to discuss the problem.

Read your information and prepare to participate in the meeting.

**Ideas person**

Your role is to come up with new ideas and creative solutions to problems.

You have the following ideas:

Use computer tracking through bar codes on all invoices and envelopes. There have been important developments in satellite tracking.

Make customers responsible for collecting their own consignments. Offer a discount for this.

Include a certificate which has to be signed by the person responsible for the packing.

## 10 Unit 5 — page 55

You are going to discuss staff confidence and morale at Frost's. Consider these questions:

1 Can you identify any problem sales people?

2 Are any other members of staff contributing to lack of morale?

3 What can be done to make Frost's seem more like a team again? Consider the following suggestions.

– Organize team-building weekends with outdoor activities such as climbing.

– Organize sales seminars from a famous sales 'guru' to inspire and re-energize people.

– Organize social activities such as parties and barbecues, where the staff and their families can get to know each other better.

4 What other types of training might work?

5 What would be most suitable for Sally's sales force?

## 11 Unit 4 — page 43

Read the criticisms of Quayside Furniture that were made in the TV documentary. Then follow the instructions on page 43.

1 There is no established system for promotion.

2 Skilled employees are only paid the minimum legal wage.

3 Quayside has failed to issue its employees with proper contracts.

4 There is no proper salary structure.

5 There is no entitlement to holiday or sickness benefit.

## 12 | Unit 7 *page 68*

Read the text and complete column B on page 68. Then follow the instructions in **3**.

**B**  People who envy top tennis players should think about their early days on the minor tournament circuit, going from competition to competition, sleeping in cars or depressing motels. I once knew a future top tennis player who had saved enough prize money to buy a second-hand camper van to make her life more comfortable. I went with her when she went to a local dealer.

When he saw us, two girls barely out of high school, he moved into his routine. He progressed from the oldest and cheapest vehicles to the most modern deluxe versions. This locked us into the logic of his pricing. Naturally, the one my friend liked best was among the most expensive. Putting on his 'favourite uncle' act he said, 'I know you've fallen in love with this, so I'd really like to help you. There is someone else who is interested, but if you paid cash I could work out a discount.'

The words 'do it now, otherwise I'll have to let the other guy have it' hung in the air like an unspoken threat. Now, if I'd been her, I'd have paid the money before he changed his mind, but she smiled sweetly, thanked him for his time and walked away. When I asked her why she hadn't bought it, she replied, 'I want it, but I don't want to discuss the price on his territory.'

The following day she rang him up and offered him $3,000, a fortune in those days but still less than the asking price. Naturally, the salesman protested, but he finally caved in and she got the van. He wished he hadn't let her leave the garage, but she had known that if she had tried to get a better price on his home ground he would have simply referred her to one of the cheaper vans. And on the phone, he couldn't do this. I wish I had such cool determination. Unless you have this gift, you will never win the big points.

I'm sure it's that which separates a champion from the rest of us. Perhaps if I'd had the same determination, I'd be as rich and famous today.

## 13 | Unit 7 *page 74*

You are a union representative. Read your information below and prepare your arguments. Follow the instructions on page 75.

**Grievance One**

Workers feel insulted by management's decision to favour its executives over blue-collar workers. Many people nowadays enjoy holidays abroad and so welcome the opportunity to study a language. It would also give ordinary workers an extra skill to help them improve their prospects. They see no reason why they have to sacrifice their free time when executives who are already much better paid get the course free and in work time. Other white-collar staff who are on the same, or an even lower grade than the blue-collar staff, have been allowed to go on the courses during work time.

**Grievance Two**

This is a clear example of the class divisions within the factory. The social club is at the heart of the factory and it gives workers the opportunity to relax after a hard day's work. It is a good facility too, for retired members of staff. A lot of important voluntary work is performed by members of the club and large sums are raised for charities and good causes. You demand that the subsidy is restored and that golfing weekends are made available to all members of staff. Someone anonymously sent you a copy of the most recent bill for a golfing weekend. You are angry about it, as this amount of money would help to keep the social club going for at least three months.

**Grievance Three**

You believe that the American manager's behaviour has been intolerable. She is arrogant and seems to treat everyone with contempt. A lot of the older men are a bit afraid of her and hate the power she has. She has no respect for other people's experience and keeps boasting about how well-qualified she is. People are afraid to say anything to her because she will accuse them of being sexist and old-fashioned. You want someone who is sensitive to different cultures and working practices.

## 14 Unit 8 *page 81*

> Options:
> Could do following:
> (i) Consolidate - reduce operation -
> concentrate on up-market coffee makers.
> (ii) Sell name and trade mark.
> (iii) Merge with similar firm.
> (iv) Create strategy to re-establish self as
> market leader.
>
> Recommendations:
> Go for option (iv) (new management team
> committed and enthusiastic).
> Short term:
> Cut costs ASAP !!!
> Advertising campaign - focus on Chivers'
> retro '60s look.
> Recruit / headhunt top designer from
> Italy / France?
> Begin Research & Development programme.
>
> Longer term:
> Launch new product in three years.
> Use transparent plastics - very
> fashionable.
> Launch economy range.
> Production abroad? (cheaper)

## 15 Unit 6 *page 65*

Read your information and then hold the meeting with Student B and Student C.

> You think that skimming the market is a bad idea because it can upset customers who have bought at the higher price. You think that you should offer the Caxton at €150. You believe that this will protect the image of the product and keep demand constant over several years. If you sell it too cheaply, this will damage the up-market image your company has been trying to develop. You do not want to export to Southland because you are afraid that this could damage the product's image and you risk the danger of the re-importation of goods into wealthier markets (the so-called 'grey' market).

## 16 Unit 5 *page 55*

You are going to discuss administration and paperwork at Frost's. Consider these questions:

1 What problems have been caused directly by the changes in office layout and general administration?

2 What impact have these problems had on performance and staff morale?

3 How can you explain the poor 'lead-to-sales' performance? How successful has the telesales team been in setting up appointments?

4 How responsible should sales people be for setting up their own meetings?

5 What changes would you like to make? Consider the following possibilities.

- Arrange for all the salespeople to work from home.

- Bring back a minimum number of administrators to deal with paperwork for the whole sales team.

- Move to smaller office premises where the whole sales team work in the same open plan office.

## 17 Unit 6 *page 61*

The quality control team at Harper's Cameras have noticed a 10% increase in costs incurred through breakages. Members of the team are now meeting to discuss the problem.

Read your information and prepare to participate in the meeting.

> **Critic / inspector**
> Your role is to make sure that the group doesn't get carried away with expensive or impractical ideas.
> You want any new idea to be thoroughly tested and analyzed before it is put into operation. You often feel that the 'ideas person' comes up with unsuitable and impractical suggestions.
> Before you spend a lot of money on tracking systems, you want to find out where breakages occur. These may happen in your own packing department, the warehouse, with the carrier, etc.

## 18 Unit 9 *page 95*

| France | |
|---|---|
| Population (millions) | 60.8 |
| Human Development index | 91.7 |
| GDP per head $ | 23,560 |
| Economic Freedom index | 2.5 |
| Annual inflation % (1990–2000) | 1.7 |
| Cost of living (NY=100) | 88 |
| Unemployment rate average % (1990–99) | 11.2 |

Recent law has introduced a 35-hour working week.
French workers tend to have longer holidays than North Americans.

**Other factors:**
- Engineering strength reflected in TGV and nuclear industries.
- Specialization in cars and telecommunications.
- Defence sector exporter.
- Strong technocratic tradition.

| Mexico | |
|---|---|
| Population (millions) | 97.4 |
| Human Development index | 78.4 |
| GDP per head $ | 4,970 |
| Economic Freedom | 2.95 |
| Annual inflation % (1990–2000) | 18.4 |
| Cost of living (NY=100) | 87 |
| Unemployment rate average % (1990–99) | 3.0 |

Part of NAFTA – the North American Free Trade Association. Theoretically easier for US and Canadian businesses to set up factories. Tourism is probably the largest employment sector of the economy.

**Other factors:**
- One of the world's largest oil producers, with substantial reserves.
- Extensive mineral resources.
- Low wage costs.
- It is in an earthquake zone.

| China | |
|---|---|
| Population (millions) | 1,249 |
| Human Development index | 70.6 |
| GDP per head $ | 790 |
| Economic Freedom | 3.55 |
| Annual inflation % (1991–2000) | 7.2 |
| Cost of living (NY=100) | 94 |
| Unemployment rate average % (1990–99) | 2.8 |

China is an extremely dynamic economy.

**Other factors:**
- Domestic market of 1.2 billion.
- Self-sufficiency in food.
- Strong mineral reserves.
- Increasingly diversified industrial sector.
- Economic reforms have led to high growth.
- Low wage costs.

## 19 Unit 10 *page 103*

You are going to make several phone calls to Ace Caterers. Unfortunately, whenever you call, Student B is not there so you have to leave a message on an answering machine. You are also busy, and when Student B returns your calls, you are not at your desk.

**Call 1**

Call Ace Caterers to organize a special staff dinner at your office to celebrate a successful year.
- Ask for a quotation.
- Give the date when you plan to have the dinner.

**Call 2**

Student B calls you back while you are at lunch. Read your recorded outgoing message.
You return to your desk after lunch to find the message from Student B. Listen carefully and note down the details.

**Call 3**

Call again. Give your address and ask if the price includes drinks and waiter / waitress service.

**Call 4**

Student B returns your call. Listen carefully and note the details.

**Call 5**

It is now the next day and you have arrived at work early.
- Decide which menu you will choose, and if you would like Ace to provide drinks.
- Call Student B and leave a message.

**Call 6**

Student B returns your call when you are in a meeting.

**Call 7**

You return from your meeting and return the call.
- Thank Student B for the information.
- Explain that there will be three extra guests.
- Ask what to do about payment once you receive the invoice.

**Call 8**

Student B returns your call almost immediately. This time you manage to pick up the phone!
- Respond appropriately to what Student B says.

## 20 Unit 4     *page 36*

Answers to quiz:

a  Hawaii is a popular honeymoon destination for Japanese couples. Couples get married on 'lucky days', which means some days flights will be full, while on others they will be less popular.

b  Two-litre bottles are too large to fit into the fridges in Spain.

c  'Finger lickin' good' was translated back into English as 'eat your fingers off'.

d  Handkerchiefs symbolize sorrow, and cutlery symbolizes the cutting of a friendship.

## 21 Unit 11     *page 114*

GEM found that 3% of British adults have set up a business, equal with Italy. This is in contrast with France and Germany, where the figure is about 1%. However, this is much worse than the US, where 8% of adults have set up a business. The figure for Canada is 7%, and for Israel, 6%. Only 16% of British people think there are good opportunities for starting a business in the next six months, compared with 56% in the US. The Japanese, at 2%, are the least optimistic. Strangely enough, the failure rate for new businesses in all industrialized countries is around 45% within the first three years.

## 22 Unit 1     *page 12*

Using the information below and the C1 features on page 12, write some advertising copy for a Sunday newspaper. Think about the interests of the target group.

Readership of this section tends to be class A1 and A2 professional people between the age of 30 and 70. They are very quality- and safety-conscious. They like the idea of being protected by the City Scooter's frame and features such as the safety belt. Elderly people see it as an economical way of getting around. Many readers with student-aged children are aware of the high accident rate among motor cyclists in their teens and welcome the scooter's safety features. However, they could be put off by its high price and would possibly buy a second-hand car instead. Parents of families living in country areas spend a lot of their time driving their children to activities in friends' houses. A reliable and safer form of two-wheel transport would lighten this responsibility.

## 23 Unit 11     *page 111*

Your mission is to make healthy lunchtime meals available to office workers. You believe that juice bars will replace coffee bars as the next fashionable concept. You think that more and more people are worried about what they eat. Use the notes below to prepare for your meeting with Hardman and Nailer. Decide which information you prefer not to divulge at this stage.

**Research**

Target market: 20–35 year-olds, young professional office workers.

You interviewed 200 office workers. 67% said they were worried about the quality of the food they eat at lunchtime. 85% said that they would buy organic food if it was priced reasonably.

Most office workers spend £5 each day on lunch. The majority said that they would pay up to £8 for an organic sandwich and drink. Your research shows that most people are getting bored with the coffee shop sandwich bar concept and want to switch to juices. People also want sandwiches and snacks with new and exciting international fillings.

**Your current business**

You have made mistakes and learnt from them. For example, in the early days, you ordered too much produce and a lot was wasted; you have learnt the importance of having good stock control and just-in-time delivery of produce and ingredients to avoid waste.

**Direct competition**

Two immediate competitors:

– Su-go is just a juice bar without the sandwiches.
– Sarnirama has been a very successful sandwich-based business but it does not use organically-produced produce. Your research shows that people are disappointed that its owners sold half its shares to a hamburger franchise.

**Companies already approached**

You want risk captial, not a bank loan with a high rate of interest.

You have been offered investment capital by Seedcorn Capital. You are tempted by their offer but they want to have direct involvement in the running of the company as a condition of their financial backing.

Another venture capital organization, Adventurecap, has expressed interest and you are going to make your pitch to them next week.

## 24 Unit 11 *page 111*

You are always looking out for potential projects but you want to examine any proposal closely and critically. Use the notes below and the information on page 111 to prepare for the meeting.

The founders of Jubiolation have approached you for venture capital of £800,000. Although this is a small sum by your usual standards, you think that this is a lot to invest in a pretentious and glorified sandwich bar.

You are polite, but extremely sceptical, and will ask searching and challenging questions. Think about what the atmosphere of the meeting should be like.

You want to find out:
- how convincing their business concept is
- the research they have carried out
- why they need the money and how much they have invested themselves
- what they are prepared to give you in return.

Think of any other questions you would like to ask them.

## 25 Unit 1 *page 12*

Using the information below and the C1 features on page 12, write some advertising copy for a business magazine. Think about the interests of the target group.

Research shows that the scooter would appeal to young professionals aged 25–35, tired of relying on public transport, which is often crowded and sometimes late. Many people in this target group perceive the City Scooter as a 'cool', fashionable form of transport. They like the idea too, of being able to wear smart city clothes, while being protected from the wind and rain. BMW is considered a very high status brand by this group.

## 26 Unit 4 *page 43*

Read the information that Quayside Furniture has provided to Carrie Phelps, in reply to the criticisms made in the TV documentary. Then follow the instructions on page 43.

### QUAYSIDE FURNITURE

A  Quayside is a small, family-run business. It cannot afford to pay its employees more. Competition is strong and the company is struggling to stay in business.

B  The company provides work in an area of high unemployment.

C  The company only employs five people full-time, who enjoy the same benefits as staff elsewhere in the industry. The other employees are not permanent members of staff, but employed as casual workers. They are taken on as needed, to fulfil orders.

D  Quayside offers flexible hours to its staff. It provides an ideal solution for people who only want to work part-time, or for students looking for holiday work.

E  The problem with the contracts is an administrative one. The secretary resigned without any warning and the company has not yet been able to replace her. There is now a backlog of typing work.

## 27 Unit 6 *page 65*

Read your information and then hold the meeting with Student A and Student C.

You want to adopt a skimming policy and offer the product at the high price for the first year, i.e. €300. There are a lot of 'early adopters' in target groups 1 and 2 who are prepared to pay a premium to have the product now. You think that you will recover your research and set-up costs quickly. You think that new competitors will appear which will force you to compete on price alone. So you should make money now.

After a year, you would like the price of the product to go down to €100–150 so that you can penetrate the market. You think that it is too risky to export to weak currency areas like Southland at the moment because their economy is weak. You also believe that business travellers could buy the Caxton abroad at the lower price.

## 28 | Unit 1 — *page 15*

Present this extra information about 'Who's there?' to your partners, and say in which part of the matrix it belongs.

**Who's there?**

– Extremely successful first two years.

Suggestions: Extend the range with different versions, famous film stars, sports people, historical characters. Develop into a computer game version.

## 29 | Unit 6 — *page 61*

The quality control team at Harper's Cameras have noticed a 10% increase in costs incurred through breakages. Members of the team are now meeting to discuss the problem.

Read your information and prepare to chair the meeting.

**Team leader / external contact**

Your role is to keep the meeting running smoothly and to encourage everyone to make a contribution. Remember to praise and encourage the group, and to be as enthusiastic as you can.

Your contacts with customers have shown that there has been an increase in the number of breakages which occur.

In addition to the breakages, some parcels have been lost on the way to the customer. Sometimes separate invoices and documents, which are sent by post, are also lost.

## 30 | Unit 1 — *page 7*

You are a journalist from *Adworld* magazine. You are interviewing Chris Rogers, one of the industry's most famous advertising people, for your magazine.

1 Find out:
   - length of time in advertising
   - number of agencies worked for
   - number of awards won
   - opinion of celebrity endorsements
   - current project.

2 Think of two further questions of your own.

## 31 | Unit 2 — *page 19*

You are going to work with Student A to complete the story. Each of you has four stages in the story.

1 Decide the order of the complete story by describing your stages to each other.

2 When you have finished, retell the story in the past using a variety of past tense forms.

Fred starts ferrying business people to Holland and Germany.

Profits fall at ABC. American rival XYZ enters European market.

ABC goes public and shares rise. Fred is now a public figure and the company is winning awards.

Fred has the idea of transporting parcels. ABC parcels is formed.

## 32 Unit 10 *page 103*

You are going to exchange several phone calls with Student A, a client. Unfortunately, you are very busy and are often not at your desk. When Student A phones, read the outgoing message on your answering machine. Student A will leave a message. When you return the call, you will also have to leave a message, as Student A is also busy and unable to answer the phone.

### Call 1

You are in a meeting and unable to answer the phone. Your answering machine plays your recorded outgoing message.

When you get back from your meeting, listen and note down the message.

### Call 2

Return the call. Say who you are and confirm the date. Give a quotation and provide details of the two menus:
- Standard menu: £23
- Special deluxe menu: £35 (includes cheese and coffee).

Offer to send a brochure and ask for Student A's company address.

### Call 3

Student A calls again while you are making a cup of tea. When you get back to your desk, listen to the message and note down any details.

### Call 4

Return the call. Explain what is included in the price:
- two members of staff who share the cooking, waiting and cleaning up.

Not included in the price:
- VAT
- drinks (£8 extra per head).

### Call 5

It is now the next day. You were disappointed that Student A did not return your call yesterday, and you are pleased to find a message waiting when you arrive at work.

### Call 6

Return the call. Confirm the date of the party and say you are sending an invoice.

### Call 7

Student A calls again when you are on another line and your answering machine takes the call. You finish your call and hear Student A's message.

### Call 8

Call back immediately. This time Student A picks up the phone!
- Thank Student A for the message.
- Confirm that there will be no problems with the extra guests.
- Say that you will expect a cheque on the day of the party.
- Thank Student A again for the business.

## 33 Unit 11 *page 113*

1 You are Mrs Sharpe's secretary from the Human Resources department. Tell the caller that Mrs Sharpe is interviewing for the rest of the afternoon. Find out when it would be convenient for Mrs Sharpe to return Jo's call.

2 You are Andy Green. You are ringing your friend Danny Roper about a homework assignment. Danny's brother / sister answers the phone.

## 34 Unit 1 *page 7*

You are Chris Rogers, a copywriter and advertising celebrity. You are being interviewed by a journalist from *Adworld* magazine. Read the information about your career and answer the journalist's questions. Invent any further information you wish.

You started your career eighteen years ago. You had just come back from a trip to Australia. You worked for the YBV agency before moving to the JK and Perkins agency. Three years ago you set up your own agency with a colleague. Over the years you have been given eleven awards for your campaigns, a number of which featured celebrities. Your current project for *Adworld* magazine is an Australian beer called Koala.

## 35 Unit 9 *page 95*

| | | **India** |
|---|---|---|
| Population (millions) | 997.5 | |
| Human Development index | 56.3 | |
| GDP per head $ | 450 | |
| Economic Freedom index | 3.85 | |
| Annual inflation % (1990–2000) | 9.0 | |
| Cost of living (NY=100) | 40 | |
| Unemployment rate average % | * | |

*\* Figure not available*

Kasada would be interested in setting up in the Bangalore region, as this is a major centre for high-tech industries.

**Other factors:**
- Massive home market of over 800 million.
- Low wage costs.
- High level of unemployment and underemployment.
- Some of the workforce possess skills for hi-tech industries such as software programming.
- Growing competitiveness on world market with high exports.
- Competition is encouraging firms to manufacture to international standards.
- Massive foreign investment.

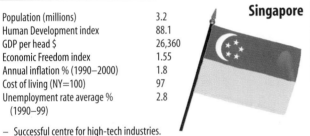

| | | **Singapore** |
|---|---|---|
| Population (millions) | 3.2 | |
| Human Development index | 88.1 | |
| GDP per head $ | 26,360 | |
| Economic Freedom index | 1.55 | |
| Annual inflation % (1990–2000) | 1.8 | |
| Cost of living (NY=100) | 97 | |
| Unemployment rate average % (1990–99) | 2.8 | |

- Successful centre for high-tech industries.
- Huge state enterprises have proved highly flexible in responding to market conditions. Singapore produces 50% of the world's computer disk drives.
- Dependence on Malaysia for water.
- All food and energy has to be imported.
- Skills shortages in some key areas, especially engineering.
- Lack of land restraining further development.
- Constructing the factory here could add 20% to building costs for Kasada.

| | | **UK** |
|---|---|---|
| Population (millions) | 59.1 | |
| Human Development index | 91.8 | |
| GDP per head $ | 24,390 | |
| Economic Freedom | 1.8 | |
| Annual inflation % (1990–2000) | 3.0 | |
| Cost of living (NY=100) | 99 | |
| Unemployment rate average % (1990–99) | 8.1 | |

Member of the EU although it has not yet adopted the Euro currency.

**Other factors:**
- Precision engineering and high-tech sectors.
- Strong energy sector based on North Sea oil and gas production.
- Flexible working practices.
- High inward investment from EU countries.
- Strong multinational sector.
- Some key manufacturing sectors in decline, particularly heavy industries.
- Much of industry still working with outmoded machinery.

## 36 Unit 6 *page 65*

Read your information and then hold the meeting with Student A and Student B.

You would like to go for a lower price straight away, i.e. €100–150. Your factory has the capacity to produce the product in large quantities, so you can benefit from economies of scale. Naturally, the product must be priced at a level where price resistance is low.

You would also like to export to Southland at €75, as this is a growing market and you could establish your brand there. If there is not a big difference between the domestic price and the export price, you will be able to avoid the danger of re-importation. You also believe that Southland is a growing economy and that this is a way of establishing your brand ahead of your competitors.

## 37 Unit 1 *page 12*

Using the information below and the C1 features on page 12, write some advertising copy for a magazine aimed at students. Think about the interests of the target group.

Even though most magazines are divided by gender, the magazine in question appeals equally to male and female students. Many students appreciate that the scooter is very economical to run and 'green'. They would feel that they were acting responsibly for the environment. Some male, and nearly all female students like the style of the scooter and the options such as the CD player. However, part of the male student population does not like to feel over-protected and enjoys the danger associated with other kinds of scooter and motor cycles. In focus groups, men said that the scooter was 'uncool' and for girls or old people! The scooter could have an image problem with this group.

## 38 Unit 6 *page 61*

The quality control team at Harper's Cameras have noticed a 10% increase in costs due to breakages. The team is now meeting to discuss the problem. Read your information and prepare for the meeting.

**Co-ordinator / implementer**

Your role is to liaise with other interested parties and to put the group's ideas into practice.

You will contact your own transport section and find out from them what they think the problems are.

You will find out from different organizations what suggestions they have for tracking deliveries.

You will find out prices and any other relevant details.

You will discover from the Accounts Department if the system can be improved, so that invoices are always ready for the despatch of goods.

## 39 Unit 12 *page 125*

Compare these cases to those on page 124–125.

1  Workers on a building site did not wear safety belts provided, so the employer (A) took them away. Sadly, A worker (B) was killed in a fall. The court decided that A had been negligent for not supplying the belt. However, this negligence was not the cause of B's death because he would not have worn a safety belt even if supplied.

2  An importer (A) contracted a delivery firm (B) to deliver goods to a chain of stores. When B realized that it had under-priced the contract it made A sign a new, more expensive one. A signed under protest but later refused to pay the invoice. When B took A to court, B lost the case because it had won the second contract unlawfully.

3  A German firm (A) gave exclusive distribution rights of its products in France to a French firm (B). When a third firm (C) imported A's products to France to sell them more cheaply, B took C to court. The European Court of Justice found that A and B's agreement went against the aims of the single European market.

4  An opera singer (A) agreed to tour England and signed a contract with an organizer (B). A promised to arrive six days before the tour began. He arrived in time for the tour but not on the agreed day, so B cancelled the contract. The court held that A had broken a minor term of the contract and was liable for damages. As he had not broken a major term of the contract he was entitled to his fee from B.

## 40 Unit 2 *page 17*

1  You are a debt counsellor. A client, Student A, has come to see you for some advice about how best to deal with his / her debts and financial problems. Find out the details and give advice about:

– how to cut monthly costs immediately, e.g. suggest approaching the finance company which set up the loan. Ask for a breathing space or reduce the amount to be paid each month.

– how to reduce the cost of any borrowing, e.g. by getting a bank loan to pay off credit cards (bank loans have a lower interest rate than credit cards), or destroying credit or charge cards.

2  You own a small business which is in difficulty. Explain your situation to Student A using the notes below, and discuss possible solutions.

Your business produces and fits double glazing for houses and office buildings. You have a severe financial crisis:

– You used to employ just six people but last summer you took on three more.

– Orders are good and there is plenty of new business but you have two or three bad debts. Your biggest customer, a hotel owner, has gone out of business owing you £30,000. You have little hope of recovering any of the debt. Two other customers owe you a total of £15,000, which you are trying to recover.

– You now have a cash flow crisis because you don't have the money to pay your suppliers or your staff.

– Last year you invested a lot of money on new vehicles for the company.

– You have a large loan from the bank and are afraid that they could demand their money back and force you into liquidation. You feel sure, however, that the business is in good shape and that this is just a temporary problem.

## 41 Unit 1 *page 15*

Present this extra information about 'Bidders' to your partners, and say in which part of the matrix it belongs.

**Bidders**

– Expensive to produce and quite difficult to play.
– Unsuccessful.
– Did fairly well in its first year but sales have fallen sharply.

Suggestions: Try selling it through museum shops and art galleries. Re-package it for other art-conscious markets like Japan. Aim at the high end of the market.

## 42 Unit 11 *page 115*

Look at the details and costings for the Puddings Galore franchise. Then follow the instructions on page 115.

### Puddings Galore

| Franchise opportunities | Costs |
|---|---|
| Target customers:<br>• Young people, before or after the cinema or the theatre.<br>• Women who want a 'treat' during a hard day's shopping.<br><br>There are currently two franchising opportunities available, both in Central London in the West End where all the main theatres are based. This location attracts shoppers and people on their way to theatres and cinemas. The area is also popular with tourists and sightseers. | • Franchise: £27,000 for three years and 10% of turnover from the second year.<br>• Lease of premises: £22,000 per year.<br>• Shop-fitting and kitchens: £30,000.<br>• Wages and charges: £9,500 per year per member of extra staff hired.<br>• There is a variable cost of £1.50 for each Puddings Galore portion and coffee.<br>• Diners pay a flat charge of £4.80. |

## 43 Unit 12 *page 121*

1 You are a letting agent. You are showing a client, Student A, some office space in a building. It is a modern block with underground parking. You represent someone who owns two floors of the building.

Student A has never rented commercial property before, so you will have to explain everything carefully. Use the information below to answer Student A's questions.

**Lease**: the contract lasts for three years and is renewable.

**Rent**: payable every three months in advance. You decide the amount. Rent increases are fixed at the rate of inflation for the three years of the contract.

**Deposits**: six months' rent. The premises to be assessed by an independent surveyor before and after the rental period.

**Notice period**: six months before the end of the contract on either side.

**Cleaning**: the occupier is responsible for the offices and landing. The rest of the cleaning is covered in the service charge.

**Car park**: the offices have four reserved spaces in the underground car park.

**Maintenance and repairs**: the landlord is responsible for the security of the building and the lift.

2 You work for a company in London. You have been asked to look after two overseas visitors for the weekend. They want to visit Shakespeare's birthplace in Stratford-on-Avon and play a round of golf. You will need a car from Friday evening to Monday morning. You will probably have to drive at least 250 miles. Your boss has told you to rent a car from Sutcliffe's Cars, a car rental firm near the office.

You want to find out as much as possible about the following:

**Price**
– weekend rental – are there special weekend rates?
– type of vehicle
– mileage – limited or unlimited?

**Insurance**
– what is included in the insurance cover?
– who can drive the car?
– where and when can you pick it up and return it?
– methods of payment?
– petrol – do you have to return the car with a full tank?

# Grammar guide

## ⓖ Adjective and adverb patterns

### Comparatives

Comparative adjectives are formed by adding *-er* to short adjectives; and using *more* or *less* with longer adjectives. Use comparative adjectives:

- to compare and contrast people or objects.

  *The new model is **smaller** and **less expensive** **than** the old one and **more convenient** to use.*

- with *the* to talk about the progressive link between actions and their results.

  ***The harder** I try, **the less** I succeed.*

- instead of the superlative.

  *Is there a **cheaper** / **less expensive** lap-top **than** this one? (= is this the cheapest?)*

Use *as* + adjective to compare the way in which two things are similar.

  *It's not **as heavy** / **comfortable as** the other one.*

### Superlatives

Most superlatives are formed by adding *-est* to short adjectives and *the most* / *least* to long ones.

  *It's **the cheapest** model but also **the least** reliable.*

Use the superlative:

- to talk about memorable experiences or events (with present perfect + *ever* / *never*).

  *It's **the most stressful** week I've ever had.*

- to state the highest possible degree of comparison.

  *I'm expecting this interview to be **the toughest**. (tougher than all the rest)*

Adverbs are generally formed by adding *-ly* to the adjective. To make them comparative, use *more* or *less*.

  *Our ordering system works **more** / **less** smoothly since we made the changes.*

Note these common exceptions:

| adjective | good | bad | hard | fast |
|---|---|---|---|---|
| comparative | better | worse | harder | faster |
| superlative | best | worst | hardest | fastest |

| adverb | well | badly | hard | fast |
|---|---|---|---|---|
| comparative | better | worse | harder | faster |
| superlative | best | worst | hardest | fastest |

## ⓖ Modifying adjectives and adverbs

Comparative adjectives and adverbs can be made stronger or weaker by using words like *quite, slightly, a little, a lot, considerably, substantially.*

  *Our chances of getting the contract are **substantially better** than two weeks ago.*

### Further patterns

*too* and *enough*

Use a positive form + *too* + adjective; or a negative form + adjective + *enough* to provide an explanation.

  *She's **too young** to do the job. She isn't **old enough** to do the job.*

*so* and *such*

Use *so* and *such* clauses to express a causal relationship between clauses.

  *He drove **so slowly that** they missed the beginning of the meeting.*
  *He was **such a slow** driver **that** they missed the beginning of the meeting.*

**Remember:**

- *hardly* is an adverb meaning 'just a little'.

  *It was so noisy I could **hardly** hear a thing.*

- When certain adverbs with a negative sense begin a sentence, the subject and verb which follow are inverted.

  ***Not only does she** speak Arabic but she speaks Russian too.*
  ***No sooner had we** left than the car broke down.*

Note that some adjectives and adverbs have different meanings despite their similarity of form.

*late* = not on time; *lately* = recently
*short* = not tall; *shortly* = soon
*hard* = difficult, not soft; *hardly* = almost none

Use adverbs:

- with verbs to show how, or to what extent an action is performed.

  *I **completely agree** with everything you've said.*
  *She **apologized profusely**.*
  *All our ingredients are **organically grown**.*

- to modify or emphasize adjectives or other adverbs.

  *I was **absolutely furious** when I heard the news.*
  *He drives **really quickly**.*

- at the beginning of phrases or sentences to comment on what comes next. They are often used in more formal speech or writing.

  ***Hopefully**, your car should be ready by this evening.* (= if there are no problems)
  ***Clearly**, we need to re-consider our credit terms.* (= it's obvious that ... )
  ***Regrettably**, your order was damaged in transit.* (= I'm sorry to say)

Adverbs such as *incidentally, consequently, understandably* are often used in this way.

## @ Conditionals

### Zero conditional

Use the zero conditional:

- to describe a simple cause and effect.
  *If you **use** that door it, **sets off** an alarm.*
- to describe a scientific truth.
  *If you **mix** blue with yellow, you **get** green.*

### First conditional

Use the first conditional:

- when you think it is likely that something will happen as the result of a future action.
  *If we **get** the contract* (condition) *we'll celebrate.* (result)
- to make a promise or threat.
  *If you **can't meet** our deadline we'll **have to** find another supplier.*

Use *when* and *as soon as* when the first action is sure to happen.
  *I'll tell you **when / as soon as** we have some news.*

Use *unless* meaning 'if ... not' in the condition clause. Use *otherwise / or else* before the likely result.
  *We'll lose the contract **unless** we give them a discount.*
  *We'd better give them a discount, **otherwise** we'll lose the contract.*

Use *provided / as long as* to make the condition stronger.
  *I'll lend you my car **provided / as long as** you fill it up with petrol.*

### Second conditional

Use the second conditional:

- to describe a future event or outcome which we think is not very likely to happen.
  *If the post **were** more reliable, we **wouldn't have to** depend on couriers.*
- to express something in the present or the future which is entirely imaginary.
  *If I **owned** the company I**'d run** it differently.* (but I'm just an employee)
- to appear more polite in making a request.
  ***Would** you **mind if** I **came** to work an hour late on Monday?*
- to make a more delicate or indirect offer.
  *What **would** you **say if** we **improved** our delivery time?*

**Remember:**

*could* can be used instead of *will* or *would* in first and second conditional sentences.

### Third conditional

Use the third conditional:

- to talk about 'unreal' or imaginary past situations.
  *If he **hadn't made** the phone call he **wouldn't have got** the contract.* (but he did make the call so he did get the contract)
- to express regrets.
  *If I**'d known** the truth about the company I **wouldn't** have taken the job.* (but I did take the job and now I regret it)

*If only ...* or *I wish ...* are commonly used when we assume the listener knows the rest.
  ***If only / I wish** I'd known the truth about the firm.*

## Mixed conditional

The mixed conditional uses the third conditional in the condition clause and the second conditional in the result clause.

Use the mixed conditional to describe a past action with a consequence in the present.

*If we'd **listened** to his advice we **wouldn't be** in this present mess.*

## ⓖ Determiners

Determiners are used to introduce nouns. They include the articles *a / an* and *the*; *some / any / much / many / little / few / each* and *several*.

Use the indefinite article *a / an* before a singular countable noun used in a general sense.

*They made us **an** offer.*

Use the definite article *the*:

- when mentioning something for the second time.

  *There was a letter in her post-box. It was **the letter** with details of her appointment.*

- when referring to a particular thing.

  *I'm still waiting for **the reply** from the bank.*

- for many (but not all) geographical names, titles, and the names of organizations.

  ***the** Amazon, **the** Managing director, **the** United Nations*

- with adjectives to refer to a particular group or class.

  ***the** jobless, **the** well-off*

- for some places and amenities.

  *I'm going to **the post-office / the hospital**. (the buildings)*

**But:**

*I'm going home / to work. (the institutions)*

Don't use articles:

- for plural countable nouns in a general sense.

  *I enjoy dealing with **customers**.*

- to refer to uncountable nouns.

  ***Money** is the root of all evil.*

- with abstract nouns like *information*, *help*, and *business*.

**But:**

For specific nouns, *the* is used.

*I hated dealing with **the customers** who came in this morning.*
***The money** she stole proves the point.*

## *some* and *any*

Use *some*:

- with plural countable nouns [C] and uncountable nouns [U].

  *We went to **some** interesting **presentations** [C] at the conference.*
  *She gave me **some** useful **advice** [U].*

- in offers and requests.

  *Would you like **some** more **copies** of our brochure?*
  *Could I have **some information**, please?*

- when we see what we want or when we expect the answer to be 'yes' .

  *Could I have **some milk** please?*
  *Are there **some** of those nice **biscuits** left?*

Use *any*:

- to express the idea of *all* or *nothing*.

  ***Any decision** (= all decisions) must be approved by the union.*
  *There isn't **any reason** (= is no reason) to be worried.*

- to check whether something exists or is available.

  *Are there **any** copies of last year's brochure left?*

## *much* and *many*

Use *many* with countable nouns, and *much* with uncountable nouns.

***Many business people** have criticized the government's economic policies.*
*The new regulations have caused **much confusion**.*

*A lot of / lots of* are used with countable and uncountable nouns and are commonly used instead of *much* and *many* in positive statements.

***A lot of / lots of business people** take the 7.30 train.*
*The mistake caused **a lot of / lots of confusion**.*

Remember:

*Lots of* is more informal than *a lot of.*

> I've got **lots of** ideas.
> He made **a lot of** suggestons at the meeting.

*Much* and *many* are more commonly used in negative statements and questions.

> How **much** time do we have before the others arrive?
> We don't have **much** time left.
> How **many** people do we expect at the meeting?
> We're not expecting **many** people at the meeting.

---

Use *few / a few* with countable nouns and *little / a little* with uncountable nouns. *A few* and *a little* mean 'some'; while *few* and *little* mean 'not much / many', or 'less than usual'.

> **A few** (= some) managers know how to inspire trust and loyalty from their employees.
> **Few** (= not very many) managers know how to inspire trust and loyalty from their employees.
> There's **a little** (= some) time left, so let's go through the figures again.
> There's **little** (= not much) time left, so we'll have to go through the figures when we next meet.

---

Use *a great / large number of* with plural countable nouns and *a great deal* of with uncountable nouns to mean 'many' or 'much'.

> **A great / large number of managers** [C] type their own letters these days.
> We have to complete **a great deal of paperwork** [U] each time we want to export our goods.

---

Use:

- *all* with countable plural or uncountable nouns.

  > **All visitors** [C] must register at reception before entering the main premises.
  > **All advice** [U] is given without prejudice.

- *several* with countable plural nouns.

  > We are going to take on **several** new trainees this autumn.

- *each / every* with singular countable nouns.

  > **Each / every participant** will receive a folder with all relevant information.

---

## ⑧ Future forms

English has several ways of expressing the future. The form we use depends on the circumstances and how we view the future event.

### Present continuous

Use the present continuous to talk about a personal arrangements and plans, particularly when we know the time and place.

> She's **leaving** for Madrid in the next few days.

### Present simple

Use the present simple to talk about schedules and timetables.

> The next flight to Amsterdam **leaves** in half an hour.

### *be going to*

Use *be going to*:

- to talk about things we plan to do, or have planned to do.

  > We're **going to** expand our overseas operation next year.

- to make predictions based on what we can see now.

  > Just look at these sales figures! We're **going to** make a loss this year.

### Future simple (*will*)

Use *will* (the future simple) for facts and predictions.

> Production of the new model **will begin** in June.
> More and more countries **will** tie their currencies to the US dollar.

- to predict the present; i.e. make a deduction based on normal behaviour

  > A: This parcel has just arrived.
  > B: That **will** be the book I ordered.

### *be to ...*

Use *be to ...* for news and announcements.
> The new terminal **is to** open in 2007.

## Future continuous

Use the future continuous (*will be* + *-ing*) to describe actions which will be in progress at a time in the future.

> *Don't worry. I'll be waiting for you at the airport.*

## Future perfect

Use the future perfect to describe something that will have happened by a point in the future.

> *We'll have had our millionth passenger by June.*

## Future in the past (*was going to*)

Use *was going to* to introduce an idea which was still in the future when viewed from an earlier event.

> *How could I have known that they weren't going to pay their bill?*

## adjectives with a future meaning

Use *bound to* when you are certain that a future event will happen.

> *He's bound to be late, he always is.*

Use *likely to* when we think there is a high probability that something will happen.

> *Unemployment is likely to rise next year.*

Use *due to* when something has been planned for, or is expected to happen.

> *Work on the office block is due to begin next month.*

## ⒢ Gerund and infinitive

## The gerund

The gerund is a noun formed from a verb by adding *-ing*.

Use the gerund:

- after certain verbs such as *detest, involve, avoid, mind.*\*
  *I detest filling in these stupid forms.*
- as the subject or object of a sentence.
  *Eating and drinking are not permitted in the computer room.*
- after prepositions, and expressions and phrasal verbs ending in a preposition.

> *Turn off the lights before leaving the premises.*
> *Are you interested in reading this report?*
> *He was forced to give up playing football after the accident.*

## The infinitive

Use the infinitive without *to* (base form of the verb):

- after modal verbs.
  *We could make the advertisement bigger.*
- after *make* (someone) and *let* (someone).
  *They can't make us accept their offer.*

Use the full infinitive (*to* + base form of the verb):

- to express a reason or purpose.
  *She went to the bank to take out some money.*
  *They took a taxi so as not to be late for the appointment.*
- after certain common verbs such as *want, manage, seem.*\*
- with verb patterns with two objects such as *encourage, request.*
  *They encouraged her to apply for the job.*

**Remember:**

Some verbs can take the infinitive or the gerund. This can produce:

- a small or subtle change in meaning.
  *I like to have a clear desk at the end of each day.* (it's a habit of mine)
  *I like helping customers find solutions to their problems.* (I enjoy it )
  *We tried to get the desk into the building.* (this was our objective)
  *We tried turning it and taking off its legs.* (this was the approach we used)
- or an important change in meaning.
  *I remembered to cancel the appointment.* (I remembered this morning, and then I did it)
  *I remembered writing down their address.* (I wrote it down, then I remembered later)
  *We hated telling her the news.* (it was difficult for us but we did it)
  *I hate to tell you this.* (I haven't told you yet but I'm going to)

\* For details of particular verbs, refer to a good dictionary such as the *Oxford Advanced Learner's Dictionary*.

## ⓖ Modals

Modals are auxiliary verbs which let us express concepts such as ability and obligation, or allow us to perform a wide range of practical tasks such as making suggestions and speculating. Each modal has a number of different uses.

### can

Use *can*:

- to talk about general abilities.

  *He **can speak** three languages fluently.*

- to ask for permission.

  ***Can I use** your phone?*

- to make simple requests.

  ***Can you take** me to the station?*

**Remember:**

The simple past of *can* is *could* or *was / were able to*; the future of *can* is *to be able*.

### could

Use *could*:

- to talk about general past abilities.

  *In the old days, a skilled worker **could produce** two shirts a day.*

**Remember:**

If we want to say we managed to do something on one occasion or after a lot of effort, we tend to use *be able to*.

  *After three hours, I **was able to make** the printer work properly.*

- to discuss possibilities or options.

  *We **could try** changing the colour of the packaging.*

- to make more polite or formal requests or offers.

  ***Could** we **have** a table by the window, please?*
  ***Could** you **speak** a little more slowly, please?*

### must

Use *must*:

- for orders we give to ourselves.

  *I **must send** in my tax form, otherwise I'll get a fine.*

- for a strong prohibition or rule.

*You **mustn't smoke** anywhere in the building.*

**Remember:**

- *must* can sound very strong. Use *have to* or *should* to describe duties, and use *could you?* to soften orders into more polite requests.

- We generally use *have to* (Not: ~~must~~) in a question.

  ***Do I have to wear** a uniform, or can I wear what I like?*

- for a strong recommendation.

  *You **must see** that film I told you about, it's brilliant.*

- for making deductions and intelligent guesses.

  *He **must be** Bill's son, they look so alike.*

**Remember:**

- For a negative deduction we use *can't be*.

  *Six thousand euros for that old car! They **can't be** serious.* (Not: ~~They mustn't be serious.~~)

- For past deductions we use *must have been / can't have been*.

  *They **can't have been** happy with the news; they **must have been** quite shocked.*

### have to

Use *have to*:

- to talk about duties or responsibilities.

  *When visitors come I **have to check** their ID and issue them with a badge.*

- to indicate an absence of obligation or necessity.

  *You **don't have to take** notes; I'll give you a hand-out at the end of the talk.*

### may

Use *may*:

- to express possibility.

  *He **may arrive** ten minutes late today.*

- to ask for permission. This is generally considered more polite than *can*.

  ***May I ask** a question?*

## might

*Might* is the past form of *may* and is used in conditional clauses.

Use *might* in the present:

- to speculate or express a more remote possibility than *may*.
  *You **might have** some trouble clearing those goods through customs.*
- to ask a polite question or make a request.
  ***Might** I **make** a suggestion here?*

## will

Use *will*:

- to express the future and make predictions. See Future forms.
- to make a spontaneous offer or decision.
  *Don't call for a taxi, I'**ll give** you a lift.*
  *I'**ll do** it straightaway.*
- to describe an habitual action. See Routines and habits.
- to make a request / give an order.
  ***Will** you **post** this letter for me?*

Remember:

- *will*, like *must*, should be used with care when giving an order.
- *shall* is only used to make offers or ask for a suggestion.
  ***Shall** I **order** the tickets? What **shall** we **do** with our obsolete computers?*

## would

Use *would*:

- to make requests or give polite orders.
  ***Would** you **bring** me the bill, please?*
- to describe past habits. See Routines and habits.
- in conditional sentences. See Conditionals.

## should and ought to

Use *should* and *ought to*:

- to give advice.
  *At an interview, you **should** / **ought to wear** clothes you feel comfortable in.*

- to talk about what we think is morally right or correct.
  *We **should help** those less fortunate than ourselves.*
- to criticize past actions.
  *You **should** / **ought to have checked** their bank references before supplying the goods.*
  *You **shouldn't have let** them come in without written permission.*
- to make predictions or predict events that happen normally or regularly.
  *If we leave now, we **should get** there on time.*
  *Jane **should be** here any minute. She usually gets in around this time.*

## need

Use *needn't* to say that something is not necessary.
*You **needn't buy** any tools; the company provides everything.*

Remember:

- *need* can also be used as a full verb.
  *You **don't need to buy** any tools.*
- In the past, there is an important difference between *need* as a modal and as a full verb.
  *I **needn't have bought** any tools because the company provided everything. (modal = I bought the tools but it wasn't necessary)*
  *I **didn't need to buy** any tools because the company provided everything. (full verb = it wasn't necessary to buy any tools so I didn't)*

## ⑧ Passive voice

The passive voice is used to indicate what happens to people, whereas the active voice says what people do. Use the passive:

- when the person / people who performed the action (the agent) is assumed, unimportant or unknown.
  *The goods **were transported** to our main warehouse.*
- to change the emphasis of a sentence.
  *Ms Meredith **was elected** salesperson of the year by her customers. (not Ms Jones)*

- to describe a process.

  *Mail is collected before midday. This is then taken to one of our sorting stations. Where necessary, it is flown by light aircraft to one of our main international distribution points.*

- for official or impersonal notices.

  *Any form of photography is strictly forbidden.*

- with a modal, without naming the agent.

  *The piracy of intellectual property should be stopped.*

Use *need* in a similar way with either the gerund or the passive.

  *My office needs decorating.*
  *My office needs to be decorated.*

Use reporting verbs and verbs of cognition to present claims and general opinions.

  *It is said that your client failed to honour the terms of the contract.*

  *The factory is known to produce the best glass in the whole of Bohemia.*

**Remember:**

- The present and past perfect continuous do not have a passive form.

  *She has been working on her report all day.*
  (Not: *Her report has been being written* ...)

- Intransitive verbs do not have a passive form. See Transitive and intransitive verbs.

- With an instrument, we often use *with* instead of *by*.

  *The drawer was opened with a screwdriver*
  (Not: *by a screwdriver*)

- Past participle adjectives have a passive sense.

  *I was really bored by the presentation.*
  (the presentation was boring)

- *get* meaning 'become' can be used with a passive sense.

  *The equipment got broken during transit.*

## *have* something *done* (causative)

Use *have* something *done*:

- to talk about services we ask other people to perform for us.

  *We had the photographs in the brochure taken by a professional.*

- to describe misadventures and accidents.

  *He had his pocket picked on the train.*

## ⓖ Past forms

### Past simple

Use the past simple to describe:

- a single past action or a series of completed past actions.

  *He signed the invoice, put it into an envelope and posted it.*

**Remember:**

We can omit repeating the subject, as in the above sentence.

- past habits and states.

  *She took the same train to work for fifteen years.*

### Past continuous

Use the past continuous:

- to set the scene at the start of a narrative.

  *Commuters were pouring off the trains, a lot of people were impatiently waiting for taxis and two stall-holders were busily selling souvenirs.*

- to show an action was in progress when another action occurred.

  *They were preparing the accounts when the computer crashed.*

- to show two or more actions were in progress at the same time.

  *While we were packing the boxes the children were writing out the labels.*

**Remember:**

We can often omit the verb *be* and use the present participle on its own.

  *Commuters were hurrying along, (they were) ignoring the street vendors (who were) trying to catch their attention.*

### Past perfect

Use the past perfect:

- to show that an action happened earlier than an action which followed.

  *When we arrived, the meeting had already started.*

- as part of a sentence expressing a past wish or regret. See Conditionals (Third Conditional).

Remember:

- Using *after* or *before* can mean we have to use the past perfect or the gerund. *After* refers to an earlier action.

  *After we had eaten / After eating we continued the negotiations.*

- *Afterwards* introduces the next action in a sequence.

  *We had lunch, and afterwards we continued the negotiations.*

## Past perfect continuous

Use the past perfect continuous:

- to show that an action had begun and was still in progress before another action or event took place.

  *He had been waiting patiently for promotion for seven years before an opportunity finally came.*

- to describe repeated actions up to a point in the past.

  *Colleagues had been taking her biscuits and borrowing her stationery for years before she finally lost her temper.*

## ⓖ Phrasal verbs

Phrasal (or multi-word) verbs consist of a verb plus one or two *particles*. A particle can either be a preposition or an adverb, although it is not always obvious which. Its meaning may not be clear from its separate parts. This course focuses on idiomatic phrasal verbs.

Compare:

*She looked up the number in the phone book.* (phrasal verb = consult)
*She looked up when her boss came into the room.* (this simply tells us about the direction in which she looked)

There are four main types of phrasal verb:

**Type 1**: intransitive. no object, e.g. *turn up*

  *He turned up.*

Intransitive phrasal verbs do not have an object but can be followed by an adverbial or prepositional phrase.

  *He turned up late for the meeting.*

**Type 2**: transitive separable, e.g. *fill in*

Transitive separable phrasal verbs have to take an object.

A full object, such as a noun or someone's name, can either go *between* the verb and the particle, or *after* the particle. However, if a pronoun is used then it must come *between* the verb and the particle.

  *He filled the application form / it in.*
  *He filled in the application form.*
  (Not: ~~He filled in it.~~)

Most type 2 phrasal verbs can be used in the passive.

  *The form was filled in incorrectly.*

Remember:

Some transitive phrasal verbs cannot be used in the passive.

  *They came across the documents.*
  (Not: ~~The documents were come across.~~)

**Type 3**: transitive inseparable. e.g. *look after*

  *Can you look after our guests / them?*

The direct object and object pronoun always follow the particle.

  (Not: ~~Can you look our guests / them after?~~)

**Type 4**: three-part transitive (phrasal prepositional) e.g. *put up with*

  *I can't put up with it / this noise any longer.*

Remember:

The same phrasal verb can have a different meaning and a different grammar.

  *The plane took off three hours late.* (type 1 intransitive)
  *They took fifty euros off the price as a discount for cash.* (type 2 transitive separable)

## ⓖ Present tenses

## Present simple

We use the present simple:

- to talk about facts, routines and habits.

  *The factory produces circuit-boards.*
  *I leave the office at half past five.*

- with adverbs of frequency or other time expressions.

  *They **often** take on extra staff at Christmas.*
  *We eat out **from time to time**.*

- with verbs of having and being; perception, opinion and thinking; and verbs expressing emotion: *be, have, need, understand, know, like, want, wish.*

## Present continuous

We use the present continuous:

- to talk about activities which are happening right now.

  *What **are** you **doing**? I'm **looking** for his phone number.*

- to talk about activities which are happening around now.

  *Peter is based at the London office but he's **helping** us out here for a few months.*

- to express a future meaning. See Future forms.

### Remember:

Some verbs generally used in the present simple (*be, have, think* are used with the present continuous when we want to emphasis their temporary nature.

  *What **do** you **think** about globalization? (general opinion)*
  *You look worried. What **are** you **thinking** about? (at this moment)*

## Present perfect

### Present perfect simple

Use the present perfect simple:

- to refer to something which started in the past and continues into the present.

  *They **have been** in business for ten years.*

- to talk about past events when no specific time is given or implied.

  *Jack **has travelled** all over the world.*

- to talk about recent events where the result is still visible.

  *The new model doesn't look the same; they **have changed** the shape of the body.*

- with adverbs such as *yet, just* and *already.* (especially in British English)

  *Have you finished that report yet?*

- to refer to results.

  *They **have taken** away six of our most important customers.*

- with stative verbs.

  *if I **have understood** you correctly ...*

## Present perfect continuous

Use the present perfect continuous:

- to describe continuous activities which started in the past and continue into the present.

  *I've **been working** hard all day.*

- to describe repeated actions up to the present.

  *I've **been trying** to send this fax all day, but each time I try it won't go through.*

- to emphasize an activity rather than a result.

  *We've **been exporting** to the USA for years.*

- to talk about a recent activity where a result is still visible.

  *Why are your clothes all dusty? I've **been looking** for some files in the basement.*

## ⓖ Routines and habits

### Adverbs of frequency

Use adverbs of frequency and frequency expressions to talk about routines and habits.

- Individual adverbs (*never, rarely, seldom, sometimes, often, always*) can go between the subject and the verb.

  *We **rarely have** complaints from customers.*

- Longer expressions (*as a rule, most of the time*) go at the beginning or end of the sentence.

  *(**Once in a while**) we have complaints from customers (**once in a while**).*

### Remember:

*Always* can be used with the present or past continuous to express annoyance or disapproval.

  *He's **always** upsetting her. (I wish he wouldn't)*

## will and used to

Use *will* to describe expected behaviour.

> A: Mr Brown kicked the photocopier.
> B: Oh yes, he **will** do that.

Use *would*, or the auxiliary *used to* + infinitive to describe past habits or routines.

> After work he **would** / **used to** sit down and read the newspaper; then he **would** / **used to** have a nap.

**Remember:**

Only use *used to* describes past states.

> He **used to be** (Not: ~~would be~~) much more enthusiastic in the old days.

Use *used to* + gerund to say someone is accustomed or is becoming accustomed to something.

> They're **used to living** in the city; the traffic doesn't wake them any more.
> I'm getting **used to working** with him.

## (g) Transitive and intransitive verbs

Intransitive verbs only involve the performer of the action (the subject) and the action (the verb).

> The train **arrived**.

Intransitive verbs include: *go, come, sleep, disappear*.

However, intransitive verbs can involve another person or thing through the introduction of a prepositional phrase.

> The train arrived **at the station**.

Many verbs which are intransitive are commonly used with a preposition.

> We **waited for** the bus.
> This bag **belongs to** me.

As intransitive verbs do not have an object, they cannot be made passive.

> He arrived last night. (Not: ~~Last night was arrived by him.~~)

Transitive verbs involve or affect another person or thing (the object).

> The president opened **the new factory**.

A transitive verb cannot stand alone and has to take an object. (Not: ~~The president opened.~~)

Transitive verbs, by contrast, can be made passive.

> The new factory **was opened** (by the president).

Transitive verbs include: *see, do, make, own, believe*.

Most transitive verbs can be used intransitively.

> What happened at the match? We **lost**.

**Remember:**

Some intransitive verbs have a transitive equivalent and should not be confused.

| die | kill |
|---|---|
| disappear | lose |
| rise | raise |

## (g) The phonemes of English

### Consonants

| Symbol | Key word | Symbol | Key word |
|---|---|---|---|
| p | price | b | bid |
| t | take | d | date |
| k | cost | g | good |
| f | few, physical | v | very |
| θ | think | ð | those |
| s | sell | z | zero, rise |
| ʃ | shop, station | ʒ | measure |
| tʃ | choose, watch | dʒ | judge, urge |
| h | here, whole | l | let |
| m | come | r | rise |
| n | sun | j | yet |
| ŋ | young | w | won |

### Vowels and diphthongs

| Symbol | Key word | Symbol | Key word |
|---|---|---|---|
| i: | sheet | eɪ | make |
| ɪ | ship | ɔɪ | boy |
| e | letter | əʊ | wrote |
| æ | bad | ɪə | here |
| ɑ: | calm | aɪ | light |
| ɒ | not | eə | their, there |
| ɔ: | course | ɜ: | third |
| ʊ | put | aʊ | now |
| u: | food | ʊə | tour |
| ʌ | cut | ə | butter |

## ⓖ Verb groups

Irregular verbs can be organized into groups which behave in a similar way. Some verbs, including some of the most common, do not follow a pattern.

| be | was / were | been |
|---|---|---|
| do | did | done |
| eat | ate | eaten |
| go | went | gone / been |
| see | saw | seen |
| win | won | won |
| write | wrote | written |

## Past simple and past participle the same

We can make sub-groups of similar verbs.

### Ending in *t* or *d*

| get | got | got / gotten (US) |
|---|---|---|
| learn | learnt | learnt |
| mean | meant | meant |
| meet | met | met |
| sit | sat | sat |
| find | found | found |
| have | had | had |
| hear | heard | heard |
| hold | held | held |
| make | made | made |
| stand | stood | stood |
| understand | understood | understood |
| lend | lent | lent |
| send | sent | sent |
| spend | spent | spent |
| sell | sold | sold |
| tell | told | told |
| pay | paid | paid |
| say | said | said |

### Ending in *-ought* or *-aught*

| catch | caught | caught |
|---|---|---|
| bring | brought | brought |
| buy | bought | bought |
| seek | sought | sought |
| think | thought | thought |

### Ending in *-eep*,*-ept*

| keep | kept | kept |
|---|---|---|
| sleep | slept | slept |

## Present and past participle the same

| become | became | become |
|---|---|---|
| come | came | come |
| run | ran | run |

## Past participle in *-en*

| beat | beat | beaten |
|---|---|---|
| break | broke | broken |
| choose | chose | chosen |
| fall | fell | fallen |
| forget | forgot | forgotten |
| give | gave | given |
| hide | hid | hidden |
| rise | rose | risen |
| speak | spoke | spoken |
| take | took | taken |
| write | wrote | written |

## Change from *-i* to *-a* to *-u*

| begin | began | begun |
|---|---|---|
| ring | rang | rung |

## Change from *-ear* to *-ore* to *-orn*

| bear | bore | born |
|---|---|---|
| wear | wore | worn |

## Change from *-ow* or *-y* to *-ew* to *-own*

| fly | flew | flown |
|---|---|---|
| grow | grew | grown |
| know | knew | known |
| draw | drew | drawn |

## No change

| cost | cost | cost |
|---|---|---|
| cut | cut | cut |
| forecast | forecast | forecast |
| hit | hit | hit |
| read /riːd/ | read /red/ | read /red/ |

# Tapescript

## Unit 1

### Part A

Interviewer  Janet White is an account [Simp. Pre] director with top advertising agency White and Springer. She's worked [Perfect] with some major clients across a range of industries, and is currently [Simple Pre] working at their New York office. So, Janet, what are the different roles in a big agency like yours?

Janet White  Well, you've got the creative side, you know, the copywriters, the people who write the ads and come up with the ideas and slogans; and the art directors who work alongside [Simp P] them to create the advertisement. And then, of course, you have the [Simp. pre] people who buy the media and plan the campaigns, and the account managers like me.

Interviewer  Mm. What exactly do you do then? [Simp. Pre]

Janet White  Erm, well, basically, I advise [Simp. Pre] the client and make sure that things go smoothly. I present the results of [simp. Pre] our research, proposals for ads and campaigns and so on.

### Part B

Interviewer  Something I've often [Pre perfect] wondered, Janet, is just how scientific advertising is, and how much is based on instinct.

Janet White  I'd say it's a mixture of both. Obviously when we start with a client we want to know what kind of customer we're dealing with, you know, which segment of the market they want to go for, because that's going to shape the form our advertising is going to take, you know, who we might choose to endorse a particular brand and so on. And very importantly, these considerations will help to determine the medium or media we choose to influence the target segment.

Interviewer  How do you mean?

Janet White  Well for instance, say you're an airline and you want to target A-B business travellers, well, we'd know what kind of magazines they are likely to read and what sort of programmes they watch on telly.

Interviewer  I see. That's the scientific bit. And what about the ads themselves?

Janet White  Well, clearly, the ads and the messages they put across have to be tailored to appeal to your target audience; but the angle, the, ah, the genius, if you like, behind the ad, is what the creative side of the agency is all about. Every successful agency needs people with that talent.

Interviewer  And what happens next?

Janet White  Well, we go back to the client and present the concept and then, if it's OK we refine and build on it.

### Part C

Interviewer  So, how do you know whether the ad has actually reached the people you were aiming at?

Janet White  Ah, good point. Basically you use tracking studies. That's where you ask a sample of viewers in the target categories if they've actually seen a commercial. If so, how many times and so on.

Interviewer  And how can you prove to a client that your campaign has been, erm, you know, successful? Presumably they expect to see increased sales.

Janet White  Well, not necessarily. Of course, I mean, the long-term aim of any campaign is obviously, to sell more of a particular product or service. But this doesn't mean that business people, say, are going to rush out and travel on a particular airline because they've seen an ad a couple of times.

Interviewer  So how can you show the client that the ad has worked, then?

Janet White  Through erm, you know, before-and-after studies. You interview say, a group of business travellers before the advertising campaign. You record their attitudes, and then afterwards, after the campaign, you carry out a similar procedure and hopefully discover that they've been favourably influenced by the ads they've seen, which, of course could help determine their choice of airline the next time they fly.

### Part D

Interviewer  Advertising is one of those fields which has the reputation of being very stressful. Is that true?

Janet White  Absolutely. Particularly when things get very last-minute.

Interviewer  I see. And have you had any difficult, you know, sticky moments?

Janet White  Well, actually I'm in the middle of one. I'm trying to sort out a problem right now. We've booked airtime for a client, for an ad on radio stations. But the actress we'd picked to do the voiceover – she was due to do the recording today – rang up a couple of hours ago to say she couldn't do it any more because of TV commitments.

Interviewer  Oh no!

Janet White  Anyway, we've been looking for a replacement. We've been playing new voices down the phone to the client all morning.

Interviewer  They must be pleased.

Martin  So what's your view on this kids' commercial, then?

Carol  I think it's absolutely ridiculous. It's a lot of fuss about nothing.

Martin  I quite agree, Carol. As far as I'm concerned, advertising is just a bit of fun.

Carol  Yes, in my opinion, we should be much more worried about the TV programmes themselves.

Martin  Mm, you're very quiet. Don't you agree, Megan?

Megan  Well, I suppose so, up to a point. I hear what you're saying, but don't you think advertisers should be more careful? Kids can be very influenced by advertisements.

Martin  Come off it! Even children don't believe everything they see on TV.

**1.3**
1  What on earth are you saying?
2  Come off it, Anna!
3  On the other hand, they could be right.
4  Wouldn't you accept that position?
5  What an awful thing to suggest!
6  There are two other points I'd like to make.

**1.4**
Laurence  Katie, there's someone I don't believe you've met. Katie Crown, this is Doctor Kowalska from the Warsaw office.

Dr Kowalska  No, but we've communicated by e-mail. How do you do, Ms Crown?

Katie  How do you do, Dr Kowalska. I'm very pleased to meet you at long last.

**Dr Kowalska** Thank you, the pleasure is all mine.

**Katie** So. Is this your first visit?

**Dr Kowalska** Well, actually, this is my third time.

**Dieter** Hi! Phil, long time no see. You're looking good.

**Phil** Hi Dieter. It's great to see you again. So, how's it going?

**Dieter** Oh, you know, I can't complain.

**Phil** I must introduce you to Sonia. Sonia, come and say hello to Dieter. Dieter is from the Munich office. You haven't met before have you?

**Dieter** No, but we've spoken on the phone. Pleased to meet you, Sonia.

**Sonia** Likewise. It's great to put a face to a voice. I've heard so much about you from Phil.

**Dieter** Good things, I hope.

**Sonia** Of course, he's a great fan of yours! So Dieter, this is your first time over here isn't it?

**Dieter** No, it's my second time, actually.

**Julia** Where do you think we should put Gangstaz?

**Ludovic** Well, it's been a disaster since the beginning. It cost us a fortune to develop but, it just never really took off.

**Alex** So, a 'dog'?

**Ludovic** Oh, definitely.

**Julia** Don't you think we could try re-launching it?

**Ludovic** I really don't think it's worth it. It didn't fit in with the rest of our range either.

**Alex** Couldn't we find a buyer for it? It's a pity not to get something for it.

**Ludovic** Well, we could try, although I'm not sure who would be interested.

**Alex** Oh, well. So, what about Wordsters? It's been out two years now, hasn't it?

**Julia** Mm, well it's done quite well already. But there are so many competitors in the word game sector. I think we need to wait and see. It's a 'question mark' for the time being.

**Alex** In that case, shouldn't we be consolidating its position?

**Ludovic** I suppose so, but we can't be sure it's going to take off. Now, we mustn't forget Sherlock. Good old Sherlock, what would we do without it?

**Julia** Absolutely, it is a mature product but people keep coming back for more. It's extremely profitable. OK it is beginning to decline, but we are planning a fiftieth anniversary edition for next year which should generate additional sales.

**Ludovic** Mm, yes, but I think the big challenge will be making it attractive for the next generation. A definite 'cash cow' at the moment.

**Alex** And last, but not least, Sketchit.

**Julia** Well, it has done very well in its first year so far. As far as we can tell, we've got forty per cent of the market.

**Alex** That's fantastic! And the market is still growing. It's easy to convert to different language editions. There's a great deal of potential here; I hope it's going to be the new Sherlock.

**Julia** Sure, but we shouldn't forget that we've had to spend a lot promoting it.

**Ludovic** Yes, we really needed the Christmas TV campaign to teach people how to play it, didn't we?

# Unit 2

**2.1**

## Interview 1

**Interviewer** So, you're an insolvency specialist, Fenella.

**Fenella** Yes, that's right. I help to wind up companies when they stop trading. I make up a list of creditors, liquidate the firm's assets, and decide who gets paid.

**Interviewer** I see. And, when businesses go broke, is this because the business idea was bad in the first place?

**Fenella** Not necessarily, even businesses based on good ideas go under if they don't have enough money to deal with their immediate financial commitments. Basically, that's what insolvency is. If they had been able to raise money to help them over cash-flow problems, it could have been another story.

**Interviewer** What's the most dangerous point for small businesses?

**Fenella** When they start to grow. They move into bigger premises, take on extra staff, and their outgoings rocket. They have a whole new level of overheads which have to be covered.

**Interviewer** So you need to generate a lot of extra business.

**Fenella** Yes, but unfortunately, firms invest heavily in equipment on the strength of one or two big customers. Then one of them finds another supplier or doesn't pay his bills, and soon, they're heading for bankruptcy.

**Interviewer** But, they could always sell the new equipment they've bought, couldn't they?

**Fenella** Well, they do, but they only get a fraction of what they originally paid.

**Interviewer** Ah. What else do small businesses need to think about?

**Fenella** They should be very aware of the business environment in which they're operating. I had some clients who owned a CD shop in a small town. They were doing well, until a big chain opened a branch next door. The independent retailer thought local people would stay loyal, but their customers deserted to the big shop, where things were cheaper. In the end, they went bankrupt. Now they should have sold up as soon as the chain arrived, and started up again in another small town.

## Interview 2

**Interviewer** James Fraser, you're a debt counsellor dealing with individuals. How do people manage to get into such a mess?

**James** Well, there are those who go mad with their credit cards or gamble; but more commonly, it's when something unexpected comes along, like losing a job. People who were managing to live within their means can't pay the bills any more.

**Interviewer** But there are plenty of jobs about, aren't there?

**James** True, but a skilled factory worker who was making good money with overtime may not be able to earn the same elsewhere. Now he can't make ends meet any more, and each month he falls further behind. He falls behind with the mortgage and the hire purchase, and ignores the unpleasant letters. In the end, he comes to me because he's receiving terrible threats.

**Interviewer** Oh dear. So what can you do, in a concrete sense, to help?

**James** Mm, well, I help them to prioritize their debts, starting with the most important things like the rent or mortgage, and electricity and water bills.

**Interviewer** And what about the things they've bought on hire purchase, or with credit cards?

**James** One option, for example, is to let the TV company take the products back. Another option is to offer a smaller repayment. Say the instalments on a washing machine are £30 a month, then you offer the company £10. Most finance companies would rather take that. After all, you can't do much with a second-hand washing machine.

**Interviewer** So do these problems mostly affect ordinary working people then?

**James** Far from it. I've dealt with managers with well-paid jobs in high-tech industries. When the recession came they suddenly found themselves out of work, and fell into exactly the same trap as the ordinary working person, except the amounts are larger.

**Interviewer** I see. And is there any other group which is particularly vulnerable?

**James** Small businesspeople like, er, builders, I'd say. I had a client who built extensions. When interest rates were low he made a fortune, but when they rose, it killed his business overnight. Most people borrow to finance a building project, and if interest rates go up, they'll wait.

**Interviewer** So what did he do?

**James** Well, in his case, he had to sell his house and the BMW to meet his liabilities It was either that or go bankrupt.

**2.2**

1 She must've been really embarrassed.
2 I'm so sorry for the misunderstanding.
3 He can't've been very pleased.
4 Oh dear, you really shouldn't've said that.
5 I do hope you'll forgive me for the other evening.
6 I'd like to apologize for what happened.
7 We ought to've briefed them better.
8 Why weren't you there?

**2.3**

1 A They've offered me the job!
  B That's brilliant news! When do you start?
2 A What a disappointment!
  B He'll get over it.
3 A How has she been since she heard the news?
  B Sad, but life goes on, you know.

4 A Alex has left me.
  B Oh, he didn't deserve you. You're better off without him.
5 A He's only forty-five.
  B Life can be so unfair.
6 A It was bad luck about your job.
  B Well, it's just one of those things, I suppose.
7 A I was sorry to hear about Felix.
  B Yes, he was a lovely cat. I'll really miss him.
8 A I finally got my promotion.
  B Well done! You deserve it.
9 A We've just had a daughter.
  B Congratulations. What are you going to call her?
10 A Oh no, I've failed the practical.
  B Oh, hard luck, I'm sure you'll pass next time.

# Unit 3

A Well, the way it works is, I do the first half of the week, and Jack takes over on Wednesday afternoons. In fact, I'm seeing him this lunchtime as usual to bring him up to date with what's been going on. Then he rings me over the weekend, to do the same thing. When we first started off, we worked shifts, you know, one of us worked mornings and the other, afternoons, but we soon gave that up because we were spending so much time travelling that we only gained a couple of hours each day, you see.

B Time is so easily wasted when you're working from home. So set yourself regular hours and realistic deadlines for completing tasks. Get into the habit of saying 'I'll do it now' to yourself, rather than 'I think I'll do it tomorrow'. Another thing to do is to resist the temptation of checking your e-mails or answering the phone whenever it rings. Let your voicemail or answering machine take the calls instead, and timetable your replies for your less productive moments. And when you do return them, treat them as a single task. And, if you can afford it, get other people to do tasks like ironing and cleaning; you'll save so much time.

C Right, I'm going to talk about the shopping centre plans. As you know, we've already fallen behind schedule, and at this rate, we'll never be ready in time. And of course, there are bound to be other problems on the way. However, all is not lost, and I've got a revised schedule, which should help us catch up. It does mean that we'll be working a lot of overtime for the next few weeks. But we'll have completed the first stage by November, and should be back on course for completion by Christmas.

D Well, I got there ten minutes early as usual, but I had to wait ages because the previous meeting was running late. By the time I finally managed to see him, I only had a few minutes. But it was a mistake really, he just wasn't paying attention, and I simply ran out of time. I really should have made another appointment, you know, where I could present our service properly. It was a complete waste of time. All the same, I expect I'll try to make another appointment to see him.

E It really is high time they paid. Their invoice is three months overdue. I could have guessed this was going to happen. I've never known a builder pay on time. I've told you before, Gareth. Before you agree to supply a new customer, we've really got to check their references with their bank first. Once upon a time, we used to do this automatically. Anyway, from now on, whenever you can, ask them to pay in advance until they've developed a history. Right, I'll send them another reminder and I just hope they pay. In the meantime, I want you to pay them a visit in person and find out what's happening.

**3.2**

1 I was wondering if you could spare me two minutes.
2 I'd like you to help me sort out these invoices.
3 Could you ask Richard to organize coffee and biscuits for the conference room?
4 Can you ring them and tell them the order is on its way?

5 Would you mind organizing the collection for Mrs Bevan?

6 So, if you'd like to deal with this straight away.

7 Do you think you could ask Anna to make this a priority?

**3.3**

1 I'll put it at the top of my list.

2 Would you like me to handle it?

3 Shall I deal with it immediately?

4 Let me take care of that for you.

5 How about if I deal with that?

6 Why don't I sort it out?

7 I'd better deal with that straight away.

**3.4**

1 I am rather busy. Could we meet later?

2 I could, but he doesn't like taking orders from me.

3 Actually, I would mind. I hate asking people for money.

4 I will, just as soon as I've finished this.

**3.5**

1 A Hi, Gerald, I haven't seen you for ages.

 B Yes, it's been years, hasn't it?

2 A Is this the first time you've been to New York?

 B No, I spent three years here as a student.

3 A I've spent hours preparing for this meeting.

 B Haven't you heard? It's been called off.

4 A How much longer do you need?

 B I should have finished it by tomorrow.

5 A How long does it take to get there?

 B Well it took me about five hours by car last time.

6 A It really is time we left.

 B But check-in isn't for another three hours.

7 A How long does it last?

 B It starts at eight and finishes at ten thirty.

**3.6**

1 Hi, are you sitting down? I've got some bad news ... Well, you'll never believe this, but Sammy Webb's agent has just rung to say that he won't be able to host the ceremony after all! Yeah, yeah, I know. He's

just been offered this multi-million-dollar role in a new comedy. Yeah. I guess we could sue him, but I'm pretty sure he won't change his mind. Mm, I think we've got to bite the bullet and look for a replacement.

2 Hello. Hi, erm, there's a little hiccup with the programmes, I'm afraid. Someone has just spotted that there is a bad spelling mistake on pages three and five. They've spelt the name of the hotel wrongly. In 'the three Kings hotel', they put an apostrophe between the 'g' and the 's' of 'Kings'... I know, I know, we should have noticed it earlier but what can we do? Do you think anyone will notice?

3 Hi, there's a snag with the fire department. We've had an inspector round and he says that the capacity of the room is six hundred and we have eight hundred guests. What do you think we should do? Can you think of any way round it?

4 There's a problem with the caterers. I've just heard that they're in real financial trouble. I'm not even sure whether they're going to stay in business. What do you think we should do about it? They've given us a really good price, but I think it's probably too good.

# Unit 4

 **4.1**

### Part A

Anne Baldwin  Now fung shui has been described as 'the art of perfect placement'. What exactly does this mean?

Nancy Chou  Well, quite simply, it's a way of achieving harmony between the natural world and our surroundings, and how we do things, like site buildings and arrange our homes and places of work.

Anne Baldwin  Mm, mm, it's quite mystical, isn't it? You know, balancing forces, and so on.

Nancy Chou  Yes, that's right, but it does have a practical side; a lot of it is based on laws of nature.

Anne Baldwin  Like what?

Nancy Chou  Mm, for example, fung

shui tells us that we should always build on the south side of a hill, but this is good practice which has developed over the centuries. People used to build on the south side of a hill; basically, this is common sense. Not only will you be protected from the north wind, but also, you'll get more light and sunshine too.

Anne Baldwin  Right, I see. And so, just how important is it in the East, then?

Nancy Chou  Very, I'd say. Some people really do believe in it. Take Hong Kong, for example. The Cantonese name for Hong Kong is Kowloon, which means 'nine dragons'. Some say it has the best fung shui in the whole of China because of these dragons which live in the mountain peaks around it.

Anne Baldwin  And do people always respect these beliefs about Hong Kong's fung shui?

Nancy Chou  Fung shui is big business in Hong Kong, but its principles may not always be followed. The building of the new airport for example, was controversial because it was built on land which had been reclaimed, you know, drained.

Anne Baldwin  Why should that have been a problem?

Nancy Chou  Well, according to fung shui practitioner Raymond Lai, this caused the dragons to be trapped; it's certainly true that there was a series of setbacks in the airport's early days.

### Part B

Anne Baldwin  So how far will property developers take fung shui into account when planning and designing new buildings?

Nancy Chou  Well, the consequences of ignoring its principles can be quite serious. For instance, several big new buildings in Taipei have stayed empty because the rules of fung shui were not followed. Prospective occupants simply were not interested.

Anne Baldwin  Goodness! So clearly any foreign developers will have to get used to following local customs.

Nancy Chou  Absolutely.

Anne Baldwin  Forgive me for asking, but what evidence is there that it actually does work?

Nancy Chou  Ah yes, people are always asking me this. Well, there was a Chinese restaurant which kept on losing money, even though its food was great and it was heavily advertised and everything. Anyway,

**155**

in the end, the restaurant owner consulted a geomancer who told him that the position of the main door made money flow out of the restaurant, rather than in. Once he changed the door, then you couldn't get a table in it any more, it was so popular.

Anne Baldwin  That's extraordinary. I know that fung shui is the latest fashion in the West, and that a lot of people have tried to apply it to their homes, but has it had any effect on business at all, do you know?

Nancy Chou  Well yes, in the US and the UK, hotels are adopting the principles of fung shui, and some even offer fung shui workshops and fung shui consultation services for weddings and meetings.

Anne Baldwin  Goodness!

**Part C**

Anne Baldwin  And what about in the workplace? What advice would you give people, you know, setting up an office.

Nancy Chou  Well, desks and work surfaces should be kept tidy and free of clutter or things like photographs and toys. Quite simply, there shouldn't be any unnecessary mess.

Anne Baldwin  I suppose so, but I'm used to working in chaos. It doesn't bother me all that much.

Nancy Chou  Yeah, but just think how much better you'd feel if you were in a tidy, well-organized environment.

Anne Baldwin  I suppose so. But where should I put the desk in the first place?

Nancy Chou  Mm, Ideally against a wall, but with a good view of the door and window.

Anne Baldwin  Mm, that makes sense. And what can we do to help ourselves work better?

Nancy Chou  Creative people should use rounded tables instead of ones with corners. And a glass paperweight can help with intuition. But don't put it too close to your computer.

Anne Baldwin  Really. Now, um, a lot of people complain about stress. What can they do to help themselves feel less stressed?

Nancy Chou  A good thing is to have water, ideally a fountain in the room.

Anne Badwin  But that might not always be practical.

Nancy Chou  True, but you could always have an aquarium, or just a goldfish in a bowl. And don't forget the plants of course. Nowadays, offices

are full of electrical charge, so plants can counteract this. It's a good idea, too, to have flowers; red flowers on the left side of the desk are best.

Anne Baldwin  Why's that, then? I mean, red flowers?

Nancy Chou  Because they're the most auspicious, you know, lucky. But overall, the best colours for a home office are green and red.

So what does the Internet really mean for our everyday working lives? It means hours wasted by junk e-mail, the loss of human contact, and drowning in a sea of information.

And as a medium for conducting business with the outside world, we could even say that it's disadvantageous. Many so-called international businesses are tiny operations with hardly any resources. I strongly believe that most natural business relationships are face-to-face, not virtual. This is surely the only way to measure and judge any future partner.

It's true that there are millions of impressive web-sites which provide useful information, but who knows what is lurking behind them? The Web is susceptible to piracy and plagiarism. It's difficult to control the flow of information. Security can be a problem. And providing personal details is risky if they fall into the wrong hands.

And finally, if we ask ourselves the question 'What does the Internet actually produce?', the answer is, 'nothing'. It's only a source of information, like a giant filing cabinet, but much less relilable.

inva**si**on
rela**ti**on**shi**p
**judg**e
approa**ch**

/ ʒ /
televi**si**on
**Asi**an
mea**su**re

/ ʃ /
**su**re
protec**ti**onism
globaliza**ti**on
informa**ti**on

/ dʒ /
encoura**ge**
ur**ge**
messa**ge**

/ tʃ /
fu**tu**re
for**tu**nately
ques**ti**on
vir**tu**al

Waiter  Are you ready to order?

Maurice  I think so, I'd like to start with the prawns. And what about you, Juliet? Do you fancy some oysters?

Juliet  I'm afraid they don't agree with me. I think I'll have the mixed starter.

Waiter  And for your main course ?

Maurice  I'll have the roast beef and Yorkshire pudding, please.

Juliet  And I'll have the breast of duck.

Waiter  How would you like it done?

Juliet  Pink in the middle, please.

Waiter  What would you like to drink with your meal?

Juliet  A glass of dry white wine, please.

Waiter  And for you, sir?

Maurice  Just mineral water. I'm driving.

Waiter  Still or sparkling, sir?

Maurice  Still is fine thank you. Is that OK with you, Juliet?

*(pause)*

Juliet  Mm, this is delicious.

Maurice  Well, actually, it's a local speciality.

Waiter  So how is your meal, madam ?

Juliet  It's really tasty, thank you.

Maurice  Can I tempt you with some cheese?

Juliet  No thank you, I really couldn't manage anything else.

Maurice  Shall I ask for the bill? We can always have coffee elsewhere.

Juliet  No, I insist, this is on me.

Maurice  Absolutely not. You can take me out when I visit you.

# Unit 5

A  Well, there is a hierarchy here I suppose, but it doesn't affect me all that much. Er, I do have a line manager I have to report to and who gives me my assignments, but I don't see her all that often. Most of the time, I work in teams on specific projects. Each member –

everyone's an expert in his or her own way, so it's quite egalitarian. Ah, we generally get on OK, but you don't bother to get to know each other because, well, you know, you, you'll be working with a different bunch of people this time next month. The main thing is that the work is really interesting and you know when you've achieved something.

B I guess I don't really have a job, it's more a way of life. I can't really tell you where my working life ends and my social life begins. Terry's the boss I suppose, I mean the one who had the original idea for the start-up, but the rest of us have bought into her dream. We certainly don't count the hours, a lot of us even have sleeping bags and mattresses which we take out at the end of the day. We send out for pizzas and keep at a problem until we've solved it. We've all got stock options, so if we do manage to launch it, then a lot of us will make a fortune.

C If you look at that organizational chart on the notice board you can see the different departments and how they relate to each other. That's me here. Everybody knows exactly what they have to do and where their responsibilities begin and end. A lot of people might find it a bit hierarchical, and, you know, stiff and formal, but to tell you the truth, I like it this way. I'd hate to work somewhere where everything depended on the wishes and moods of one person. And working relationships which get too familiar usually finish in tears, you know what I mean?

D It would be an exaggeration to say that we are a big happy family, because some of the time there is some fighting and things can get very unpleasant, but it's really Mr Jones who keeps everyone together. I suppose you might say we're all part of his gang and it's very paternalistic. He's quite authoritarian, and I'd never dare to use his first name to his face, but people here really do care about each other. It's quite hard for newcomers but once you're trusted, that's it. There's quite a lot of

socializing outside work and there are always little celebrations on birthdays and things like that. Sometimes, it can be too intense, almost suffocating, I suppose.

**5.2**

Gavin Wilson  So, what's the dress code then? I had to wear a jacket and tie in my last job.

Judith Parker  Really? Well, you won't have to here. It's smart casual, I suppose.

Gavin Wilson  Oh no! And I even bought a suit for the interview.

Judith Parker  Oh dear, you needn't have spent your money. Oh but you've really got to wear your ID tag. In fact, you're expected to challenge anyone who isn't wearing one.

Gavin Wilson  Oh! I didn't need to do that in my old job.

Judith Parker  Maybe not, but we were made to tighten up on security. We had some unwelcome visitors. Now this is the staff restaurant.

Gavin Wilson  Mm, it looks very nice. And is there a smoking area at all?

Judith Parker  Actually no. You're not allowed to smoke on the premises. It's also banned outside the building as you come into reception.

Gavin Wilson  So where do people go then?

Judith Parker  You're meant to go to a shelter in the car park.

Gavin Wilson  The car park! I've never had to do that before. There's always been a smokers' room.

Judith Parker  Well, things are different here. Oh and another thing, there's a pay phone on each floor for staff.

Gavin Wilson  So they won't even let us phone from our workstations?

Judith Parker  Well you're supposed to use the pay phones; but nobody makes a fuss if you keep calls short. Anyway, now we're coming to Research and Development. Access is limited and you mustn't ever bring anyone in without permission.

**5.3**

1 Someone sent you a CV with their application form. Tell them it wasn't necessary to send their CV.

2 Tell someone that boots and hard hats are essential for all visitors.

3 Tell someone that the canteen is a no-smoking area but that a lot of people do it anyway.

4 Tell someone that long hair and beards are against the rules.

5 Tell someone that staff are

completely prohibited from taking home confidential documents.

6 Someone asks why you aren't wearing an ID tag. Explain that you didn't think it was necessary.

**5.4**

1 I had to wear a jacket and tie in my last job.

2 You're supposed to use the pay phones.

3 I didn't need to do that in my last job.

4 You're not allowed to smoke on the premises.

**5.5**

1 You mustn't ever bring anyone in without permission.

2 It's smart casual I suppose.

3 I even bought a suit for the interview.

4 You're expected to challenge anyone who isn't wearing one.

**5.6**

Simon Jones  I'm really fed up, Andrea. We've got this no-smoking policy but nobody seems to respect it. You know, in June 75% of staff were for a total ban. But the other day I noticed that there were lots of cigarette ends around the front door and even in the plants at reception.

Andrea Fox  Yes, you're right, it really does create an awful impression.

Simon Jones  And the toilets smell of smoke too. There are some people who are ignoring the rules completely. Do you have any idea who it could be?

Andrea Fox  I've got my suspicions. We've taken on quite a few people lately and there are one or two serious smokers among them. We didn't make our no-smoking rules all that clear when we were recruiting.

Simon Jones  Well, there's always the parking lot.

Andrea Fox  Come on, Simon, you can't expect people to go all the way to the parking lot for a smoke. Think of all the time it wastes, as well.

Simon Jones  I suppose so. We can't carry on like this. What shall we do?

Andrea Fox  There's a small room next to the coffee lounge. How about setting that aside for smokers?

Simon Jones  How will it affect the insurance?

Andrea Fox  I don't know, but it'll be a lot less risky than having people smoking in places where there could be a real fire hazard.

Simon Jones OK then, but from now on, people who don't respect the new rules will really have to go! And I don't care who it is. I'll get Jo to do a letter for all the notice boards and to e-mail everyone too.

**5.7**

Paul Did you watch House Guests last night?

Jenny Yeah, wasn't it great? Would you have voted for Paula as well, Maggie?

Maggie Actually, I didn't even see it. To tell you the truth, I just don't understand what the attraction of programmes like that is.

Paul Basically, it's fun to see how ordinary people react, you know, in real life.

Maggie Real life? But it's all in front of the cameras!

Jenny So what? The people are real.

Maggie Anyway, what I hate most is how they're forced, you know, to fight each other. Basically, it's so humiliating.

Jenny Yeah, yeah, but the thing is, they volunteered. You know, nobody forced them.

Paul And after all, it's a lot more interesting than your soap operas.

Maggie My soap operas! Huh! You know, it's you who watches them, not me.

Jenny Mind you, Paul, I have to say, I like watching them too.

**5.8**

A I used to look forward to coming into work but the old team spirit has disappeared. It's hardest for the newer staff. We used to have a mentor system – you know, an experienced member of staff would look after a less experienced person. But nowadays all we really care about is meeting the sales targets. And paperwork's a nightmare since we lost the back-up staff. OK, I'm earning a lot more money, but money isn't everything you know.

B Some of the older staff can be quite intimidating, particularly Paula! I'm still learning the ropes but I find it hard to approach some of the others. And when I'm on my own, in my little cubicle, I feel really quite isolated. I'm selling better as I gain experience, but I don't know how much longer I'll last.

C Sales is a grown-up job for grown-up people and my role is to get the best from them. If my salespeople want to cry on someone's shoulder, they'd better not come to me. They should spare a thought for all the people in the factory whose jobs depend on them. Most of them earn a quarter of what a good salesperson can make.

D Now they've taken away the basic salary, I never know if I'll be able to pay the bills. I'm finding it difficult to make ends meet – I've got a young family too. I also preferred it when we set up our own meetings with customers. You could get a better feel for the client and build up more of a rapport. I can't seem to close the sales any more. And the harder I try the worse it gets.

E We used to achieve an average of one sale for every four leads, but now it's fallen to one in six. Sickness and absenteeism is up. Morale among the sales force is low. Staff turnover has risen dramatically. Other than that, everything's great!

# Unit 6

**6.1**

### Part A

Jay Thomas What do you think of this idea that there is a fair price for everything?

Tara Williamson Well, as an ordinary person, I tend to agree. But as an economist I would say it all depends on the market.

Jay Thomas How do you mean?

Tara Williamson Well, do you remember the fuel crisis of a few years ago?

Jay Thomas The petrol shortage?

Tara Williamson Yes, well, the owner of our local petrol station doubled his prices. Now, as a motorist I was furious, but as an economist I admired him.

Jay Thomas Admired him!

Tara Williamson Yeah, because he acted in a rational way. It was the law of supply and demand in action. He got the maximum income from his remaining stock. Look, just think, if he had sold at the normal price, he'd have run out in a couple of hours. By raising his price, he controlled demand. It was a good

example of price elasticity in action.

Jay Thomas But weren't his prices predatory, you know, unfair?

Tara Williamson Predatory, no. It wasn't a captive market, and people could go elsewhere. But, his old, regular customers have never forgiven him. I certainly haven't been back since.

### Part B

Jay Thomas What determines how a company sets the price of a new item?

Tara Williamson Well, obviously a lot depends on the price of competing articles. But after that, the price is basically what they think the market will bear.

Jay Thomas I must say I was upset last year when I bought a new computer. I paid full price for it, round about €1500. Six months later it was down to about €800, virtually half the price.

Tara Williamson Ah well, with articles such as the latest high-tech equipment, they'll use a two-stage strategy. They'll skim the market first …

Jay Thomas Skim the market?

Tara Williamson Yeah, they'll set the price as high as they dare, knowing there are customers, early adopters, who will happily pay the asking price to be the first to enjoy the benefits of the new product, particularly if it's scarce, you know, in short supply.

Jay Thomas I see. I suppose at the time, I was prepared to pay a high premium to do that.

Tara Williamson It makes good business sense too; it lets the manufacturer break even and recover his development costs early on. Once this level of demand has been satisfied they can attract the next level of consumer by putting it into a more affordable price range. That way, they can achieve greater market penetration.

### Part C

Jay Thomas But how much control do manufacturers have over the retail prices of their goods?

Tara Williamson Well, big brand names are keen to dictate the price at which their goods sell. Department stores can be made to respect the price lists and guidelines. And the image of designer labels and other luxury goods can be damaged if they're sold, at discounted prices say, through supermarkets.

Jay Thomas But how could a

supermarket get hold of them in the first place?

Tara Williamson Through the grey market. Most branded goods will fetch different prices in different markets. So, the supermarket will locate a supply in a lower cost country, and then import them to sell at a cut price. The big brands don't like it because it makes a mess of their pricing structure and upsets the exclusive retail outlets. They may even take the supermarket to court.

Jay Thomas So what's in it for the supermarket, then?

Tara Williamson Well, it gets people into their store, where they'll buy other goods at regular prices.

Jay Thomas So, do they sell these luxury brands at a loss?

Tara Williamson No, but they'll work at a much lower margin than a department store, much less than the list price. Other products, like washing powder, can be loss-leaders, which they'll sell at cost price or even at a small loss, to get the customers through their doors.

Jay Thomas OK, but if that's the case, why do most retailers all seem to charge around the same price for some goods? I remember shopping around for kitchen appliances, and finding very little variation.

Tara Williamson Well, retailers won't actually sit around a table and fix prices with their competitors. But what they will do, is keep an eye on each other's prices and try to match them. It's not in their interest to get involved in a price war.

### 6.2

1 So, to re-cap, we all feel that transport costs have risen too high.
2 Can I just finish off what I was saying?
3 Wouldn't it be a good idea to contact the supplier again?
4 We haven't heard from you yet, Chantal.
5 It's an interesting point, but I'm not sure how relevant it is to our discussion.
6 I'd just like to say that I think we should keep the schedule in mind.
7 Do you mind if I say something here?
8 Could you just run through that again, as I'm still not quite clear.
9 Does anyone have anything further to add?
10 So what you're suggesting is waiting until next month before making a final decision.

11 To return to my earlier point, I still think we should reject their proposal.
12 The point I'm trying to make is if we don't act now, it will be too late.

### 6.3

| | |
|---|---|
| 1 **re**fund | re**fund** |
| 2 **wel**come | **wel**come |
| 3 re**port** | re**port** |
| 4 **con**tract | con**tract** |
| 5 su**pport** | su**pport** |
| 6 **in**voice | **in**voice |
| 7 **pro**ject | pro**ject** |
| 8 **tran**sport | tran**sport** |
| 9 **re**search | re**search** |
| 10 **pro**gress | pro**gress** |

### 6.4

1 A What size are you?
   B Forty two; I think it's size twelve over here.
2 A Do you think it goes with this shirt?
   B Well actually, the patterns really clash.
3 A Could I try it on?
   B Of course, the changing room's through there.
4 A Would you like it gift-wrapped?
   B Yes please, it's for a present.
5 A Do you need any help?
   B Yes please, I'm looking for a walkman.
6 A How would you like to pay, madam?
   B Is VISA all right?
7 A They don't fit; they're much too tight.
   B I'm sure they'll stretch.
8 A What do you think of the green one?
   B The colour really suits you.
9 A Do you have any more in stock?
   B I'm afraid we only have what's on display.
10 A Do you have this in any other colour?
   B No, but we're expecting an order next week.

### 6.5

Caroline Yes, we're very proud of it. It's the old cloth hall where merchants used to sell their wares. It dates from the Middle Ages.

Luke I'm looking for something for my son. He's 12.

Caroline How about one of these T-shirts?

Luke The ones with the dragon on the front? Yeah, they look fun. What's with the dragon?

Caroline Well, there is a legend associated with the city. A dragon drank up all the water in the Vistula you see.

Luke He'll love that. This'll be fine for him. Medium would do, I think. I'd like something for my wife. That glassware looks nice. This vase is amazing.

Caroline It's very reasonable. It's all handmade by craftsmen.

Luke Mm, magnificent, but I don't think I'll get home without breaking it. I wouldn't be able to get it into my suitcase. I'll find her something at the airport, some of those chocolate-covered plums. She loves those. Hey, now my daughter would really like this. It's amber, right?

Caroline Yes, silver and amber jewellery is really famous in this region. Amber is fossilized resin, you know. There is a lot of it in the Baltic. It's been getting more expensive lately but it's still extremely good value for money.

Luke Yeah, it's really unusual too. I think I'll get her one of these necklaces. Caroline – is one supposed to haggle here?

Caroline No, not really, but I'll get him to give you a discount.

# Unit 7

### 7.1

**Part A**

Interviewer What do you think the key to a successful negotiation is?

Eric Perrot Well, first of all, to understand the buyer's expectations and to be as well prepared as possible.

Interviewer Mm. Prepared in what sense?

Eric Perrot Well, obviously you have to know exactly what is and isn't negotiable. You have to know how far you can go to reach a compromise, or overcome an objection.

Interviewer Oh, I see.

Eric Perrot Never forget that a customer will always try to beat you down on price. So you need to know what your final figure is, and must never ever make a deal which is against the interests of the firm, for the sake of getting an order.

**Interviewer** I see. So what's your immediate aim when you are negotiating with a client?

**Eric Perrot** In the short term, the ideal outcome is to walk away with an order – not at any price, but one that both sides will be satisfied with.

**Interviewer** But doesn't there have to be a winner and a loser?

**Eric Perrot** That's the worst kind of deal if you want to develop a longer-term relationship. Your customers will never forgive you if they feel they've been treated badly. It's not like talking someone you'll never see again into buying a car.

**Interviewer** I see. So what is your longer-term aim then?

**Eric Perrot** Simply to make the transition from supplier to partner. When you've dealt with the same person for a while you can trust each other and work together well. You can do business more quickly too. For instance, the other day, I negotiated a one-million-euro contract in less than four minutes.

**Interviewer** But what happens if the person changes, you know, someone else takes over?

**Eric Perrot** You have to start all over again. Most big companies will insist on changing or rotating the buyer. They don't want the relationship between the supplier and buyer to get too cosy.

**Part B**

**Interviewer** So what skills do you think a good negotiator or salesperson needs?

**Eric Perrot** Well first and foremost, you need to be a good listener. You also need to be a bit of a psychologist to gain an insight into the type of person you are dealing with. And you need to recognize the 'buy signs' when you see them so you can take the initiative and close a deal.

**Interviewer** You haven't mentioned being persuasive. Why's that?

**Eric Perrot** Well, it's the facts and figures of the overall proposal which have to be persuasive, not you. If what's on the table will meet their needs, then they'll go for it.

**Interviewer** Right. And you've talked about types of customers. Now tell me Eric, what kind do you find the most difficult to deal with?

**Eric Perrot** The quiet ones, the ones who don't speak. They can be very hard work, particularly when you are meeting them for the first time. If there is no dialogue it's hard to build a rapport and reach an agreement.

**Interviewer** Mm, so how do you get round that?

**Eric Perrot** Well, I leave doors open.

**Interviewer** Doors open?

**Eric Perrot** Yes. I don't tell them the whole story. I leave out information, or put some obvious holes in my presentation, which will get them to ask a question I can answer and build on.

**Interviewer** I see. And what about aggressive customers?

**Eric Perrot** They are easy. Usually, when people come over as aggressive, it's because they feel insecure. They're terrified of losing face. So I give them recognition and reassurance, and make them think that they are the boss. Things go better after that.

**Interviewer** And you never get angry or upset yourself?

**Eric Perrot** Absolutely not. Losing your temper or bursting into tears are signs of weakness. Confrontation gets you nowhere. It's always much better to settle one's differences in a calm and civilized way.

**Part C**

**Interviewer** And what other things are negotiable in a contract, other than just the price, I mean?

**Eric Perrot** Most importantly, the quantity of the order and the length of the contract. It could be a single delivery. Or it could be for three, or even six months.

**Interviewer** And do clients ever ask for an incentive, you know, a sweetener?

**Eric Perrot** Oh yes, all the time. For instance, last month, a big supermarket chain asked for help with an advertising campaign. So I said something like, 'We'll contribute €20,000 provided you order an extra two tons a month.'

**Interviewer** I see, so a bit of give and take. So you'll never give something for nothing?

**Eric Perrot** Absolutely not. You really leave yourself open to abuse if you make concessions without getting something in return. There are always strings attached.

**Interviewer** I understand. But tell me, I've often wondered what happens if market conditions change, you know, how flexible is a contract?

**Eric Perrot** Well, let me tell you about last year. There was a terrible harvest we could never have predicted, and the price of potatoes rocketed. Unfortunately, I'd already undertaken to supply a major customer for three months.

**Interviewer** And could you go back to the buyer and renegotiate the terms, or get out of the contract?

**Eric Perrot** No, no, of course not. We just had to live with it. But basically it meant that we lost nearly a euro on every kilo we sent that customer. But at no time did we try to get out of the deal, and I'm certain that they respected us for it.

**7.2**

**Receptionist** Hello, Outdoor Sports.

**Customer** Could you put me through to Customer Services, please?

**Customer Services** Customer Services, can I help you?

**Customer** Yes please, it's about a waterproof jacket I bought last year.

**Customer Services** And what seems to be the problem?

**Customer** I washed it according to the instructions on the label and now it's leaking.

**Customer Services** Hmm. How long have you had it?

**Customer** I realize it's no longer under guarantee but I don't think a quality item should wear out so quickly.

**Customer Services** Well, you'll need to bring it into the branch so that we can have a look at it, and give you a credit note or a refund.

**Customer** I bought it in your branch but I don't live in the area. Can I return it to my local branch?

**Customer Services** Yes, that's no problem at all, just so long as you've kept the receipt.

**Customer** Thank you for your help.

**Customer Services** Thank you. Goodbye.

**7.3**

1 I can fully appreciate your frustration, Mr Miller.
2 Do you happen to have your reference number?
3 I'm just accessing your details on my screen.
4 If you'd like to bear with me a moment.
5 I'll credit your account straight away.
6 I do apologize for any inconvenience you've suffered, Mr Hall.

**7.4**

1 I can really understand why you're unhappy, Mr Miller.
2 Have you got your reference number?
3 Can you hold on while I find your file?

4 Hold the line, please.
5 Don't worry, I'll cancel the bill.
6 I'm very sorry for what's happened, Mr Hall.

**7.5**

a The sales manager promised me a **25%** discount if we pay within 30 days.

b The sales manager promised me a 25% discount if we pay **within 30 days**.

c The **sales** manager promised me a 25% discount if we pay within 30 days.

d The sales manager **promised** me a 25% discount if we pay within 30 days.

**7.6**

Call handler  Frisby Furnishings.

Mrs Smith  Hello, this is Mrs Smith here. I'm expecting a delivery of a new sofa and chairs. Now, I'm really fed up, as I've been waiting around all morning for a delivery and your van still hasn't turned up. I can't hang around all day for this. They promised me they'd be here in the morning and haven't ...

Call handler  Just a moment. What's your name?

Mrs Smith  It's Mrs Smith.

Call handler  Could you spell that?

Mrs Smith  S-M-I-T-H.

Call handler  Mrs Smith. This isn't my department.

Mrs Smith  Oh! Well ...! Whose department is it then?

Call handler  I need your reference number.

Mrs Smith  Right, I've got it here. Er, yes, it's LR23/65.

Call handler  LR23/65. Right ...

Mrs Smith  Hello, hello ... Is there anyone there?

Call handler  Hello. Look, I can't find the transport manager. Give me your number and I'll call you once I've spoken to him. All right?

Mrs Smith  I suppose so. It's 0202 876539. How long will that take?

Call handler  I really don't know, I'll call you as soon as I can.

Mrs Smith  Yes, but what am I supposed to do? I've been waiting here all ... Hello?

**7.7**

1 A I stayed in this awful hotel once. The food was terrible and the traffic was so noisy, I couldn't sleep at night. It was dreadful, but I've stayed in some terrible hotels in my time ...

B Me too, that reminds me of the time when I stayed in a youth hostel in the Lake District. It was so cold that I didn't sleep a wink all night. There were sixteen people in the dormitory and if you could have seen ...

2 A I really hate this weather, don't you? I find it so depressing ...

B I know what you mean. I get really miserable in the winter too, I think it's because there isn't any sunlight ...

3 A I was absolutely furious at the way they treated me. It was so rude and unkind ...

B You poor thing. I'll never forget the time when I was flying to Munich. We had to wait for five hours because of fog. And do you know, they didn't even give us anything to eat ...

4 A Oh I love animals. We've got two dogs you know. Sometimes I think that they're more faithful and reliable than any human being ...

B Really! There was this book I read which was all about heroic animals. There were some incredible stories in it ...

5 A Have you ever seen a cricket match? It's a marvellous game ...

B Well, I don't know much about cricket, but I'm really into basketball. In fact our team is leading the junior league at the moment ...

6 A ... and in the final minute of the competition I managed to get the ball and I scored from twenty feet ...

B That's amazing. Now, as I was saying, cricket is a fascinating game. We could go and watch a game on Sunday if you like ...

**7.8**

1 A Well, our price is $100.
  B What if I offered you $70?
  A I'm afraid I can't do that, but we can split the difference if you like.
  B What $85? That sounds fair, I suppose.

2 A I'm afraid we've hit a stumbling block with your loan application.
  B Oh!

A We need to get a letter from your employer before we can go ahead with it.
  B I'll phone her straight away.

3 A If you give me a discount, I can think about increasing the order.
  B OK, I'll scratch your back if you scratch mine.

4 Government subsidies to help companies to export are an important bone of contention between members of the EU.

5 Don't you understand anything? She's trying to play us off against each other so that she can appear like the answer to all their problems.

6 Management and unions have been at loggerheads over the payment of overtime for the last three months.

7 A I offered him 10% discount, but then he insisted on an extended guarantee and free delivery.
  B That's typical of Julius, if you give him an inch he'll take a mile.

8 A There's nothing we can do, we have to honour the contract or else they'll take us to court.
  B You're right, they've got us over a barrel this time.

# Unit 8

**8.1**

### Part A

Interviewer  So are organizations really that blind to their own problems, that they need to call in consultants?

Bill Watts  Well, it's certainly true that when you call in consultants, it's because you've already identified that something needs to be done. Perhaps you realize that your competitiveness has started to suffer, that your market position is being challenged, and so on.

Interviewer  So in fact, they could really do most of it themselves. Be their own consultant, I mean.

Bill Watts  Possibly, but many senior managers understand that their company could benefit from the objective look of outsiders, people who aren't, say, involved in inter-departmental rivalry and company politics. Their own people are often too busy to stop to think about strategy. They're too close to the day-to-day running to take a broader look. And also, you may need expert advice when strategic decisions have to be taken.

Interviewer  Like what?

Bill Watts  Like purchasing another company, deciding whether to move into different markets, and so on. Sometimes consultants will give management the courage to follow a course of action by confirming what it already suspected.

### Part B

Interviewer  But how did it feel, when you started out in your late 20s, going into a company and advising people who'd been in the business all their lives, and who knew it inside out?

Bill Watts  Well, it could be quite intimidating, given that McKinsey has always specialized at the highest level of management. Most of the clients were much older than me.

Interviewer  So how did you cope?

Bill Watts  Well, I was trained in the techniques the company used which, incidentally, were often quite unknown in Britain, and this gave me self-confidence. We were experts in management theories and gathering market intelligence.

Interviewer  And how did people react to this?

Bill Watts  Well, I'll never forget going to some companies and being looked at like a man from Mars.

Interviewer  And did companies believe your findings, or follow your recommendations?

Bill Watts  Well, yes. When you're trying to formulate a strategy, you work closely with the client. If you're trying to introduce change, it is essential that the key people are involved in the process. This means working closely with them. A consultant can't impose anything, but only advise. But what we are always doing is asking the question 'What if?', or 'Why don't we try doing it this way?', and developing different plans to meet changing circumstances.

Interviewer  So the clients, they're closely involved in the process then, and formulating the plan.

Bill Watts  Yes. It's absolutely essential if it is going to work, or gain the commitment of the people within the organization.

### Part C

Interviewer  Now, one of the other things that McKinsey is famous for,

is its up-or-out policy. What exactly does that mean?

Bill Watts  Basically, if it doesn't look as though a consultant is going to become a partner, then they are told to leave the company.

Interviewer  That's a bit, brutal, isn't it?

Bill Watts  It sounds more brutal than it is. Don't forget, that in the first place, recruitment is only ever from among the very best people; and by the time someone has spent a couple of years at McKinsey they've gained some extremely useful and marketable experience.

Interviewer  And what happens to them?

Bill Watts  Frequently they're head-hunted or else return to an organization which they've already advised.

Interviewer  Right, so they haven't been discarded.

Bill Watts  No, not at all. I didn't mean to give that impression. In fact a lot of consultants quite welcome the change of having a conventional job and escaping the constant pressure.

Interviewer  What form does this pressure take?

Bill Watts  Incredibly long hours and lots of travel. Running training sessions and giving presentations which require an enormous amount of preparation. Clients pay very high fees and expect complete professionalism in return.

Interviewer  Do you have any regrets in your career at all?

Bill Watts  No, not at all. The compensations are tremendous. You get a fascinating insight into all sorts of different organizations, far more so than anyone would have in a normal working life. It's incredibly stimulating and challenging, and of course, the money's extremely good. Being a consultant is also a remarkably good way of getting yourself noticed by some of the top firms in the world.

1  Let's take a look at the evidence, shall we?
2  If you'd like to open the report at page 4.
3  As you can see, this pie chart reveals two other worrying features.
4  I'd like to draw your attention to the following market intelligence.
5  Right, I'm going to begin by running through our main findings.
6  So what can we learn from all of this?

7  I'd like to hand you over to my colleague, Sylvie Grey.
8  Sylvie will be talking you through our short-term recommendations.
9  This brings me to the other key issue, namely, the company's image.
10  Finally, I shall attempt to outline a longer-term strategy for growth.

Good morning everybody. As you know I'm here today to present our findings, and share our suggestions with you. First of all, I'll outline the firm's current position, and talk you through the evidence. Next, I'll propose some immediate steps it should take. Finally, we shall put forward some recommendations for the longer term, and discuss the alternatives. However, before I begin, on behalf of the entire team I'd like to thank you all for your openness and co-operation. We all appreciate how difficult it is to be under the microscope.

1  Woman  So tell me, how did you find this restaurant?
   Man  A friend recommended it to me.
2  Woman  I've worked here for thirty years.
   Man  Thirty years! I expect you've seen lots of changes.
3  Man  I've got a new job.
   Woman  Really? How wonderful! Congratulations!
4  Woman  We're from Italy.
   Man  Oh are you? Whereabouts exactly?
5  Man  They didn't get the contract.
   Woman  Oh, what a pity! What went wrong?

# Unit 9

### 9.1

### Part A

Peter Fagin  What is the biggest problem of doing business internationally?

Sheena Savage  One of trust, I'd say. Exporters would like to have cash in advance, when an order is placed. Buyers, of course, would rather pay once they've got the goods.

Peter Fagin  Right.

Sheena Savage  However, if the buyer pays in advance, there's no guarantee that the goods will be sent. Similarly, if the exporter sends the goods, they have no guarantee that they'll be paid, or that the order won't be cancelled once the goods are half way across the world.

**Peter Fagin** So basically, you've got to find a way in which neither side is made to run an unfair risk.

**Sheena Savage** Exactly. This is why such a lot of transactions are carried out with documentary letters of credit.

**Peter Fagin** Right, so how does this help the exporter?

**Sheena Savage** Essentially, it adds a bank's promise to the buyer's promise, that the seller will be paid.

**Peter Fagin** So, what's in it for the buyer?

**Sheena Savage** Well, for the buyer, the terms of the letter of credit guarantee that they'll get the goods. Ah, also, they're protected because payment will only happen after the bank has received all the documents relating to the shipment.

## Part B

**Peter Fagin** I see, so what kind of documents have to be supplied?

**Sheena Savage** Ones that prove the goods have been sent, like a bill of lading and invoices signed by the shipping company.

**Peter Fagin** So, who does what?

**Sheena Savage** Well, after the two sides have agreed a deal, the buyer has a letter of credit set up. It's the buyer's bank which does this, by the way, not the seller's, and it's generally the buyer who pays the fees.

**Peter Fagin** Right.

**Sheena Savage** Anyway, so the bank produces the letter of credit which contains all the buyer's terms and conditions.

**Peter Fagin** Terms and conditions ...?

**Sheena Savage** Yes, such as when the goods have to be received; er, how they should be packed and so on.

**Peter Fagin** Right.

**Sheena Savage** The letter of credit is sent to the exporter's bank, where its details need to be checked. And if the exporter is willing to accept them, then they'll appoint a freight forwarder, you know, a specialist firm, to deal with the practicalities of exporting the goods – finding a carrier, obtaining a bill of lading, and so on.

**Peter Fagin** It sounds a long and complicated process.

**Sheena Savage** True, but it's generally believed to be the best way of doing things. Both sides are made to think

carefully before committing themselves. Anyway, to cut a long story short, there is a lot of correspondence between the two sides' banks, but, once all the documents are in order, they're sent to the bank which issued the letter of credit and payment is authorized.

**Peter Fagin** So, how does the buyer get the goods?

**Sheena Savage** Well, they go off to the port with all the documents, where they're exchanged for the goods. They won't let the buyer take the goods without all the documents and proof of payment from the bank.

## Part C

**Peter Fagin** And how should exporters price their products, er, in their own currency, or in the currency of the country they're exporting to?

**Sheena Savage** Well, my advice is, whenever possible, quote your prices in your own currency. After all, this is what most of your own costs are based on. You can leave yourself extremely vulnerable by quoting in the importer's currency, especially if it's subject to inflation, or is volatile.

**Peter Fagin** Yes but, this can't always suit the buyer, can it? I mean, what happens if they've agreed to pay US dollars, and their currency all of a sudden devalues?

**Sheena Savage** Quite simply, if large sums of money are involved, they should buy their currency forward. That is, they agree to purchase currency at a given rate, at a date in the future.

**Peter Fagin** So, you agree to buy at a known rate later on.

**Sheena Savage** That's right. Of course it means that you could lose out if the exchange rate moves in your favour, but you won't have a nasty surprise if say, your currency devalues in the meantime. Doing business is complicated enough, without having to worry about movements in the currency markets.

**9.2**

Good afternoon everyone. On behalf of Xu Silks, I'd like to welcome you to our factory. My name is Mei and I'm going to be your guide today. As you can see, we're standing in the Information Centre. Now, before we begin our tour, I'd like to tell you a little about the history of silk and its production. If you'd like to gather round the display, I'll tell you about

the silkworms which produce it.

**9.3**

First of all, silk moths lay hundreds of thousands of eggs, which hatch into worms. After a month, the worms are large enough to weave a cocoon of fine thread. Once they have woven their cocoons, the silkworms go to sleep. After that, the cocoons are brought to a smoking chamber where the worms are painlessly destroyed. Next, each cocoon is carefully examined. Only those which are perfect are chosen. Afterwards they are thoroughly washed to remove the glue which holds them together.

Then, each cocoon is carefully unwound and spun into thread. Finally, the thread is ready to be dyed or woven into material.

**9.4**

### Conversation A

**Karen** Hi Matt, is your back a bit better?

**Matt** Oh, thanks for asking, Karen, It is now; but before it was absolute agony and I had to go to an osteopath.

**Karen** An osteopath? So what did he do then?

**Matt** She, actually. Well, first of all, she massaged my back to relax the muscles. Then just when I wasn't expecting it, she made my back go 'click' a couple of times.

**Karen** Oh, wow, and did it hurt?

**Matt** No, not at all. I was surprised more than anything, that this incredibly tiny woman could do something so violent. It was astonishing.

**Karen** So it's better now, your back, is it?

**Matt** Well, it's still a bit sore, but it's such a relief, I can't tell you. You know, being able to walk again, at last.

### Conversation B

**Sonia** So, how did your weekend go, Steffi?

**Steffi** Oh, I had a great time, which is quite amazing, really. Particularly when you think how much I was dreading it. You know, all that outside stuff, climbing and canoeing. I've always been completely useless at it.

**Sonia** Right. And er, what about the instructors. Don't they use these, er, ex-army types?

**Steffi** Oh, well yes. Ours was called Danny – an ex-marine.

Sonia  Oh, a brute!

Steffi  Yeah, well at first I was absolutely terrified of him. But in fact, he was a really gentle guy. I managed to do things I had never believed were possible before.

Sonia  So it was worth it, then?

Steffi  Oh yes, definitely. In the end, I was quite sad to leave. Anyway what did you do?

Sonia  Me? Oh nothing so exciting unfortunately.

# Unit 10

**10.1**

A  Well, I got a mysterious phone call from an agency asking if I was interested in a job with better prospects and more money. I felt quite flattered. Anyway, so I met the person in a hotel and we discussed the proposition over a drink. Basically, she made me an offer I couldn't refuse and there was a marvellous 'golden hello'.

B  Well, I guess it was expected really. My parents had always assumed that one day I would end up joining them, and so I did.

C  On the erm, grapevine, if you like. I have to go to most of the medical congresses and conferences, and eventually you get to know everyone on the circuit. So when this person I'd known asked me if I'd be interested in joining his sales team I didn't hesitate. It's hard to find good medical representatives, you know.

D  Well, I'm part of the Indian brain drain, I suppose. It's so easy for IT professionals with the Internet. Anyway, what I did was to target ten companies that I was interested in working for, and then I found out about them from their websites and so on. Then I did a CV and e-mailed it to them. People were quite impressed that I'd used my initiative, and I got lots of job offers.

E  Well, at college I had this work experience to do as part of the course, and so they sent me here for a term last year. And they must have liked my attitude because they offered me a permanent job. But without the college I wouldn't have thought of applying.

F  I know that some people have contacts who can pull strings for them, but I had to go through the interview process to get this job. There was an ad which said it was looking for talented people for a rewarding career and well, here I am.

**10.2**

A  Well, it's an extremely demanding job. I'm head of the legal department and I have a lot of responsibility. Sometimes you have to make personal sacrifices. I hardly see my daughter, and last month I had to cancel a holiday that I'd had planned for ages. Then again, we have good fringe benefits, such as health insurance, and if the company does well, then we get big annual bonuses.

B  There isn't really a pay scale or career structure or anything like that, and I just do what needs to be done. I have insisted though, that they let me finish off my accountancy course. I see this as a stepping stone to something outside the family business. I'm fairly certain though, that my parents secretly want me to stay and take it over from them one day.

C  I genuinely feel it's a really worthwhile job. Our products really do make people's lives better. I enjoy dealing with doctors and building a relationship with clients by listening to what they need. And of course, the money is very good and I get a brand new company car every two years, and a great expense account. Something else I like is the pension scheme. I'm not getting any younger!

D  Brilliant. It's the most challenging thing I've ever done, that's for sure. I've just learnt about website design, which goes together well with my programming experience. And if you've got the right talent and the right attitude, then the possibilities are fantastic, as there's such a skills shortage. The salary's good too, but what I like best are the stock options, you know, shares in the company.

E  It really suits me. I've always had an aptitude for handicraft and technology. The basic salary's not bad and there's the chance of overtime. I see myself moving up in a few years. I could get on the next rung of the ladder and be a supervisor or something like that.

F  I've got to say, I haven't really been stretched at all. If anything, it's a bit of a dead-end job. However, it pays the rent and it's allowing me time to look around for something better. It certainly beats being unemployed.

And it'll look good on my CV.

**10.3**

a  Mm, I think I'd much rather be out on the road visiting customers. I prefer travelling around to being stuck in an office all day.

b  Let me think, erm ... ah! There was a time when a lot of important documents were lost. I simply made another set and delivered them personally.

c  Mm, that's an interesting question. I'm good at picking up languages, I suppose. And I'm good at remembering names.

d  My qualities? Well, I'm thorough and methodical and have a very good eye for detail. This is very important when you're filling in airway bills and bills of lading.

e  To tell you the truth, I haven't really thought about it. It's still early days and I need to gain experience. But perhaps I might start my own import-export business one day.

f  I'd prefer not to talk about money at this stage if you don't mind.

g  From my student placement? That I regard myself as a team player, not just an individual.

h  Well, I tend to be slow at dealing with paperwork, although I'm working hard to improve on this area.

**10.4**

1  Although they thank you for a job well done or send you a birthday card, what do they really think of you?

2  To tell you the truth, I think you should think through their offer, as it's a worthwhile job with good prospects.

3  Rather than cutting costs, some companies think there are advantages in offering perks such as health schemes.

4  Have you had any further thoughts on those three documents for the meeting this Thursday?

5  I think you'll agree, Mr Smith is thorough and methodical, and is therefore the right person for this job.

**10.5**

This is HYS. There's no one to take your call right now. Our switchboard is open from 8 a.m. to 5.30 p.m. Monday to Friday. However, if you would like to leave a message with your name and number, or send a fax, please do so after the beep, and we will return your call as soon as possible.

**10.6**

Er, this is Patrick Donovan from Elite Repairs calling at 5.45 on Thursday evening. I'm ringing about an order reference, number MT/4721. I was expecting delivery this afternoon but it still hasn't arrived. I desperately need it for the weekend. Er, please could you ring me on 0705 65465 to tell me what has happened to it. Thank you.

**10.7**

You are through to Patrick Donovan's voicemail. Please leave a message giving the time of your call and a contact number. I shall do my best to return your call within four working hours.

**10.8**

Hello, Mr Donovan, this is Sabine Robert from HYS here returning your call at 9.05 on Friday morning. This is simply to inform you that your order was despatched by courier yesterday evening, and ought to be with you before midday. Should you need to contact me again, my mobile number is 07207 675551. If I don't hear from you, I shall assume the parts have arrived. Goodbye.

# Unit 11

**11.1**

## Part A

Interviewer  So, what are the advantages then, of a franchise over setting up your own business, say?

Anthea Fowler  Well, first and foremost a franchise is the best way of going into business for yourself, without being by yourself. Lots of entirely new businesses, struggle and eventually go under in the first few years, but a franchise – with a tried and tested concept– has more chance of survival. It's much less risky.

Interviewer  So just how popular are they, then?

Anthea Fowler  Well, in actual fact, about thirty per cent of British businesses are franchises. They're worth around ten billion pounds and they employ half a million people.

Interviewer  Goodness. So what kind of business know-how do you need?

Anthea Fowler  Not a lot, but you have to be totally committed, at least until the business is up and running. You also need to develop a certain mental toughness. For instance, hiring and firing is always hard. But all said and done, there isn't a better way of going into business for someone with limited experience.

Interviewer  So, in short, you don't have to be a real entrepreneur then?

Anthea Fowler  No, quite the opposite in fact, someone who wanted to do their own thing might not be suited to a franchise where you have to follow hard and fast rules, you know, a kind of recipe.

Interviewer  So, who are they best for then?

Anthea Fowler  Well, I work a lot with middle-aged people who have been made redundant. Now, they may not feel young enough to set up a business from scratch, but they have a lot of experience to build on. Now, one of the big pluses of a franchise is that shortly after you've made your decision, you can get started again really quickly. The other day, for instance, I helped fix up a couple with a franchise opportunity; the ink on the agreement was hardly dry before they were making plans.

Interviewer  I see, and should people, you know, work in an area they already know well?

Anthea Fowler  Well, many franchisers say it hardly makes a difference – having previous experience – because they provide you with such a thorough training. But personally, I think you should always go for an area you know, because you're much more likely to know the kind of problems which can arise.

Interviwer  So if you've worked in a restaurant, then you might consider a fast food franchise.

Anthea Fowler  That's right.

## Part B

Interviewer  So how do franchisers make their money?

Anthea Fowler  Firstly, from the joining fee. This varies enormously, from a few hundred, to hundreds of thousands of pounds. But basically the bigger the business, the higher the fee.

Interviewer  Mm, wow. And then there's a percentage of your profits too, isn't there?

Anthea Fowler  Actually, it's based on your turnover, not on your profit.

Interviewer  And what do you get in return for all of this?

Anthea Fowler  Goodness! The list is long. Training and know-how, management systems, a name, a logo. Erm, national advertising. Help and expert advice with any eventual problem. And of course, franchises have big buying power and can pass on important reductions in the goods you consume because they buy in bulk. But most of all you're buying into their reputation.

Interviewer  Their reputation?

Anthea Fowler  Yes, let's say you need to buy new tyres for your car. Now, there could well be a good independent tyre shop over the road whose prices aren't as expensive as a franchise, but most of us will automatically go to a big name.

Interviewer  Which happens to be a franchise. OK.

Anthea Fowler  You see a franchise, is essentially like a brand, and brands make customers promises and provide guarantees.

## Part C

Interviewer  To be honest, I wouldn't know what kind of opportunity to go for. There's nothing I think I'm immediately cut out for.

Anthea Fowler  You're not alone; choosing a franchise can be such a difficult choice for a lot of people. Personally, though, I'd go for a sector which is up and coming, where there's not too much competition. Some areas are so saturated that it's difficult to get established. Then I'd visit exhibitions, buy magazines, and talk to people, so you can select well and wisely.

Interviewer  And what should you ask when you find one that interests you?

Anthea Fowler  Well, find out how long they've been operating, what back-up they provide, where they advertise, and so on. Before you commit yourself, talk to people who have already operated the franchise. The franchisers will probably give you contact details for a couple of people you can talk to, but I'd ask for a list so I could make my own choice.

Interviewer  Right. And what if the franchiser asks you to sign up and pay the joining fee immediately?

Anthea Fowler  Quite frankly, if it's too easy to join I'd be suspicious. In some cases, no sooner do you sign up, than you realize there were complications and conditions that weren't explained beforehand. By and large, you see, a good franchise will have more applicants than territories. If it's worth having, it'll be you who has to convince the franchisers that you can make a success of it, and not the other way round.

**11.2**

1 What are your objectives for this meeting?
2 Could you leave your prototype with us?
3 How much are you personally prepared to invest?
4 So you'd like our help, would you?
5 Don't you think your sales forecast is too ambitious?
6 These figures are rather unrealistic, aren't they?
7 You did carry out a feasibility study, didn't you?
8 Would you mind telling us who else you have approached?
9 Aren't you forgetting the competition?
10 Would it not be better to manufacture abroad?

**11.3**

1 Not at all; it's quite viable, given the uniqueness of the product.
2 I can assure you that they're based on detailed marketing research.
3 Naturally, so we feel confident that we can meet these targets.
4 I'm afraid their identity has to remain confidential.
5 If you don't mind, we'll discuss the competition later.
6 Unfortunately, we're not prepared to do that before we've received a firm commitment.
7 Actually, we've already raised money from our families and friends.
8 Obviously, we'd like to go away with your financial backing.
9 Certainly, but we believe that other backers would welcome the opportunity to invest.
10 I'm glad you asked us that, but at this stage, we'd like to keep a close watch on quality.

**11.4**

1 A What are your objectives for this meeting?
  B Obviously, we'd like to go away with your financial backing.
2 A Could you leave your prototype with us?

B Unfortunately, we're not prepared to do that before we've received a firm commitment.
3 A How much are you personally prepared to invest?
  B Actually, we've already raised money from our families and friends.
4 A So you'd like our help, would you?
  B Certainly, but we believe that other backers would welcome the opportunity to invest.
5 A Don't you think your sales forecast is too ambitious?
  B Not at all; it's quite viable, given the uniqueness of the product.
6 A These figures are rather unrealistic, aren't they?
  B I can assure you that they're based on detailed marketing research.
7 A You did carry out a feasibility study, didn't you?
  B Naturally, so we feel confident that we can meet these targets.
8 A Would you mind telling us who else you have approached?
  B I'm afraid their identity has to remain confidential.
9 A Aren't you forgetting the competition?
  B If you don't mind, we'll discuss the competition later.
10 A Would it not be better to manufacture abroad?
   B I'm glad you asked us that, but at this stage, we'd like to keep a close watch on quality.

**11.5**

1 What does your factory produce?
2 Does your factory produce components?
3 Doesn't your factory produce components?
4 It produces components, doesn't it?
5 It produces components, doesn't it?

**11.6**

Gemma Michael  New Affiliates. Gemma Michael speaking.
Philip Hawkins  Good morning, could I speak to Juliet Winters, please?
Gemma Michael  May I ask who's calling, please?
Philip Hawkins  Yes, certainly. My name's Philip Hawkins; I spoke with Ms Winters at the franchise fair last week.

Gemma Michael  I see. And could I ask what it's in connection with, Mr Hawkins?
Philip Hawkins  Well, yes. It's regarding some literature she gave me about your franchise scheme. I have a few queries.
Gemma Michael  I see. If you'd like to hold the line I'll see if she's available. Hello, Mr Hawkins. I'm terribly sorry, but I'm afraid she's with another client at the moment.
Philip Hawkins  Oh dear, what a pity.
Gemma Michael  Would you like to try again later, or would you rather she phoned you?
Philip Hawkins  Erm, perhaps it would be better if she rang me when she's free.
Gemma Michael  When would be a good time to speak to you?
Philip Hawkins  After lunch; er, shall we say between two and three?
Gemma Michael  Certainly, so if you'd just like to give me your details, I'll make sure that she returns your call as soon as she's available.

**11.7**

Assistant  Hello, Design.
Jerry  Hi, can I speak to Maria, please?
Assistant  Who's calling?
Jerry  Oh, sorry, it's Jerry from Truscott's Travel here.
Assistant  Hi Jerry, so what can we do for you ?
Jerry  Well, Maria gave me some sketches for the new brochure and there are a few details I need to check out with her.
Assistant  Oh right. Ah, hang on a moment and I'll see if she's free ... Hi Jerry, I'm sorry, but she's going to be tied up all morning.
Jerry  Oh no!
Assistant  Do you want to try again later on. Or shall I get her to call you back?
Jerry  Maybe it's better if she gives me a ring when she's got a few minutes to spare.
Assistant  So when would suit you?
Jerry  Ah, any time after lunch would be fine.
Assistant  You'd better give me your number again, just in case. I'll get her to ring you back the moment she's free.

# Unit 12

## Part A

**Interviewer** What legal advice would you give firms about setting up their own website?

**Stella Moss** Well, the first thing I'd say is that, contrary to what people think, the Internet, or cyber-space, is not a law-free zone. The claims you make on your website must be true. The terms and conditions of your contracts have to be legal in the countries where you hope to do business. I'd also tell them to protect their systems from hackers.

**Interviewer** People who break into computer systems.

**Stella Moss** Yes, a determined hacker could get into your customer base and find details such as credit card information. Businesses have a legal duty to protect their clients' confidentiality, and you need to prove that you've done everything to keep this information secure.

**Interviewer** I see.

**Stella Moss** Having said this, in my experience, the most serious Internet-related problems are caused by a firm's own employees, which then involve the firm in legal action.

**Interviewer** For instance?

**Stella Moss** Well, an employee may deliberately transmit confidential information. Or unknowingly download a virus which can wreck your system. This could be a quite innocent mistake, the kind of thing anyone could do. They could also be infringing copyright – either deliberately or inadvertently – by downloading software or games. They could also create problems with other members of staff by sending them insulting messages or offensive material. This, of course, is quite deliberate.

**Interviewer** So, what would be the consequences of this last problem?

**Stella Moss** Well, the person receiving it could complain that they have been forced to work in a hostile environment and claim compensation from their employer.

## Part B

**Interviewer** And what about cyber-libel, which we've heard such a lot about lately?

**Stella Moss** Well, this is simply libel published through e-mail or the Internet. A large number of people are extremely naïve about what they put in e-mail messages. Few people realize that legally, there's little difference between sending an e-mail and writing a letter on your firm's headed notepaper.

**Interviewer** I see.

**Stella Moss** Another problem is that many of us confuse the informality of the medium with intimacy and privacy. If anything, the opposite is true. You have little control over what others do with it. Once received, any document can be sent on to as many people as you like.

**Interviewer** Could you give us some concrete examples of cyber-libel in action?

**Stella Moss** Oh, right. Well, let's say there are two companies bidding for a contract, the same one. Now, imagine there's a person in company A who sends an e-mail message to a colleague saying that if company B doesn't get the contract, it is likely to go bankrupt. Now, let's say the colleague reads the message and passes it on to outsiders. If the story is untrue or malicious, there could be a case to answer.

**Interviewer** So it only becomes libel once it leaves the company?

**Stella Moss** Ah, sorry, no, not at all. It's still libel, even if it's circulated within the company, but it's only likely to be recognized as such once it's read by the victim of the libel.

**Interviewer** Goodness – it's quite complicated.

**Stella Moss** Now if company B can prove that A had won the contract by damaging B's reputation, the consequences could be serious. British courts tend to award comparatively small amounts in damages, but if you are taken to court in the States, then you could be forced to pay millions.

**Interviewer** And how is this different from slander?

**Stella Moss** Well, legally there's hardly any real difference – other than, of course, slander is spoken while libel is written. However, in practical terms, the physical evidence from libel – the written document in black and white, which can form the basis of a case – may be absent. Someone accused of slander could simply deny having said anything offensive, or claim that witnesses had misheard them.

**Interviewer** Unless, of course, it was recorded on TV or something like that.

**Stella Moss** Indeed.

## Part C

**Interviewer** So is there any way that a firm can protect itself against its employees?

**Stella Moss** Well, there are a few steps it can take. The first is to educate its staff.

**Interviewer** Educate?

**Stella Moss** Yes. To tell people exactly what they can and can't do using the firm's e-mail.

**Interviewer** So, not being allowed to transmit gossip or download games. That sort of thing.

**Stella Moss** Yes. And I'd explain the company's policy on the use of e-mail to each employee. And I'd get them to sign a declaration which says they undertake to use e-mail responsibly.

**Interviewer** I see.

**Stella Moss** And I'd make this a condition of employment for any new employee.

**Interviewer** Right, but erm, how can you make sure that they follow it, the policy I mean?

**Stella Moss** Well, ask any lawyer, and they'll tell you that a policy on its own won't provide protection against legal action unless it's properly policed. It won't make any difference at all, unless the firm can show that it actively monitors Internet use.

**Interviewer** A bit sinister, isn't it? So what, if after all this, someone is caught using it improperly?

**Stella Moss** You make an example of them and fire them.

**Interviewer** Ouch! And finally, will any of this make much of a difference if, say, the firm is involved in litigation because of an employee's actions?

**Stella** Well, normally, a company is liable for any act carried out by its employees. But if it can show that it took all reasonable steps to prevent the abuse, it could argue that the employee acted beyond the scope of his, or her, responsibilities. It just may be able to escape liability.

### 12.2

**Alan Judd** So what do you think of the premises, Ms Brewer?

**Sally Brewer** Well, I think they're quite nice really. They're fairly well situated and the reception area is lovely. The offices are nice and light too. Ah, one thing I'm worried about, though, is visitors.

**Alan Judd** Visitors? I'm afraid I don't quite follow you.

Sally Brewer  Sorry, what I meant was, we're likely to have a number of visitors who'll need to be able to park.

Alan Judd  Oh yes, I see, I'm sorry. Ah, yes, well, ah, as you know, parking space is at a premium in this area but you are entitled to a number of spaces in the underground car park as part of the lease. Erm, any more than that will cost extra.

Sally Brewer  Extra! Ah, as I understood it, parking was included in the lease.

Alan Judd  Yes, but not unlimited parking, I'm afraid. Would you like me to run through the relevant part of the contract with you?

Sally Brewer  Erm, not just yet, Perhaps we can sort that out if I decide to go ahead. Ah, so tell me, when, erm, exactly are they available, the premises, that is?

Alan Judd  Well, the existing tenants have to vacate them by the end of the month. Then of course there are the dilapidations to make good.

Sally Brewer  Dilapidations? What exactly do you mean by dilapidations?

Alan Judd  Ah, basically, it's damage which goes beyond fair wear and tear, you know, normal use. And putting the premises back into the state they were in when they were first let.

Sally Brewer  Oh, I see. So if I've understood you rightly, the current tenants are responsible for putting that right. But what if …

**12.3**

1 You have just explained the terms of the lease to the tenant, but he doesn't appear to have understood. Offer to explain them again.

2 The agent has just given you a complicated explanation about the terms of the contract. You haven't understood very much of it at all.

3 You believed that decoration of the hall and reception area was included in the rent. Now you are told that it is an additional charge.

4 The letting agent has just told you that he can only guarantee you a two-year lease. Re-phrase this, to check that you've properly understood what was said.

5 The letting agent mentions that 'dilapidations' are assessed at the end of the letting period. You don't know what 'dilapidations' means.

**12.4**

1 The building is quite well situated …
2 The building is quite well situated …

**12.5**

1 It's fairly close to the station …
2 The reception area is really nice …
3 The meeting is important …
4 The lift is quite slow …
5 It's up to you …

**12.6**

1 It's fairly close to the station; it's just a two-minute walk.
2 The reception area is really nice, but it's spoilt by a really awful carpet.
3 The meeting is important, so please be there on time.
4 The lift is quite slow; we could waste a lot of time going up and down.
5 It's up to you, but I hope you'll take our views into consideration.

**12.7**

Conversation 1

A  I've heard an interesting whisper.
B  No, what?
A  Well, I don't like to spread gossip, but Tanya Wilkes, Mr Wilson's secretary, is leaving.
B  Oh really? I can't say I'm surprised. But do you know why?
A  Well, it's all hush-hush, but apparently they're going to start up a business together.
B  Oh, you can count on me. I won't breathe a word.

Conversation 2

B  Do you want to hear an interesting piece of gossip?
C  Go on. I'm all ears!
B  This is between the two of us, but Tanya's leaving. She's going off with Mr Wilson.
C  No, never!
B  I swear it's true. And they're setting up in business together.
C  Where did you get that from?
B  Let's just say a little bird told me. And don't let the cat out of the bag, will you?
C  Oh, no! My lips are sealed!

Conversation 3

C  You'll never guess what I've just heard on the grapevine.
D  No, what's that?
C  Promise you won't tell anyone.
D  Of course I won't. Come on, spill the beans.
C  This is in the strictest confidence. But apparently, Tanya is running away with Sam Wilson. They're starting a new life together.
D  Well, well. Who would have believed it? Still waters run deep.
C  Don't tell anyone, will you?
D  Oh, I won't tell a soul!

# Glossary

## a

**absenteeism** /ˌæbsən'tiːɪzəm/ n (158) the act of staying away from work often without a valid reason

**account director** /ə'kaʊnt daɪˌrektə(r)/ n (152) the person in an advertising company with overall responsibility for a particular client, or account

**accountant** /ə'kaʊntənt/ n (26) a professionally trained and qualified person who is responsible for keeping financial records for an organization

**added value** /ˌædɪd'væljuː/ n (59) a product's extra value following its treatment or transformation

**advertising agency** /'ædvətaɪzɪŋ ˌeɪdʒənsi/ n (6) a business which produces advertising and promotional material on behalf of other businesses and organizations

**affiliate** /ə'fɪliət/ n (113) an organization which is all or partly owned by a larger organization

**airtime** /'eətaɪm/ n (152) the amount of broadcast time a story or promotion receives on radio or TV

**allege** /ə'ledʒ/ v (118) a legal term meaning to make a claim or accusation before it has been proved; *allegation* /æləˈgeɪʃn/ n (118) public statement made without proof

**annual bonus** /ˌænjʊəl 'bəʊnəs/ n (164) an extra payment received by workers once a year which is often connected to company or individual performance

**appeal** /ə'piːl/ v (12) to attract, interest; v (118) a legal term meaning to make a claim against a decision or judgement; *court of appeal n* (118) a higher court where an earlier judgement made in a lower court can be challenged and overturned; *appealing* /ə'piːlɪŋ/ *adj* (7) attractive or interesting

**aptitude** /'æptɪtjuːd/ n (97) natural ability for learning something or acquiring a skill

**arrears** /ə'rɪəz/ n (32) money owed; *in arrears* to be late in paying an invoice or account

**articulate** /ɑː'tɪkjələt/ *adj* (104) able to express thoughts and ideas clearly and well in speech

**aspirational brand** /æspəˌreɪʃnl 'brænd/ n (38) a brand which creates a strong desire in consumers who believe it gives

higher status to those who acquire it

**assemble** /ə'sembl/ v (64) to construct something from individual parts; *assembly line n* (64) area of a factory where parts of a product are assembled

**assertive** /ə'sɜːtɪv/ *adj* (104) able to express opinions and beliefs strongly and with self-confidence

**assets** /'æsets/ n (17) the items belonging to a company which form part of its wealth

**astute** /ə'stjuːt/ *adj* (104) able to make clear and accurate judgements of people and opportunities

**attitude** /'ætɪtuːd/ n (7) the way someone thinks or feels and how this affects their behaviour

**authoritarian** /əˌθɒrɪ'teəriən/ *adj* (47) describes a person who expects their laws and decisions to be obeyed without question or discussion

**award** /ə'wɔːd/ v (117) to make an official decision to give someone an amount of money

## b

**back (someone) up** /ˌbæk 'ʌp/ v (75) to openly agree with somebody's opinion or provide help and support; backup /bæk'ʌp/ n U (54)

**backing** /'bækɪŋ/ n (112) support, especially financial, necessary to perform a project

**backlash** /'bæklæʃ/ n (89) a strong negative reaction or opposition to an event or unpopular decision

**bad faith** /ˌbæd 'feɪθ/ n (116) dishonest intentions, e.g. act in *bad faith,* see **good faith**

**bankrupt** /'bæŋkrʌpt/ *adj* (17) unable to pay off debts; *bankruptcy n* (153) the state of being bankrupt

**basic salary** /ˌbeɪsɪk 'sæləri/ n (54) regular payment for a job, not including extra payments such as overtime or bonuses

**batch** /bætʃ/ v (29) to group similar items and tasks in order to deal with them efficiently during a given time

**beat (someone) down** /biːt 'daʊn/ v (67) to persuade someone to reduce the price of goods after a lot of forceful argument

**bid** /bɪd/ v (15) to offer to pay a particular price for something, often in competition with other buyers; *bidder n* (15) the person who makes a bid; *bid n* (78) an offer to buy something, especially in an auction

**blessing** /'blesɪŋ/ n (40) a special gift or favour which brings advantages to the person who receives it

**blue-collar worker** /'bluː kɒlə(r) ˌwɜːka/ *adj* (74) a worker who does manual work, usually in a factory, which requires physical effort; see **white-collar worker**

**board of directors** /ˌbɔːd əv daɪ'rektəz/ n (109) the group of directors responsible for supervising and running a company

**board member** /ˌbɔːd 'membə(r)/ n (62) one of the directors on the board

**board meeting** /ˌbɔːd 'miːtɪŋ/ n (62) meeting of directors at which decisions about a company are made

**bond** /bɒnd/ n (122) a document from a company or government promising to repay with interest a sum borrowed from an investor

**bone of contention** /ˌbəʊn əv kən'tenʃn/ n (161) an important topic of disagreement

**booming** /'buːmɪŋ/ *adj* (17) enjoying a period of growth or prosperity

**brain drain** /'breɪn dreɪn/ n (164) the movement of well-trained or educated people from their home country, to countries where they can earn more or enjoy a better standard of living and better opportunities

**brainstorm** /'breɪnstɔːm/ v (15) to work together as a group, suggesting ideas and solutions to solve a particular problem

**brand** /brænd/ n (8) a product or service which is easily recognized by its name, design and packaging

**brand conscious** /'brænd ˌkɒnʃəs/ *adj* (8) aware and able to recognize a particular brand

**breach** /briːtʃ/ n (75) a legal term for the failure to keep to an agreement; *breach of contract n* (118) the failure to keep to the conditions of a contract

**break down** /ˌbreɪk 'daʊn/ v (29) to reduce a task to its individual elements to make it easier to complete

**break even** /ˌbreɪk 'iːvn/ v (64) to be at the point where income from sales equals costs

**breakthrough** /'breɪkθruː/ n (48) an important development or discovery which solves a problem or changes the way we do something

**brochure** /'brəʊʃə(r)/ n (49) a small magazine-like book, which presents products or

services through text and pictures

**budget** /'bʌdʒɪt/ n (9) a plan of money available and how it will be spent over a given period

**buoyant** /'bɔɪənt/ *adj* (94) successful and stable due to good business

**buy into** /ˌbaɪ 'ɪntuː/ v (157) to accept a particular idea or philosophy, e.g. to *buy into* somebody's dream

## c

**call in** /kɔːl 'ɪn/ v (161) to invite someone to your organization for their professional advice or service

**campaign** /kæm'peɪn/ n (7) a programme of planned activities to achieve a commercial objective

**candidate** /'kændɪdət/ n (61) someone who has applied for a position in a company

**capital project** /'kæpɪtl ˌprɒdʒekt/ n (92) a project requiring a large investment

**captive market** /ˌkæptɪv 'mɑːkɪt/ n (158) buyers who can only deal with a single seller or who have no choice over goods

**caravan** /'kærəvæn/ n (88) a group of merchants travelling together across the desert for mutual safety and protection, with camels or other animals

**career structure** /'kəriə ˌstrʌktʃə(r)/ n (97) a career path for employees within an organization offering opportunities for promotion within a clear time-scale

**cargo** /'kɑːgəʊ/ n (87) goods carried on a boat or plane

**carrier** /'kæriə(r)/ n (86) the commercial company given the responsibility of transporting goods

**carry on** /ˌkæri 'ɒn/ v (157) to continue

**carry out** /ˌkæri 'aʊt/ v (87) to perform a task or duty

**cartel** /kɑː'tel/ n (59) a union of often international companies or producing countries which agree not to compete with each other

**case** /keɪs/ n (116) a question which is decided by a court of law

**cash and carry** /ˌkæʃ ənd 'kæri/ n (45) a large shop or warehouse where in return for favourable prices, customers buy goods in large quantities and take them away

169

**cash cow** /kæʃ 'kaʊ/ n (14) mature product which produces an important and regular income; see **dog**; **question mark**; **star**

**cash flow** /'kæʃ fləʊ/ n (17) the movement of money in and out of a business

**catalogue** /'kætəlɒg/ n (84) a book listing the ranges and specifications of goods offered by a firm or supplier

**catch up** /ˌkætʃ 'ʌp/ v (29) to make up for time wasted earlier

**catering** /'keɪtərɪŋ/ n (24) the service of providing food and drink for social events

**challenging** /'tʃælɪndʒɪŋ/ adj (97) difficult and testing in an interesting way

**claimant** /'kleɪmənt/ n (118) a person who makes a claim against another person or organization; or who claims under the terms of an insurance policy

**clear** /'klɪə(r)/ v (32) to gain official permission for payment

**client** /'klaɪənt/ n (6) a more formal word for a customer, someone receiving professional services

**clinical trials** /ˌklɪnɪkl 'traɪəlz/ n (48) closely monitored tests and experiments that new pharmaceutical products must undergo before they can be exploited commercially

**close a deal** /ˌkləʊz ə 'diːl/ v (160) to move from negotiation and discussion to a final agreement or sale

**collapse** /kə'læps/ v (62) to fall down suddenly and dramatically

**come over as** /ˌkʌm 'əʊvə(r)/ v (67) to give an impression to others of what you are like

**commercial** /kə'mɜːʃl/ n (10) a TV or radio advertisement

**commission** /kə'mɪʃn/ n (54) a percentage of the selling price which a salesperson or agent receives for successfully completing a sale

**commodity** /kə'mɒdəti/ n (59) raw materials in their un-transformed state, e.g. crude oil, coffee beans

**commute** /kə'mjuːt/ v (12) to travel regularly from home to your place of work by train, bus or car, usually some distance away; **commuter** n (12) a person who commutes

**competitive edge** /kəmˌpetətɪv 'edʒ/ n (62) the decisive advantage that one company or product has over others

**competitiveness** /kəm'petətɪvnəs/ n (26) the capacity to compete effectively against one's rivals

**component** /kəm'pəʊnənt/ n (64) a piece or part of something like a machine or engine

**compromise** /'kɒmprəmaɪz/ n (67) an agreement acceptable to both sides, where you accept less than you originally hoped for; *reach a compromise* v (67)

**computer-literate** /kəm'pjuːtə ˌlɪtərət/ adj (104) describes a person who uses a computer effectively without necessarily being a computer expert

**concession** /kən'seʃn/ n (58) an agreement to do something you did not intend to do as the result of a discussion or negotiation; *make a concession* v

**conscientious** /ˌkɒnʃi'enʃəs/ adj (104) careful to do things thoroughly and as well as you can

**consortium** /kən'sɔːtiəm/ n (92) a temporary association of different businesses or groups of people who work together to achieve a common aim

**consultant** /kən'sʌltənt/ n (42) someone who can give expert advice in management, law, public relations, etc.

**consumer** /kən'sjuːmə(r)/ n (8) a customer who buys goods or services

**consumer base** /kən'sjuːmə ˌbeɪs/ n (38) the group of customers that a company depends on for its sales

**copywriter** /'kɒpiˌraɪtə(r)/ n (7) a person who writes the copy, i.e. the texts used in advertisements and commercials

**costings** /'kɒstɪŋz/ n pl (115) the calculations of money required for a particular project or service

**counsel** /'kaʊnsəl/ (118) a legal term for a lawyer, or team of lawyers that speak in a law court

**count on** /'kaʊnt ɒn/ v (168) to rely or depend on someone or something

**court** /kɔːt/ n (116) the official place where legal matters are decided

**craftsman** /'krɑːftsmən/ n (159) someone skilled at making things with his hands

**crafty** /'krɑːfti/ adj (104) clever in a secretive and not always honest way

**crane** /kreɪn/ n (87) a piece of mechanical equipment used for lifting or unloading heavy objects

**credit note** /'kredɪt ˌnəʊt/ n (160) a document provided when you return goods to a shop, so you can exchange them for something else of the same value

**creditor** /'kredɪtə(r)/ n (32) a person or organization which is owed money

**creep up** /ˌkriːp 'ʌp/ v (62) to increase slowly and unnoticeably

**critical path analysis** /krɪtɪkl 'pɑːθ əˌnæləsɪs/ n (34) a way of studying the stages of a complicated operation in order to decide how to achieve it as quickly as possible

**crude oil** /'kruːd ɔɪl/ n U (58) petroleum in its most basic state before it is refined

**cubicle** /'kjuːbɪkl/ n (51) a small private area created by putting up partitions in a large room

**currency** /'kʌrənsi/ n (65) the official money of a country or area; the US dollar , euro, and yen are all currencies

**curse** /kɜːs/ n (40) something that will cause great harm

**cut out** /kʌt 'aʊt/ v (78) to remove or avoid

**cut out for** /kʌt 'aʊt fɔː(r)/ adj (165) to be suitable for, e.g. if you are *cut out for* a job, it suits your skills and personality

**CV** /siː 'viː/ n (96) (British English) **c**urriculum **v**itae: a document written by job applicants giving their personal, educational and professional details; (American English) *resumé*

**cyber-libel** /'saɪbə ˌlaɪbl/ n (116) libel which is committed using the Internet

**cyberspace** /'saɪbəspeɪs/ (116) the idea of an environment where communication between computers takes place

## d

**dam** /'dæm/ n (92) a barrier built across a river to create a lake or reservoir, often used in the production of hydro-electricity

**damages** /'dæmɪdʒɪz/ n pl (117) money awarded by a court as compensation for a personal or professional injury

**dead-end** /'ded end/ n (164) with no prospects and little hope of a better future, e.g. a *dead-end* job

**deadline** /'dedlaɪn/ n (28) the date by which an application has to be submitted or a task completed

**deadlocked** /'dedlɒkt/ adj (68) describes negotiations which can't progress because neither side is prepared to compromise or make a concession

**deal with** /'diːl wɪð/ v (152) to handle or take charge of a task or problem

**debt** /det/ n (16) money which is owed to a person or organization

**debtor** /'detə(r)/ n (32) someone who owes money

**default** /dɪ'fɔːlt/ v (92) a legal term meaning to fail to do what is required by law or contract

**defendant** /dɪ'fendənt/ n (118) a person or organization accused of a crime in a court of law

**delegate** /'delɪgət/ v (28) to give someone a task or responsibility which you would otherwise have to do; *delegator* n a person who delegates

**demanding** /dɪ'mɑːndɪŋ/ adj (97) something that requires a lot of time, energy and effort

**devalue** /diː'væljuː/ v (163) to decrease in value, e.g. if a currency *devalues* it reduces its buying power on the international market

**diplomatic** /dɪplə'mætɪk/ adj (104) able to handle delicate or difficult situations tactfully and without offending people

**discounted** /'dɪskaʊntɪd/ adj (158) reduced in price, often because the customer is buying in bulk

**discount warehouse** /'dɪskaʊnt ˌweəhaʊs/ n (45) a large supermarket with a basic range of goods where people buy in bulk, usually at a reduced price

**disposable income** /dɪ'spəʊzəbl 'ɪnkʌm/ n (38) the income you have left to spend after you have paid taxes

**distribution channel** /dɪstrɪ'bjuːʃn ˌtʃænl/ n (38) the route by which a manufacturer's products reach the end consumer

**diversify** /daɪ'vɜːsɪfaɪ/ v (78) to move into selling a wider range of goods and services

**dog** /dɒg/ n (14) a product which is reaching the end of its life-cycle or which never realized its potential; see **cash cow**, question mark, star

**double** /'dʌbl/ v (158) to multiply by two

**download** /daʊn'ləʊd/ v (65) to receive programmes or information electronically via computer

**downturn** /'daʊntɜːn/ n (94) a drop in sales, profits or the amount of business done

**draw up** /drɔː 'ʌp/ v (29) to prepare something in writing, e.g. a document for a meeting or a legal document such as a contract or insurance policy

**drawback** /'drɔːbæk/ n (122) a disadvantage

**dress code** /'dres kəʊd/ n (157) the way that employees are expected to dress, either officially or by custom

**drum** /drʌm/ n (21) a large cylindrical container for carrying oil or chemicals

**dynamic** /daɪˈnæmɪk/ *adj* (104) forceful, energetic and very active

**e**

**early adopters** /ˌɜːlɪ əˈdɒptəz/ *n* (158) consumers who are among the first to buy or try new products

**e-commerce** /ˌiː ˈkɒmɜːs/ *n* (84) business conducted via the Internet

**economies of scale** /ɪˌkɒnəmɪz əv ˈskeɪl/ *n* (38) the principle that unit costs fall, the greater the number of units which are produced

**economist** /ɪˈkɒnəmɪst/ *n* (56) an expert on economics

**efficient** /ɪˈfɪʃnt/ *adj* (54) works well, achieving aims with little waste of time or effort

**egalitarian** /ɪˌɡælɪˈteərɪən/ *adj* (46) based on the principle that people have similar rights and are entitled to express their opinions openly

**e-mail** /ˈiːmeɪl/ *n* (22) a message sent electronically via computers

**emerging market** /ɪˌmɜːdʒɪŋ ˈmɑːkɪt/ *n* (38) a new market which is likely to become more important in the future

**end up** /end ˈʌp/ *v* (164) to finish or arrive somewhere at the end of a journey or career(s)

**endorse** /ɪnˈdɔːs/ *v* (7) to use or approve of a product which is being advertised; it's usually a famous and respected person who does this

**enthusiasm** /ɪnˈθjuːzɪæzm/ *adj* (102) keen interest; *enthusiastic* /ɪnˌθjuːzɪˈæstɪk/ *adj* (102)

**entrepreneur** /ˌɒntrəprəˈnɜː(r)/ *n* (6) an adventurous businessperson willing to take risks and supply the capital needed for a new business

**estate** /ɪˈsteɪt/ *n* (119) the money and property which is left by someone when they die

**ethical** /ˈeθɪkl/ *adj* (42) morally right or correct

**exchange rate** /ɪksˈtʃeɪndʒ ˌreɪt/ *n* (44) the amount at which different currencies are traded

**exclusive outlet** /ɪksˌkluːsɪv ˈaʊtlət/ *n* (39) where luxury or designer goods are sold, e.g. expensive departments stores

**executor** /ɪɡˈzekjʊtə(r)/ *n* (119) the person, often a lawyer, responsible for administering a dead person's will or estate

**expatriate** /ˌeksˈpætrɪət/ *n* (86) someone who lives outside his own country, usually for the purposes of work

**expense account** /ɪkˈspens əˌkaʊnt/ *n* (164) the record of money spent by someone while working, travelling, or entertaining for his company, and which is re-paid by the employer

**expertise** /ekspəˈtiːz/ *n* (112) knowledge and professional advice

**export credit guarantee** /ˌekspɔːt ˈkredɪt ɡærənti:/ *n* (92) a way for governments of developed countries to stimulate export trade with less developed and higher risk markets

**extension** /ɪkˈstenʃn/ *n* (22) a telephone line within a business, linked to a switchboard

**f**

**fall behind** /ˌfɔːl bɪˈhaɪnd/ *v* (29) to lose time on a schedule or performing a task

**feasibility study** /ˌfiːzəˈbɪləti ˌstʌdɪ/ *n* (110) the careful analysis of the practical costs, risks, and benefits of a commercial scheme

**fees** /fiːz/ *n pl* (115) the money paid to someone, e.g. a lawyer, for a professional service

**filing-cabinet** /ˈfaɪlɪŋ ˌkæbɪnət/ *n* (156) a large metal cabinet with drawers used to organize documents

**findings** /ˈfaɪndɪŋz/ *n pl* (80) the results and discoveries of research

**fix up** /ˈfɪks ʌp/ *v informl* (165) to arrange

**fixed costs** /ˈfɪkst kɒsts/ *n* (17) the costs borne by a business such as rent, wages, lighting

**flowchart** /ˈfləʊ tʃɑːt/ *n* (91) a diagram used to provide a clear visual representation of a process

**fluctuate** /ˈflʌktʃueɪt/ *v* (62) to rise and fall quickly or change suddenly

**follow up** /ˌfɒləʊ ˈʌp/ *v* (96) to take further action on something

**fork-lift truck** /ˌfɔːklɪft ˈtrʌk/ *n* (21) a vehicle often used in a warehouse for lifting and moving heavy items

**franchise** /ˈfræntʃaɪz/ *n* (25) the authorization given by a company to others who wish to use its name when selling its goods or providing a service; *franchiser n* (106) owns the franchise and sells its rights under licence to *franchisees n* (106)

**freight forwarder** /ˈfreɪt ˌfɔːwədə(r)/ *n* (87) a business used by exporters to organize the transportation of goods to their destination

**fringe benefit** /ˌfrɪndʒ ˈbenɪfɪt/ *n* (164) advantage such as a car, or health insurance given to employees in addition to their salary

**from scratch** /frəm ˈskrætʃ/ *phr* (165) from nothing

**g**

**get into** /ɡet ˈɪntuː/ *v* (153) to become involved in; (167) to enter; *get into the habit v* (154) to develop the habit

**get on with** /ɡet ˈɒn wɪð/ *v* (29) to have a good or satisfactory relationship with someone

**get out of** /ɡet ˈaʊt əv/ *v* (67) to avoid or escape from a duty, e.g. *get out of* a contract

**get through to** /ɡet ˈθruː tuː/ *v* (67) to successfully make contact with someone by telephone

**globalization** /ˌɡləʊbəlaɪˈzeɪʃn/ *n* (38) the process where a company does business or sources its supply and production of goods around the world

**go for** /ˈɡəʊ fɔː(r)/ *v infml* (152) to choose or select

**go under** /ɡəʊ ˈʌndə(r)/ *v infml* (153) to fail, go bankrupt

**golden hello** /ˌɡəʊldən həˈləʊ/ *n* (98) a sum of money given to a newly employed person in a company as an incentive to join

**good faith** /ɡʊd ˈfeɪθ/ *n* (26) honest intentions, e.g. sign a contract in *good faith*; see **bad faith**

**goods** /ɡʊdz/ *n pl* (8) objects for sale

**goodwill** /ɡʊdˈwɪl/ *n U* (72) positive and co-operative feelings

**graduate** /ˈɡrædʒueɪt/ *v* (11) to earn a qualification by completing a course of study at a higher education institution; *graduate* /ˈɡrædʒ uət/ *n* (98) a person who has graduated

**grey market** /ˌɡreɪ ˈmɑːkɪt/ *n* (159) a situation where goods in short supply are traded legally but without the approval of the manufacturer

**grievance** /ˈɡriːvəns/ *n* (74) a situation that is seen as unfair and the source of disagreement

**guarantee** /ɡærənˈtiː/ *n* (70) formal promise e.g. *under guarantee* describes a product which is sold with a promise that it will be of a certain quality; *guarantee v* (78)

**guidelines** /ˈɡaɪdlaɪnz/ *n* (11) a set of rules which outline what an organization or business can or should not do

**h**

**hacker** /ˈhækə(r)/ *n* (116) someone who, without permission, accesses or interferes with information held on computers

**haggle** /ˈhæɡl/ *v* (68) to argue over the price of something

**handover** /ˈhændəʊvə(r)/ *n* (109) the passing of power or responsibility to another person

**hang around** /hæŋ əˈraʊnd/ *v infml* (161) to waste time uselessly by waiting for something to begin or happen

**headed notepaper** /ˌhedɪd ˈnəʊtpeɪpə(r)/ *n* (167) official writing paper on which is printed the name, logo and contact information of an organization

**headhunt** /ˈhedhʌnt/ *v* (54) to actively search in other companies for a well-qualified person for a job in your company

**headquarters** /ˈhedkwɔːtəz/ *n* (46) the offices from which an organization is controlled; *abbr* HQ

**hierarchy** /ˈhaɪərɑːkɪ/ *n* (46) a system with clearly defined grades of status and authority from the highest to the lowest; *hierarchical* /ˌhaɪərˈɑːkɪkl/ *adj*

**hire purchase** /haɪə ˈpɜːtʃəs/ *n* (17) a way of buying expensive goods where the buyer makes a series of regular payments over a pre-arranged period of time

**hold** /həʊld/ *v* (62) to stay at a certain level; *hold* /həʊld/ *n* (87) the space on a ship or a plane where cargo is stored

**hot-desk** /hɒtˈdesk/ *v* (51) to take any available working space on arrival at work, instead of having one's own desk or office

**human resources** /ˌhjuːmən rɪˈzɔːsɪz/ *n pl* (98) the department in an organization which handles its workforce's needs, such as recruitment and training

**i**

**ID tag** /aɪ ˈdiː tæg/ *abbr* (50) **Id**entity / **Id**entification **T**ag: a badge which is worn to prove who you are or to authorize access to a building or area

**image** /ˈɪmɪdʒ/ *n* (7) the overall impression that the public receives of a product, person or service

**incentive** /ɪnˈsentɪv/ *n* (45) an extra benefit that aims to encourage someone to buy something, e.g. a discount, or that encourages someone to work harder, e.g. a bonus

**income** /ˈɪnkʌm/ *n* (9) money received as payment for work, or as a return on investment

**incompetence** /ɪnˈkɒmpɪtəns/ *n* (22) the inability to perform a job or task to an adequate standard

**incur** /ɪnˈkɜː(r)/ v (16) to suffer the unpleasant results of a situation you have created yourself

**industrial tribunal** /ɪnˌdʌstrɪəl traɪˈbjuːnl/ n (46) a court where work-related matters, e.g. unfair dismissal, sex-discrimination, are heard and judged

**inflation** /ɪnˈfleɪʃn/ n U (7) the general rise in costs and prices

**influence** /ˈɪnfluːəns/ v (11) to affect someone or have the power to make them change their mind

**infrastructure** /ˈɪnfrəstrʌktʃə(r)/ n (88) the essential systems and services which countries, cities or organizations need to function effectively

**infringe** /ɪnˈfrɪndʒ/ v (118) to break a law or invade the rights of another person or organization; *infringement n* (119)

**initiative** /ɪˈnɪʃətɪv/ n (67) personal quality of accepting responsibility and take decisions without help or approval; *take the initiative* (160) use your initiative

**innovation** /ˌɪnəˈveɪʃn/ n (112) the transformation of inventions into commercially viable new products and services

**insight** /ˈɪnsaɪt/ n (9) a deep understanding of what someone or something is really like

**insolvent** /ɪnˈsɒlvənt/ adj (17) (formal) not having the money to pay one's debts

**instalment** /ɪnˈstɔːlmənt/ n (17) one of a series of regular payments, e.g. under a hire-purchase agreement

**insurance** /ɪnˈʃɔːrəns/ n (12) a form of risk management based on a contract which guarantees compensation in the event of loss, damage or injury

**intellectual property** /ˌɪntəˌlektʃuːəl ˈprɒpətɪ/ n (116) the legal concept that an idea, piece of software or writing is owned by a person or company and cannot be sold or copied without their permission

**interest rate** /ˈɪntrest reɪt/ n (122) the percentage amount a bank or lender charges borrowers

**invoice** /ˈɪnvɔɪs/ n (32) a document requesting payment for the supply of goods or services

**iron out** /aɪən ˈaʊt/ v (68) to solve or eliminate the problems that are affecting something

## j

**joint venture** /dʒɔɪnt ˈventʃə(r)/ n (39) a business enterprise in which two or more people or organizations work together

**junk mail** /dʒʌŋk ˈmeɪl/ n (156) unwanted advertising delivered by post or through the Internet

## l

**launch** /lɔːntʃ/ n (6) the introduction of a new product or service into the market using advertising and other promotion

**lead** /liːd/ n (158) information about, or a request from, a potential customer which, if followed, could result in a sale

**leak** /liːk/ n (94) the giving away of sensitive or secret information by a member of a business or organization

**lease** /liːs/ n (121) a legal contract for the rental of a property or business premises

**level off** /levl ˈɒf/ v (62) to stay at a constant level after a period of rises or falls

**liable** /ˈlaɪəbl/ adj (117) financially or legally responsible *liability* /ˈlaɪəbɪləti/ n (117)

**liaise** /lɪˈeɪz/ v (7) to work closely and co-operate with someone by sharing information and by keeping each other up-to-date

**libel** /ˈlaɪbl/ n (116) printed malicious or untrue stories which damage someone's reputation

**line manager** /laɪn ˌmænɪdʒə(r)/ n (156) the person directly in charge of another employee or responsible for a particular process

**liquidate** /ˈlɪkwɪdeɪt/ v (153) to sell a company's assets for cash in order to pay its creditors

**literature** /ˈlɪtrətʃə(r)/ n U (113) written information about a company or its products

**litigation** /lɪtɪˈgeɪʃn/ n (116) the process of taking legal action

**long-term** /ˈlɒŋ tɜːm/ adj (17) unlikely to have an immediate or medium-term result

**lose face** /luːz ˈfeɪs/ v (160) to be in a situation where you appear foolish and experience a loss of honour or status

**lose out** /luːz ˈaʊt/ v (8) to miss an opportunity

**loss leader** /lɒs liːdə(r)/ n (57) an item which is offered at cost price or less to attract customers into the store

**Ltd** /ˈlɪmɪtɪd/ abbr (16) limited company, a company whose members are only liable for debts up to a determined amount

## m

**make up** /meɪk ˈʌp/ v (29) to replace or compensate for something, e.g. *make up the time*

**margin** /ˈmɑːdʒɪn/ n (159) the difference between the cost price and the selling price of goods or a service

**market leader** /ˌmɑːkɪt ˈliːdə(r)/ n (78) the company that sells the most of a particular product in a market

**market penetration** /ˌmɑːkɪt penɪˈtreɪʃn/ n (158) the act of trying to obtain a greater share of a market by advertising and promotion

**market share** /ˈmɑːkɪt ˌʃeə(r)/ n (7) the amount of the overall market taken by a product or company

**marketing mix** /ˈmɑːkɪtɪŋ ˌmɪks/ n (44) the combination and interaction of the four Ps of marketing

**mass market** /mæs ˈmɑːkɪt/ n (39) the market consisting of large numbers of customers

**mass production** /ˌmæs prəˈdʌkʃn/ n (112) the manufacture of large numbers of identical products through the use of fast mechanical processes

**matrix** /ˈmeɪtrɪks/ n (14) a diagram made of rows and columns

**maturity** /məˈtʃʊərɪti/ n (14) point of full development in a product's life; (122) the date on which a bond has to be paid

**MD** /em ˈdiː/ abbr (20) **M**anaging **D**irector

**means** /miːnz/ n pl (17) the money or income that a person has; v (17) *live within your means* manage with the money you have

**media** /ˈmiːdɪə/ n pl. (6) means of communication including newspapers and magazines, TV and radio

**medium** /ˈmiːdɪəm/ n (9) means by which something is communicated or expressed; adj (95) of average size, between large and small

**menial** /ˈmiːnɪəl/ n (108) describes a job not requiring much skill and therefore of low status

**mentor** /ˈmentɔː(r)/ n (158) an experienced person given the role of advising and training a new member of staff

**merge** /mɜːdʒ/ v (78) (of companies) to join together in order to reduce and share costs and to become more efficient or competitive; *merger n*

**methodical** /meˈθɒdɪkl/ adj (100) describes a person who completes a task in an orderly and thorough fashion

**monitor** /ˈmɒnɪtə(r)/ n (114) a means of observing and recording something; *monitor v* (167) to control and check that a task is being performed correctly

**monopoly** /məˈnɒpəlɪ/ n (59) a situation where one person or supplier controls or dominates the supply of goods to a market

**morale** /məˈrɑːl/ n (55) the confidence or mood of a person or group at a particular time

**mortgage** /ˈmɔːgɪdʒ/ n (17) a loan from a bank or building society specifically designed to allow someone to buy a flat or a house

**multinational corporation** /mʌltɪˌnæʃnəl kɔːpəˈreɪʃn/ n (38) a large business or organization with companies and production facilities in many different countries

## n

**negligence** /ˈneglɪdʒəns/ n (22) not taking the expected or sufficient amount of care or attention

**negotiate** /nəˈgəʊʃɪeɪt/ v (66) to attempt to arrive at an agreement through discussion and compromise; *negotiation* /nəˌgəʊʃɪˈeɪʃn/ n (42) the process of negotiating; *negotiator* /nəˈgəʊʃɪeɪtə(r)/ n (66) the person involved in negotiation; *negotiable* /nəˈgəʊʃɪəbəl/ adj (159)

**networking** /ˈnetwɜːkɪŋ/ n (96) the process of making business contacts with people who may be influential or prove useful

**niche market** /niːʃ ˌmɑːkɪt/ n (85) a business opportunity provided by a narrow and specific part of a market

**numerate** /ˈnjuːmərət/ adj (104) describes a person who has a good operational knowledge of basic mathematics

## o

**on-line** /ɒnˈlaɪn/ adj (22) connected to the Internet

**optional** /ˈɒpʃənl/ adj (12) not compulsory; as you wish; *option* n (15) a choice

**organic** /ɔːˈgænɪk/ adj (42) describes farming methods or food produced in a more traditional way, avoiding the use of chemicals

**organizational chart** /ɔːgənaɪˌzeɪʃənl ˈtʃɑːt/ n (157) a diagram which presents the different activities, hierarchy and chain of responsibility within an organization

**outcome** /ˈaʊtkʌm/ n (42) the end result of something

**outgoings** /'aʊtgəʊɪŋz/ n pl (17) the amount of money spent by a person or company

**outline** /'aʊtlaɪn/ v (72) to give the general picture of a situation without going into detail

**outperform** /aʊtpə'fɔ:m/ v (79) to perform significantly better than a rival

**output** /'aʊtpʊt/ n (91) the production, or rate of production

**outstanding** /aʊt'stændɪŋ/ adj (32) not yet paid, e.g. an *outstanding* invoice; (38) exceptional, e.g. an *outstanding* candidate

**over-capacity** /ˌəʊvəkə'pæsəti/ n (62) having a greater production capacity than you require

**overcharge** /ˌəʊvə'tʃɑ:dʒ/ v (20) to charge more than the official or set price for something either deliberately or accidentally

**overcome** /ˌəʊvə'kʌm/ v (67) to succeed in finding a solution to a problem or difficulty

**overdue** /ˌəʊvə'dju:/ adj (32) late, not paid by the required time

**overheads** /'əʊvəhedz/ n pl (17) the regular costs of running a business usually divided into fixed costs and variable costs

**overtime** /'əʊvətaɪm/ n (51) extra hours worked in addition to normal working hours

## p

**partnership** /'pɑ:tnəʃɪp/ n (16) the association of two or more people who join together to run a business

**patent** /'peɪtnt/ n (49) an official document which gives the holder exclusive rights over an invention and prevents others from copying it

**paternalistic** /pəˌtɜ:nə'lɪstɪk/ adj (47) describes a system in which an employer acts like a father figure

**peak** /pi:k/ v (62) to reach the highest point or value

**pension scheme** /'penʃn ˌski:m/ n (164) a system in which employees can qualify for a company pension when they retire by paying contributions into the company's pension fund

**perks** /pɜ:ks/ n (100) fringe benefits

**persuasive** /pə'sweɪsɪv/ adj (41) has the ability to make people do or believe something

**philanthropic** /ˌfɪlən'θrɒpɪk/ adj (48) helping the poor or weak through the gift of money, aid or medicine from a feeling of kindness and concern

**pick up** /pɪk 'ʌp/ v (99) to learn a foreign language informally by seeing or hearing it often; (99) to improve; (115) to take hold of and lift

**pie chart** /'paɪ tʃɑ:t/ n (80) a diagram in which a circle is used to represent the whole of something, e.g. a company's sales, with individual sections representing percentages of the whole

**pioneer** /ˌpaɪə'nɪə(r)/ v (76) to develop a new way of doing something

**piracy** /'paɪrəsi/ v (119) the deliberate and illegal act of reproducing copyright material and selling it as the genuine article

**pitfall** /'pɪtfɔ:l/ n (109) a danger or trap which is hidden or not obvious

**plagiarism** /'pleɪdʒərɪzəm/ n (156) copying another person's ideas or writing and pretending that it is one's own work

**plant** /plɑ:nt/ n (38) a living thing growing from the ground; (44) a factory or production facility

**play (someone) off against (someone)** /ˌpleɪ 'ɒf əgenst/ v (161) to arrange for others to compete with each other to your eventual advantage

**plc** /ˌpi: el 'si:/ abbr (16) public limited company, a registered company whose shares can be traded on the stock exchange

**pledge** /pledʒ/ v (75) to make a sincere and serious promise

**plummet** /'plʌmɪt/ v (62) to fall suddenly and dramatically

**policy** /'pɒlɪsi/ n (9) a plan of action or statement of ideals

**poll** /pəʊl/ n (8) the process of asking a large number of people for their opinions

**portfolio** /pɔ:t'fəʊliəʊ/ n (14) a collection of documents showing examples of the range of what a company has to offer, e.g. a product *portfolio*; (122) a range of shares held by an investor or investment company

**positioned** /pə'zɪʃnd/ adj (39) how a product or service is placed in a market

**postpone** /pəʊst'pəʊn/ v (28) to delay something until a later time or date

**potential** /pə'tenʃl/ n U (38) possibilities which promise much which have not yet been exploited

**predatory price** /ˌpredətri 'praɪs/ n (57) price which exploits the weakness of a situation, e.g. a situation of short supply, to the advantage of the seller

**premises** /'premɪsɪz/ n pl (17) the buildings used by a business for its activities

**premium product** /ˌpri:miəm 'prɒdʌkt/ n (45) a product which people are prepared to pay more for because it is perceived as special; *at a premium* (115) of high value because it is in short supply

**pressure group** /'preʃə(r) ˌgru:p/ n (11) a group of people which works together to influence what a government or business does on a particular issue

**price elasticity** /'praɪs iˌlæsˌtɪsɪti/ n (56) the relationship that exists between the demand for a product and its price

**price list** /'praɪs lɪst/ n (158) a list of goods for sale and their prices

**price sensitive** /'praɪs ˌsensɪtɪv/ adj (45) describes a situation where demand for a product would be greatly affected by a change in price

**pricing structure** /'praɪsɪŋ ˌstrʌktʃə(r)/ n (159) the way prices are set by a business for its products or services

**prioritize** /praɪ'ɒrətaɪz/ v (29) to place tasks or problems in their order of importance so you can decide which to deal with first; *priority* /praɪ'ɒrəti/ n (39) considered the most important thing in a given situation

**product placement** /ˌprɒdʌkt 'pleɪsmənt/ n (9) an advertising technique where advertisers arrange for products to be shown or used by characters in a film or TV programme

**production facility** /prɒ'dʌkʃn fəˌsɪləti/ n (38) a factory or plant where something is produced

**promotion** /prə'məʊʃn/ n U (9) method used to make people aware of a product or service and make them want to buy it; n (123) being raised to a higher position in a company

**prototype** /'prəʊtətaɪp/ n (110) an earlier version of an invention in the course of its evolution to a final product

**proven** /'pru:vn/ adj (122) tested and shown to be true

**psychometric test** /ˌsaɪkəmetrɪk 'test/ n (102) a test devised and carried out by psychologists or recruitment professionals to reveal the intelligence, motivation and character of the people who take it

**public relations** /ˌpʌblɪk rɪ'leɪʃnz/ n (108) the management of information so that a person's or organization's image is seen favourably by the public and media; abbr PR

**publicity** /pʌb'lɪsɪti/ n U (21) attention from the media

**publicity stunt** /pʌb'lɪsɪti ˌstʌnt/ n (9) something which is deliberately done to attract media attention and raise awareness of a product or service

**pull strings** /pʊl 'strɪŋz/ v (97) use your connections with influential people to gain advantages for somebody

**purchase** /'pɜ:tʃəs/ n (9) something bought; v (32) to buy; *purchaser* n (38) person who purchases

**put off** /pʊt 'ɒf/ v (29) to delay until a later time

**put (someone) through** /ˌpʊt 'θru:/ v (160) to connect somebody by telephone

## q

**question mark** /'kwestʃən ˌmɑ:k/ n (14) a product which is in the early stage of its life cycle, with high growth but low market share; see **cash cow, dog, star**

**questionnaire** /ˌkwestʃə'neə(r)/ n (16) a written list of questions meant to be answered by a number people as part of a survey

**quote** /'kwəʊt/ v (163) to give the price a company or person will charge to do a particular job or task

## r

**rally** /'ræli/ v (62) to become stronger after a period of difficulty or weakness

**range** /reɪndʒ/ n (152) a variety of things of a similar type

**rapport** /ræ'pɔ:(r)/ n (67) a close relationship; *build a rapport* develop a close relationship

**raw materials** /ˌrɔ: mə'tɪəriəlz/ n (59) the basic elements, e.g. cocoa beans and sugar, which manufacturers transform into finished products

**re-cap** /ri:'kæp/ v (60) to summarize briefly what was said earlier

**receipt** /rɪ'si:t/ n (73) a paper which proves payment for goods or a service

**recession** /rɪ'seʃn/ n (17) a period when there is a slowing down in business activity and the economy

**redundant** /rɪ'dʌndənt/ adj (76) not in employment; *to be made redundant* to lose one's job because there isn't enough work or because the job has disappeared

**reference** /'refrəns/ n (96) a statement of a job candidate's character and ability to do a particular job, written by somebody who knows the candidate well

**reference number** /'refrəns ˌnʌmb(ə(r)/ *n* (70) the numbers and letters used to refer to a particular document so that it can be found again easily

**refund** /'riːfʌnd/ *n* (60) money which is returned to a customer because a product or service was faulty or unsatisfactory

**relevant** /'reləvənt/ *adj* (22) obviously connected or related to something

**relocate** /ˌriːləʊ'keɪt/ *v* (95) to move a business to another place

**remittance** /rɪ'mɪtəns/ *n formal* (32) a sum of money sent in payment of an invoice

**reputable** /'repjətəbl/ *adj* (121) respected, having a good reputation

**resign** /rɪ'zaɪn/ *v* (46) to give up one's job or position in order to take up a new position, or sometimes as the result of a conflict or scandal

**retail** /'riːteɪl/ *n U* (57) the business of selling small quantities of goods to the general public; *retailer* /'riːteɪlə(r)/ *n* (57) a shopkeeper

**retail outlet** /'riːteɪl ˌaʊtlət/ *n* (21) a shop that stocks and sells a manufacturer's products

**revenue** /'revənjuː/ *n* (58) the money which is received from the sale of services or goods

**rewarding** /rɪ'wɔːdɪŋ/ *adj* (97) giving personal satisfaction, particularly when you think an activity is useful

**rival brand** /'raɪvl ˌbrænd/ *n* (8) a brand which is in competition with another

**rotate** /rəʊ'teɪt/ *v* (160) to move from one person or company to another in order to give each one a turn

**round** /raʊnd/ *n* (68) a stage in a competition, e.g. a *round* of golf; (96) one complete part of a process, e.g. a first *round* of interviews

**ruling** /'ruːlɪŋ/ *n* (119) an official decision

**run away with** /ˌrʌn ə'weɪ wɪð/ *v* (168) to leave secretly or unexpectedly with someone to start a new life together

**run through** /rʌn 'θruː/ *v* (60) to explain or discuss something quickly in order to clarify or check it

**rung on the ladder** /ˌrʌŋ ɒn ðə 'lædə(r)/ *n* (97) a level in an organization or career structure

**ruthless** /'ruːθləs/ *adj* (104) hard and pitiless towards other people in achieving your aims

**S**

**sacked** /sækt/ *adj* (22) dismissed from one's job often because of poor performance or conduct

**salary** /'sælərɪ/ *n* (26) a regular payment for work or services, usually paid monthly into a bank account

**sample** /'sɑːmpl/ *n* (152) a small number of people or things, used to obtain information about a larger group

**scapegoat** /'skeɪpgəʊt/ *n* (21) someone who carries the blame for a mistake even though they may be innocent or no more guilty than others

**schedule** /'ʃedjuːl/ *n* (60) a plan of events

**segment** /'segmənt/ *n* (152) a part of an overall market where consumers have shared characteristics

**set up** /set 'ʌp/ *v* (29) to organize something; *v* (54) to start a new business; *v* (39) to become established, e.g. foreign businesses *set up* in the new economic development zone

**setback** /'setbæk/ *n* (108) a problem or difficulty which prevents you from progressing as quickly as you wish

**sexual discrimination** /ˌsekʃuəl dɪskrɪmɪ'neɪʃn/ *n* (46) a situation where someone suffers harm or prejudice because of their gender

**shareholder** /'ʃeəhəʊldə(r)/ *n* (49) the person or institution which holds shares in a company

**shift** /ʃɪft/ *n* (154) the period of time that one group of employees works before being replaced by another group

**shipment** /'ʃɪpmənt/ *n* (163) a consignment of goods sent by sea

**shop around** /ʃɒp ə'raʊnd/ *v infml* (159) to search different shops or suppliers to obtain the best price or value for money

**short term** /ʃɔːt 'tɜːm/ *n* (160) now and the immediate future; see **long term**

**shortlist** /'ʃɔːtlɪst/ *v* (94) to narrow down a choice to a small number of possibilities; *shortlist n* (96) a small number of candidates chosen from a larger number of applicants for a job

**showroom** /'ʃəʊruːm/ *n* (54) a place where goods are displayed at their best advantage for customers to see and examine

**side with** /'saɪd wɪð/ *v* (118) to choose to give your support to somebody who is engaged in an argument or dispute

**sign up** /saɪn 'ʌp/ *v* (165) to join or enrol

**skilled** /skɪld/ *adj* (49) having a talent or ability

**skim the market** /ˌskɪm ðə 'mɑːkɪt/ *v* (57) to put a high price on a new product in order to realize high short-term profits from sales to consumers keen to own the product immediately

**slander** /'slɑːndə(r)/ *n* (117) a spoken statement which is untrue or malicious and designed to damage another person's reputation

**slogan** /'sləʊgən/ *n* (8) a memorable phrase or sentence associated with a product or company

**slump** /slʌmp/ *n* (62) a general drop in the level of business or business confidence

**small print** /'smɔːl ˌprɪnt/ *n* (122) the details and finer points of a written contract

**soar** /sɔː(r)/ *v* (62) to rise up steeply and suddenly

**software** /'sɒftweə(r)/ *n* (45) the programmes used by a computer

**sole trader** /səʊl 'treɪdə(r)/ *n* (16) a businessperson who works on his own account

**solicitor** /sə'lɪsɪtə(r)/ *n* (118) a type of British lawyer

**sort out** /sɔːt 'aʊt/ *v* (99) to organize or establish order; to find a solution to a problem

**split the difference** /ˌsplɪt ðə 'dɪfrəns/ *v* (74) to compromise and meet somebody halfway in a negotiation

**sponsorship** /'spɒnsəʃɪp/ *n* (9) the payment of sporting or arts events by an organization as a way of advertising its products or services

**staff turnover** /stɑːf 'tɜːnəʊvə(r)/ *n* (99) the rate at which employees leave a company and new ones join

**star** /stɑː(r)/ *n* (14) a product with a high market share and high growth, but whose costs are also high; see **cash cow**, **dog**, **question mark**

**start up** /'stɑːtʌp/ *ph v* (168) to begin a new business; *start-up n* (102) a new business starting from nothing

**stepping stone** /'stepɪŋ ˌstəʊn/ *n* (97) an intermediate step which allows you to achieve your final objective

**stereotype** /'steriətaɪp/ *n* (28) a fixed idea that people may have of something, e.g. of a particular person, profession or nationality, and which may not be true in reality

**stock** /stɒk/ *v* (45) to keep extra goods in reserve ready for when people want to buy them

**stock option** /'stɒk ˌɒpʃn/ *n* (157) an incentive offered to employees who have the opportunity to buy shares in the company where they work at a favourable rate

**stockbroker** /'stɒkbrəʊkə(r)/ *n* (83) someone who buys and sells on the stock exchange on behalf of other people

**strategy** /'strætədʒɪ/ *n* (38) a long-term objective with a plan of action to achieve it

**strike** /straɪk/ *n* (76) action when people refuse to go to work because they want more money or better working conditions

**stumbling block** /'stʌmblɪŋ ˌblɒk/ *n* (74) a problem or difficulty that gets in the way of achieving what you want

**sub-contractor** /ˌsʌbkən'træktə(r)/ *n* (94) a person or company carrying out work on behalf of a main contractor on a large project

**subordinate** /sʌ'bɔːdɪnət/ *n* (29) someone under the authority or orders of someone else

**subsidy** /'sʌbsɪdɪ/ *n* (74) money paid by the government or an organization to help a business keep its prices low; *subsidize* /'sʌbsɪdaɪz/ *v* (74)

**subtle** /'sʌtl/ *adj* (9) using indirect ways to achieve something

**sue** /suː/ *v* (119) to take legal action against someone in a court of law

**surge** /sɜːdʒ/ *v* (62) to increase suddenly and strongly

**survey** /'sɜːveɪ/ *n* (7) a way of finding out the general public's opinions on a topic by asking them carefully chosen questions

**sweetener** /'swiːtnə(r)/ *n* (160) something extra offered as an incentive to make a deal or offer more acceptable to someone

**switchboard** /'swɪtʃbɔːd/ *n* (164) the central panel controlling an organization's telephone system, where incoming calls are answered and directed to the right person or extension

**synergy** /'sɪnədʒɪ/ *n* (78) the working together of two or more activities to produce a combined effect greater than if they acted separately

**t**

**take on** /teɪk 'ɒn/ *v* (29) to accept a task or responsibility; (124) to employ

**takeover** /'teɪkəʊvə(r)/ *n* (78) gaining control of a company by buying it or controlling enough of its shares; *take over v* /teɪk 'əʊvə(r)/ (109) to take on the responsibility that somebody else used to have for something

**talented** /'tæləntɪd/ *adj* (97) possessing a natural skill or ability

**talk sb into** /tɔːk ˈɪntuː/ v infml (67) to persuade someone to do something

**target** /ˈtɑːɡɪt/ n (6) a particular market or segment of the population at which you are aiming your product

**task** /tɑːsk/ n (6) a piece of work which needs to be done

**tenacious** /təˈneɪʃəs/ adj (104) describes a person who continues despite difficulties until an aim is achieved

**territory** /ˈterətri/ n (166) the area which is allocated to a franchise or to a salesperson to exploit as their own

**test case** /ˈtest keɪs/ n (118) a court case which is selected to be judged as typical and representative of other possible cases

**tied up** /taɪd ˈʌp/ adj (122) describes money which is invested and therefore not immediately available for use; adj infml (166) describes a person who is busy, occupied with another task or person

**timetable** (154) /ˈtaɪmteɪbl/ v to prepare a list which shows the times at which things should happen

**tough** /tʌf/ adj (64) strong and not easily damaged; (104) mentally strong enough to make hard decisions or handle difficult situations

**track record** /ˌtræk ˈrekɔːd/ n (122) reputation earned from past actions

**tracking study** /ˈtrækɪŋ ˌstʌdi/ n (7) a technique for assessing the effectiveness of an advertising campaign

**trademarked** /ˈtreɪdmɑːkt/ adj (116) carrying a legally registered symbol or words which represent a company or product

**transaction** /trænˈzækʃn/ n (68) a piece of business

**transit** /ˈtrɑːnzɪt/ n (87) being transported from one place to another, e.g. the goods are in transit

**trend** /trend/ n (9) the general movement or development in a particular direction

**trial period** /ˌtraɪəl ˈpɪəriəd/ n (102) an agreed period of time that a new employee has to complete satisfactorily before being confirmed in his position

**troubleshooter** /ˈtrʌblˌʃuːtə(r)/ n (74) an expert who is sent to an organization to sort out its problems

**tumble** /ˈtʌmbl/ v (62) to fall suddenly

**turn up** /tɜːn ˈʌp/ v infml (161) to arrive somewhere

**turnover** /ˈtɜːnəʊvə(r)/ n (38) the amount of money in a given period, coming into a business from its sales

**two-tier** /ˈtuːtɪə(r)/ adj (58) with two clear and separate levels

**tycoon** /taɪˈkuːn/ n (98) a successful and rich businessperson

**u**

**undermine** /ˌʌndəˈmaɪn/ v (119) to weaken or reduce confidence in someone or something

**understaffed** /ˌʌndəˈstɑːft/ adj (72) not having enough staff for an organization to function well

**undertake** /ˌʌndəˈteɪk/ v (24) to agree and commit oneself to do something

**up-front** /ˌʌpˈfrʌnt/ adj (115) paid in advance before receiving the goods or service

**uphold** /ʌpˈhəʊld/ v (116) to support an earlier decision or judgement

**urge** /ɜːdʒ/ v (41) to encourage strongly

**USP** /juː es ˈpiː/ abbr (12) Unique Selling Proposition (or Point): the key feature of a product or service which makes it different from its competitors

**v**

**value** /ˈvæljuː/ n (125) what something is worth; value for money, worth the money something costs

**variable costs** /ˌveəriəbl ˈkɒsts/ n (64) the costs, e.g. materials, labour, which vary according to the number of units produced; see **fixed costs**

**vending machine** /ˈvendɪŋ məˌʃiːn/ n (56) a machine where customers use coins to purchase snacks, soft drinks cigarettes, etc

**venture capital** /ˌventʃə ˈkæpɪtl/ n (111) the money required to support a business enterprise which has an element of risk

**venue** /ˈvenjuː/ n (66) the location where an organized event takes place

**vessel** /ˈvesl/ n (88) a ship tanker or large boat

**viable** /ˈvaɪəbl/ adj (49) capable of being successful and profitable

**virtual** /ˈvɜːtʃuəl/ adj (88) not in a digital form, but in a computer's memory or on the Internet; almost

**virus** /ˈvaɪrəs/ n (116) computer code sent accidentally or deliberately over the Internet which stops a computer from working properly

**voicemail** /ˈvɔɪsmeɪl/ n (103) an electronic system recording telephone messages

**voiceover** /ˈvɔɪsəʊvə(r)/ n (152) the spoken commentary by an unseen actor on a television commercial

**volatile** /ˈvɒlətaɪl/ adj (104) unstable

**voucher** /ˈvaʊtʃə(r)/ n (72) a piece of paper which can be used instead of money to pay for something

**voyage** /ˈvɔɪdʒ/ n (88) a sea journey

**w**

**warehouse** /ˈweəhaʊs/ n (21) a large building where materials or finished goods are stored before being distributed or exported

**wares** /weəz/ n (159) old-fashioned term for goods to be sold

**wear out** /ˌweər ˈaʊt/ v (160) to become damaged through use

**website** /ˈwebsaɪt/ n (40) an Internet location which carries the electronically-stored web pages for a person or organization

**white-collar worker** /ˈwaɪt kɒlə ˌwɜːkə(r)/ n (74) someone who works in an office or professional environment; see **blue-collar worker**

**wholesaler** /ˈhəʊlseɪlə(r)/ n (39) the business which buys large quantities of goods from a manufacturer to sell on to a retailer

**will** /wɪl/ n (119) a document which contains details of how a person would like to distribute their wealth after their death

**wind up** /waɪnd ˈʌp/ v (153) to close a company down and deal with its affairs, usually as a result of going bankrupt

**withdraw** /wɪðˈdrɔː/ v (42) to take something away; (105) to no longer take part in something; (122) to take out money from a bank account

**workstation** /ˈwɜːkˌsteɪʃn/ n (50) the computer and desk area where someone works

**worthwhile** /ˌwɜːθˈwaɪl/ adj (97) something worth the time, money, and effort spent on it

**y**

**yearly planner chart** /ˌjɪəli ˈplænə ˌtʃɑːt/ n (29) a large calendar showing an entire year on which people write important events such as deadlines, examination dates and holidays

**youth** /juːθ/ n (111) time of life before, or at the beginning of, adulthood

**z**

**zone** /zəʊn/ n (98) an area with a particular feature or use; economic development zone n (38) a region with incentives such as tax advantages to encourages businesses to locate there

# OXFORD
### UNIVERSITY PRESS

Great Clarendon Street, Oxford OX2 6DP

Oxford University Press is a department of the University of Oxford. It furthers the University's objective of excellence in research, scholarship, and education by publishing worldwide in

Oxford  New York

Auckland  Bangkok  Buenos Aires  Cape Town Chennai  Dar es Salaam  Delhi  Hong Kong Istanbul  Karachi  Kolkata  Kuala Lumpur  Madrid Melbourne  Mexico City  Mumbai  Nairobi São Paulo  Shanghai  Singapore  Taipei  Tokyo Toronto

with an associated company in Berlin

Oxford and Oxford English are registered trade marks of Oxford University Press in the UK and in certain other countries

© Oxford University Press 2002

The moral rights of the author have been asserted

Database right Oxford University Press (maker)

First published 2002

ISBN 0 19 457346 X

Printed and bound by Grafiasa S. A. in Portugal.l

**Acknowledgements**

The authors and publisher are grateful to those who have given permission to reproduce the following extracts and adaptations of copyright material:

p6 Adapted from 'A breath of fresh air – that will be nine quid please' by Colin Grimshaw, The Independent 26 March 2001. Reproduced by permission of Independent Newspapers (UK) Ltd.

p8 'Generation Y' by Ellen Newborne & Kathleen Kerwin, Business Week 15 February 1999 © The McGraw-Hill Companies, Inc. Reproduced by permission.

p11 Extracts from www.adbusters.org. Reproduced by permission of Adbusters Media Foundation.

p12 Information about BMW C1 from www.bmw.co.uk . Reproduced by permission of BMW UK Ltd.

p12 Review of BMW C1, Evening Standard. Reproduced by permission of Evening Standard / Atlantic Syndication.

p18 'Santa inspires Gadget Shop founder' © Rupert Steiner / The Sunday Times 14 September 1997. Reproduced by permission of Times Newspapers Ltd.

p19 'Switched on, the computer games queen' © Rupert Steiner / The Sunday Times 5 October 1997. Reproduced by permission of Times Newspapers Ltd.

p28 'Beat the clock' © Professor Cary L. Cooper / The Sunday Times 5 March 2000. Reproduced by permission of Times Newspapers Ltd.

p38 'China wipes the smile off western lips' © Catherine Wheatley / The Sunday Times 31 October 1999. Reproduced by permission of Times Newspapers Ltd.

p46 'Golf pros in hole over dress code' by Paul Kelso, © The Guardian 21 January 2000. Reproduced by permission of Guardian Newspapers Ltd.

pp46–7 Extracts from Riding the Waves of Culture, 2nd Edition by Fons Trompenaars and Charles Hampden-Turner. Reproduced by permission of Nicholas Brealey Publishing.

p48 Extracts from www.merck.com. © 1995 – 2001 Merck and Co. Inc., Whitehouse Station NJ, USA. All rights reserved. Adapted and used with permission of Merck and Co. Inc.

p58 Adapted from 'Big oil faces pump protest' by Leo Lewis, Independent on Sunday 20 May 2001. Reproduced by permission of Independent Newspapers (UK) Ltd.

p61 Extracts from The Essential Managers Manual by Robert Heller and Tim Hindle. © 1998 Dorling Kindersley, text © 1998 Robert Heller and Tim Hindle. Reproduced by permission of Penguin Books Ltd.

p66 Interview with Eric Perrot. Reproduced by permission of Eric Perrot.

p68 Extract from Mark H. McCormack on Negotiating by Mark H. McCormack. Published by Arrow Business Books. Reproduced by permission of The Random House Group Ltd.

p76 Interview with Bill Watts. Reproduced by permission of Bill Watts.

p79 'Merger most foul' by Andrew Leach, Financial Mail on Sunday 21 January 2001. Reproduced by permission of Mail on Sunday / Atlantic Syndication.

p93 'Internet tutorial: How the Internet works' from http://english.unitechnology.ac.nz. Reproduced by permission of the New Zealand Ministry of Education. All rights reserved.

p96 Adapted from 'White collars felt in war on CV Fraud' by Jonathan Thompson, The Independent 10 December 2000. Reproduced by permission of Independent Newspapers (UK) Ltd.

p97 Extracts from The Seven Habits of Highly Effective People: Powerful Lessons in Personal Change by Stephen R. Covey. Reproduced by permission of Simon & Schuster.

p98 'Perk practice' © Anita Chaudhuri, The Guardian 30 August 2001. Reproduced by permission of Guardian Newspapers Ltd.

p108 'How to join the family business' © Tola Awogbamiye, The Guardian 3 June 2000. Reproduced by permission of Tola Awogbamiye.

p109 'Anguish of telling a son he will never run family firm' © John O'Donnell / The Sunday Times 5 August 2001. Reproduced by permission of Times Newspapers Ltd.

p116 'Net call to protect top names' by Wendy Grossman, The Telegraph 18 July 2001. Reproduced by permission of Telegraph Group Ltd.

p118 'Damages for actress over 'dog's birthday' story', The Telegraph 22 May 2001. Reproduced by permission of Telegraph Group Ltd.

p118 'Judges limit rise in personal damages awards to a third' by David Graves, The Telegraph 24 March 2000. Reproduced by permission of Telegraph Group Ltd.

p119 'Share and share alike post-Napster' by Jonathan Lambeth, The Telegraph. Reproduced by permission of Telegraph Group Ltd.

p119 'Dealer who sold violin to pay £3m damages' by Will Bennett, The Telegraph, 27 February 2001. Reproduced by permission of Telegraph Group Ltd

Sources:
pp38, 67, 59, 89, 94, 95, 106, 132, 137 Information and statistics taken from; Economist Pocket Negotiation, Economist Pocket International Business Terms & Economist Pocket World in Figures.
p 49 Information from The Sunday Times 4 February 2001.
p89 Information from The New Oxford Dictionary of English.
p 98 Information from The Evening Standard, 23 November 2000.

Although every effort has been made to trace and contact copyright holders before publication, this has not been possible in some cases. We apologize for any apparent infringement of copyright and if notified, the publisher will be pleased to rectify any errors or omissions at the earliest opportunity.

The publishers would like to thank the following for the use of photographs:
©Courtesy www.adbusters.org p11; The Advertising Archive p44; ©BBC p53 (Weakest Link); The Anthony Blake Photo Library p91; ©BMW p12; CEPHAS/Stockfood p35, /TOP/Pierre Hussenol p134; ©Bohemian Nomad Picturemakers/CORBIS p38; ©Foodpix/Eric Futran p114, 139; Format Partners/Paula Glassman p124 (male); ©Fourth Room p98, 99; ©The Gadget Shop p18; Getty/FPG International/V.C.L p8, /Barry Rosenthal p40, /Phil Boorman p55 (Jenny), /Ryanstock p61, /Antonio Mo p111; Getty/Hulton Archive/Lambert p81 (woman); Getty/Imagebank/Barros & Barros p21, Britt J.Erlanson-Messens pp28, 105 (female), Ezio Geneletti p81 (silver espresso), /Marc Romanelli pp83, 86, /Bob Scott p93, /Ghislain & Marie David de Lossy p103, /Romilly Lockyer pp105 (male), 125 (waiter), /G.K. & Vikki Hart p124 (magic); Getty/Stone/ Ken Fisher p6, /Robert Daly p9, /Peter Correz p42 (family), /Jon Riley p80, /Ian Logan pp81 (two cups), 131, David Hanson p90, /Catherine Ledner p105 (Asian woman), Shuji Kobayashi p105 (black male), /Paul Chesley p115, /Tony Craddock p116, /Moggy p125 (jeans); Nicholas Brealey Publishing p46 (males); PA Photos/John Stillwell p46 (J.Owen); ©Eric Perrot p66; ©PhotoDisc p96, /Keith Brofsky p54; Pictor International Ltd p55 (Sally, Raymond); Popperfoto/Reuters p53 (Big Brother), /Reuters NewMedia Inc. p53 (ER); ©Powerstock pp13, 55 (Paula), 68, /Zefa/Visual Medi Fastforward pp117, 55 (Toby); Rex Features p66 (parliaments), /Jeroen Oerlemans p58; ©Superstock pp25, 71, 128.

Commissioned photography by:
Trevor Clifford p42 (bottle).

The publishers would like to thank the follow for the use of copyright cartoons:
"Ralph Harrison, king of salespersons" (Release date 01/22/90). The Far Side® by Gary Larson ©1990 FarWorks, Inc. All Rights Reserved. Used with permission on page 6.

Illustrations by:
Stefan Chabluk p43; Mark Duffin pp54, 64, 112; Richard Duszczak pp127, 135; Sarah Jones pp18, 26 (leisure), 76, 88, 108, 121; Tim Kahane p36; Satoshi Kambayshi pp15, 32, 56, 74, 97, 101, 113, 119; Malcolm Livingstone pp16, 20; Katherine Walker pp23, 26 (door), 51, 57, 73, 126, 130, 136; He Yuhong p36 (symbols).

Design by:
Shireen Nathoo Design

The author and publisher would like to thank the following individuals for their advice and assistance in the preparation of this book:
Alan K Costerisan, Michael Frankel, Blanka Klimová, Anna Kucala, Jon Kear, Dorota Miller, Andrew Preshous